AASMAH MIR was born ⟨…⟩
Her parents emigrated ther⟨…⟩
a furiously shy teenager she ⟨…⟩
anything or speak to anyon⟨…⟩
has spoken to complete str⟨…⟩ ⟨…⟩ radio, including
BBC Radio 5 Live and Radio 4, and won a few awards
for it too. Life, eh? She co-presents the *Breakfast Show* on
Times Radio and writes a column for *The Sunday Times*.

'Full of beauty, wit and inner strength, this unique dual voiced
memoir moved me deeply. Aasmah Mir's childhood may have
been bittersweet but her writing, like her broadcasting, is
pure gold' – SAMIRA AHMED

'Honest and powerful' – IAN RANKIN

'I will be thinking of Aasmah's story for a very long time.
She writes with such richness of her life, such detail of her
time at school and the love for her young brother. This book
will resonate with many people no matter that they be Christian or Muslim, British or Pakistani. A treasure of a book'
– FERN BRITTON

'Young Aasmah bursts into life in this lovingly evoked por-
trait of a Scottish childhood, complicated by the challenge
to fit in when the shade of your skin seemingly sets you
apart. Exuberant, warm, funny and wise, just like its author'
– MARIELLA FROSTRUP

'I loved this book partly because Aasmah Mir has such a
good way with detail that she can with conjure Glasgow in
the 80s or Pakistan in the 60s so vividly and economically

it's like looking at snapshots in a photo album; but what I loved most were the moments when you sense her – and her mother – understanding that the world and their place in it is not what was advertised and they are going to have to work and sometimes fight to secure that place. I found it incredibly moving and it made me think and rethink how the narratives that shape who we are and how we fit in are not givens but negotiations and always up for revision' – THE REVEREND RICHARD COLES

'An exquisite memoir, revealing how the wheels of progress have turned across two generations – but how they have also got very stuck. It is at times heart-breaking and poignant but also so very funny and clever and full of small moments that you want to pause and reread' – FI GLOVER

'[A Glasgow Girl] will leave your heart in your mouth. Writing about a culture that values compliance in women and encourages silence, Aasmah Mir's book does the exact opposite. Moving between her and her mother's life, it reveals parts of the Pakistani immigrant experience that are rarely seen on our bookshelves. Aasmah's raw and honest account of her family life will blow you away!' – SAIMA MIR

'An incredible memoir on culture and finding your voice that will stay with you long after you have read it' – *The Sun*

'An interwoven tale of love, loss and life in Glasgow and Pakistan across multiple generations' – *The Sunday Times*

'Evocative and vivid' – *The Scotsman*

'A gorgeous book about family and identity' – *The i Paper*

Aasmah Mir

A Glasgow Girl

A memoir of growing up and finding your voice

HEADLINE

First published as *A Pebble in the Throat* in 2023 by
HEADLINE PUBLISHING GROUP

First published in paperback in 2024 by
HEADLINE PUBLISHING GROUP

1

Cataloguing in Publication Data is available from the British Library

ISBN: 978 1 4722 8855 4

Designed and typeset by EM&EN
Printed and bound in Great Britain by Clays Ltd, Elcograf S.p.A.

HEADLINE PUBLISHING GROUP
An Hachette UK Company
Carmelite House
50 Victoria Embankment
London EC4Y 0DZ

www.headline.co.uk
www.hachette.co.uk

For my mum and dad, who gave us everything.

And for my daughter R, who is my everything.

ONE

Glasgow, Scotland, 1985

From the car to the door of the shop lies a distance of barely a few metres but it feels as long and twisty as the Karakoram Highway and just as perilous. It is May and the air still feels sharp. But there is a softness to the cold that suggests the approach of summer and all that it will never hold.

I sit inside the car searching for kindness in the faces of passers-by. No. No. Maybe. Absolutely not. After a while I start to fret. The ugly clock on the dashboard ticks over to 3:48 p.m.

Twisting at the strap of the school bag on my knees, I press it against the inside of my hand until a raspberry-coloured stain forms. I do this unthinkingly, not intending to cause pain. I open my palms and stare at them as if seeing them for the first time. Bringing the thumb of my right hand up to my mouth, I begin to chew the curve of the nail.

My mother sits in the driver's seat. She is always waiting for me with an undiminished amount of patience. How long have we been sitting like this? How many times? The same face, the same hair, the same name; I sprang from her body and yet we could not be more different.

The door to the shop opens and two girls tumble out, screeching and shoving sweets in their mouths, elbowing and backing into each other.

'Fuckin' shut it Morvern, ya eejit HAHAHAHAAA.'

My heart flips, a coldness starts to build in my stomach. I shrink back in my seat wishing myself invisible. They must not see me. But there's a flash of blazers and hair and they are gone. I gaze after them – wretched, relieved, envious.

We both know how this is going to go. How it always goes. I break the silence, forcing the air out of my shrinking throat.

'It looks . . . very . . . busy inside, Mum,' I say doubtfully, looking out of the car window again. 'It'll take . . . ages.'

Every time I hear my voice it surprises and infuriates me. It sounds pathetic. This is not who I am supposed to be; who I was born to be.

Out of the corner of my eye I see my mother's chin dip slightly. The silence envelops us.

'I don't really need the magazine. Let's just go home.'

I try to sound breezy. I want this to end. But I hear her sigh, so softly that it disappears like thin smoke from the candles on a birthday cake. Disappointment sketches its name in the air.

'Don't worry *beti*. I'll get it. I'll leave the keys in.'

The door slams, the keys dance in the ignition and she is gone. I hold my breath, my eyes following her. But the Karakoram Highway holds no fear for my mother. She walks along the pavement with a quick, efficient stride; the narrow, treacherous path widens and flattens with every step. She is in a hurry, there are so many things to do and a life to lead. She pushes the door of the newsagents and disappears inside.

I click on the radio switching from Radio 1 to Radio Clyde and back again searching for the right song. The one with the perfect amount of sweetness or saltiness; the one that tastes just right. I want to let its sugariness explode on my tongue before it turns to thorns in my throat; to gulp down its salty water then let the liquid slowly flood my lungs. I want to leave this place and to plunge headfirst into it at the same time.

I think about the chocolate bar she will buy me along with my magazine. I have a ridiculously sweet tooth, always ready to splinter a Highland Toffee on my soft molars or chew furiously on a Mars Bar. Thin paper bags of boiled sweets grow damp in my blazer pockets as the rain soaks into me. I bolt my lunch and dinner and immediately start to crave the vanilla heights of caramel and cocoa. I dump huge spoonfuls of sugar on to Frosties; I eat bread and jam like it's nothing; I rub Polos on to my teeth at night in bed because they taste of mint so must essentially be toothpaste. I am so obsessed by sweet things that I take to stealing small change from my father's vast suit pockets to fund my habit and hasten the rotting of my teeth. Once my mother took radical steps to wean me off sweet things; now she connives in my addiction.

And I receive my hit gratefully. Because sweet is simple. A slice of apple pie is forever buttery and chewy and sticks to your teeth in a pleasing way. A square of iced gingerbread always lies like a snow-topped castle on a moat of technicolour custard. Food like that leaves your tongue sweet and your mood high; it never turns to ashes in your mouth.

My mother is coming back. This time I can see her face. She looks preoccupied; something is twisting like a fish in her head. But as soon as she spots me she smiles in her compact way. She waves the magazine and some chocolate and punches the air in triumph. I've seen that gesture many times before. She did it when my little brother finally started walking at the age of three, motoring his chubby legs across the grass, his rosy tongue sticking out with the effort. She did it when I won the one hundred metres at Sports Day, her chin dipping into her chest, the wind blowing the curls into her soft face.

My mother, my champion, my betrayer.

She pulls open the door and puts the magazine and the chocolate on my lap and turns the key. Folding her body forward she checks her rear-view mirror for traffic. It took my mother three attempts to pass her driving test, her tiny feet getting tangled in the ends of her sari as she tried to locate the clutch.

Soon we're speeding along the Great Western Road. The radio is up high and occasionally I pass a Malteser to her and she eats it off her palm as if she is checking a curry for salt. I eat mine from between my forefinger and thumb because that is how you should eat in this country.

In this car in this perfect moment I feel almost happy. Here I can pretend that it never happened. My mother and I could drive and drive until we reach some sunny place where everyone's face is open and smiling; where people don't whisper poison in your ear while you wait to cross the road or queue for your lunch in the canteen. If we keep going it would just be the two of us. If we keep going, I'd never have to go to school again and she would promise to never ever leave me again.

Gujranwala, Pakistan, 1965

I lock eyes with Maqsooda before I let the plate fall from a height. It shatters and lies in five hideous pieces on the floor.

The noise finally sends home the family sitting in the drawing room before they have even had a chance to complain that the tea was not quite hot enough, the samosas a bit too oily or the laddoos not sufficiently round. They are already thrusting their feet back into their shoes and gathering their veils around them when I pop my head around the door. On top of all the swearing and the incident with the tea this really is too much. They hurry out of the house and into the street in appalled silence.

My brother Khalid had already done the detective work. He had slipped into the university and sat in on one of Iqbal's lectures. Without even a pen he had lolled at the back with his hands in his pockets and waited, unchallenged and entitled, my father's sole male heir. He already had low expectations but when Iqbal appeared, Khalid sat forward and blinked slowly. No, this man really wouldn't do. A 'dry roti' – no oil, too much flour – he chuckled to himself. He left after just five minutes, the door slamming monstrously behind him.

But my father was adamant. He had given his word and there was to be no going back. Iqbal would be a strong match. His family was solid, he was highly educated and not a businessman, just as I had stipulated he must not be. There was not a whiff of scandal or deceit around him – not like the last one. But I did not want to marry this dry-sounding man whose world only extended to the city limits of Gujranwala; whose sleepy eyes as described by my brother promised neither love nor adventure; whose family seemed a collection of thin eyebrows and even thinner hearts.

I slam the tea tray down on the table – a bit harder than I had meant to. The saucers leap and dance and my mother jumps in her chair.

'Hey auntie, how many sugars?' I ask loudly.

The woman looks aghast. Her eyebrows travel to the middle of her huge forehead, which is caked in white powder. She readjusts her shawl around her body.

'How many . . . ?' She looks at my mother for guidance, her voice drying up in her throat.

'Sugars. How many do you take?' I am brandishing the spoon in my hand, my head casually cocked to one side as if I were serving her in a roadside dabba.

'I . . . I . . . three?'

'Three? My God! Do you want to die?'

My mother shifts in her seat. Out in the street a hawker is selling matches, his voice rising and falling in a hopeless crescendo.

'Here, just have one. It's better for your figure,' I decide.

I swish the spoon around briskly and thrust the cup at her which she takes in two shaky hands.

Her sour-faced daughter who has not spoken once cannot shift her gaze from me, slowly calculating whom she will tell first about this creature, this jungli. She narrows her eyes and moistens her thin lips. I hand a cup to my mother, our eyes not meeting. Then I walk back to the kitchen without a backwards glance, my hips swinging, my sandals flip-flopping loudly, adjusting my tumbling dupatta as I go.

Maqsooda is clanging pots as I reach the kitchen. I raise an eyebrow at her and issue a few curses in her direction. Then she passes the plate to me silently, stands well back and watches with her huge beautiful eyes as I dash it to the floor.

Days pass and my father grows puzzled as to why there has been no word from the Maliks. He pivots from confusion to humiliation then anger. But he is too proud to ask. After two weeks have passed they and their unsuitable son are never mentioned again.

*

Eight months later, I am awakened by my brother's voice.

'Baby! Oh – baby! Get up!'

It is just 6 o'clock. I am rubbing the sleep from my eyes and trying to pat down my hair when the door opens and my older sister Naz bundles in.

'Quick, you have to go downstairs. Khalid says he needs to take your photo!'

'My photo? Why?'

'For the rishta. They need a picture. But you have to go now.'

'I need to comb my hair at least, wash my face. I've just woken–'

'Baby! No time for that. Come – now!' thunders my brother from downstairs. He must have woken the whole of Gujranwala. He has most certainly disturbed our buffalo in the field next door.

I slowly descend the stairs desperately trying to smooth my hair. My sister Koukab and I have the tightest, curliest hair in the family. No amount of massaging sunflower oil into it makes any difference. In the morning it looks as if we have been electrocuted.

'Come on, why can't I even wash my face?' I protest, walking into the living room. 'This is silly. I look half-asleep!'

But my brother is already impatiently gesturing to the chair opposite him. I notice a bored-looking man with a camera standing silently so I sit down huffily and as I look up he releases the shutter. Before I can ask for another they are striding out of the room, out of the front door and into the street, carrying with them the sleepy photograph that will send me to a city thousands of miles away whose name I have neither heard nor uttered before.

TWO

Baljaffray, Scotland, 1976

My little brother has disappeared. One minute he was in the back garden playing with my Sindy dolls, methodically placing them upright in his old pram; the next my mother is shouting for him, the panic rising in her voice. My mother is always shouting for one of us – she starts at the eldest or youngest and lists us all until she gets to the right one – but my brother is only three and has just begun to walk. The pram has gone too; the Sindy dolls lie on the grass, their limbs sticking out at odd angles. We stare at each other wondering which one of us should have been watching him; then we start to search nearby, our steps quickening, his name echoing around the estate.

'Imran? Imraaaan? Immi?'

Our house sits at the top of a hill – brand new, identikit, the colour of nothing – a cardboard box that has been blown there and settled, disgruntled, biding its time. Everything is new. When we moved here the tarmac on the streets was so new it looked like treacle, the road markings had not yet been etched on to the sticky black road. The man who painted them one sunny morning shouted and shook his fist as my dad absent-mindedly drove over them, ruining his fresh lines and stamping white tyre tracks where they should not have been for years to come.

We are the first house at the bottom of the street so we gain an extra strip of grass at the side where my dad and brother are always playing cricket. I never understand how such a dull game can elicit so many emotions. They scream and shout in frustration and joy; they grow high-pitched and giggly; they argue over distances and angles I cannot see. They enjoy a secret language that I do not comprehend and which is never fully explained to me, yelling bewildering things like 'PLUM! PLUM!' and 'L-B-W!' I am always in the field, never trusted to bat or bowl, huffing and puffing up and down steep hills to retrieve the scuffed red ball. Neighbours watch this strange subcontinental sport played by the raucous family of six. Skinny freckly boys pass by clutching footballs in the crook of their arms. Their mouths hang open slackly and they slow down.

'Whit ye playin' mister?' one boy asks my dad, scratching the back of his head like Stan Laurel.

My dad tells him and gives him the cricket ball to hold. He stares at it in wonder, weighing it in his hands like a cannonball before theatrically knocking it against his head.

'Jeezo . . . That could fuckin' kill ye, big man!'

*

I find my first best friend at the bottom of my garden. Her name is Heather and our tiny lawns back on to each other. She clocks me one day and ducks under the fence and into my garden before her mum can stop her. She has light brown hair, close-set blue eyes and a crooked smile. We stare into each other's mouths and nostrils. We torment the neighbourhood cats, fence each other with knitting needles and garden canes and uproot prize blooms to make sickly perfume from their petals. She is never out of my house and I am never out of hers.

The estate sprawls up and over a steep hill; I have a friend in virtually every street. Mary – the upstairs of whose house I never see because she has an open tread staircase that I am too scared to climb for fear of plummeting through the gaps to my death; Jonathan, whose family is Czech and always sound like they are shouting at each other; Claire who eventually emigrates to Canada, making me cry for days.

But I have also made my first enemy. Scamp, a shaggy terrier that looks like the head of a mop. He lives in the next street, patrolling it for errant children with chubby thighs. I try to creep past number 16 but he always spots me and chases me across the busy road at the top of the hill and down the steep bank into the nettles below. I run so fast from him so many times that I become the fastest runner at my primary school. But I still carry a deep fear of him, taking huge diversions to avoid walking past that house. When someone casually mentions that he has been run over by a lorry, I silently rejoice. His tyranny is over; my thighs are safe.

Across the road from our house is the brow of a thick grassy hill that falls away into the burn, a magical place of stepping stones through shallow bubbling water, of shady dens and ropes hung from trees for swinging on and breaking limbs. We spend hours there every day, sharpening sticks, burrowing into the red stony earth, making mud pies, floating makeshift crafts and tossing flowers and leaves into the frothy water. As the light fades, my mother sends a sibling to stand on the bank, arms folded, and tell me to come home for dinner.

As I climb the hill, coated in dust and scratches, I hear the unmistakeable wail of the siren signalling the end of the day for the workers of the big factory in Clydebank. The first time I hear it I am terrified. It starts like a low growl from a wounded animal then becomes a loud unforgiving single note. Even after it ends you can still hear it ringing in your ears. After many years I come to anticipate its familiar mournfulness bookending the day; and when it stops for ever I miss it.

The houses on our street are set so close together that it is impossible to ignore whatever drama is unfolding that day. A dog escapes into someone's garden and is eating their fat begonias or gnawing at a small child; someone has shot headfirst over their handlebars on to the concrete and knocked their front teeth out; a group of boys is swinging bicycle chains at each other. Sometimes children run down the hill to gawp at the mulletted shirtless boys delivering crates of drinks from the Alpine lorry. The liquid stains our tongues and leaves us hyper. Some girls stare after them long after they have gone, twisting a strand of hair or sucking their thumbs.

But today the drama in our street is that my little brother is nowhere to be found. My sister is dispatched north on her yellow-gold bike. My dad phones my uncle who lives three streets away and can mobilise a few of my many cousins. My older brother ambles off, hands in pockets, towards the burn. My mum and dad tip me into the car and we speed down the hill scanning the pavements and fields, the neighbouring streets and gardens shooting by. My dad's hand is on my mother's knee, he is reassuring her in Urdu, telling her not to worry, that they'll find him. My heart is beating faster through either fear or excitement. I think of Scamp squashed beneath the wheels of a lorry and I am convinced that I am being punished for celebrating his death. I look out of the window, sure that I will spot him – my roommate, my little buddy, my everything – somewhere on these dangerous roads.

In that house in a narrow front-facing bedroom I sleep above my little brother on a bunk bed. It squeaks and rocks as he waves his hand in front of his face like a manic pendulum, focusing on something – a pattern, a face, a grid – that none of us ever see. I lean over the edge of the top bunk and hiss at him to stop or I shout for mum. He does this for an hour every night until exhausted he falls asleep, slipping into a more peaceful world where he looks contained, angelic – miles from the torment that pursues him all day. Despite this pantomime every night I still feel as if I am his protector, floating above, warding off the spiteful djinns that gather to plague him. When he eventually falls asleep I lean over again and stare at him. His square head is slightly turned to the side, his mouth open, his little arms lying on either side above his head like he has surrendered to sleep or dozed off while dancing. I take in his long eyelashes, his brown velvety curls, the tiny mouth that is capable of ear-splitting screams, the full cheeks always blotchy with anger, the chubby palms I love to tickle.

'*Round and round the garden, like a teddy bear.*'

'Ahaaa, again!' he laughs, lifting his little pink chin up to me, his dimples perfectly symmetrical.

My love for him is ridiculous. I want to carry him everywhere, give him his bottle, hold his hand at all times. I want him all for myself and I bribe him to stay with me with whatever I can – a stolen biscuit, a lollipop I had been saving. I cut up a plate of white bread and cheddar cheese and lure him on to the garden swing, where I feed it to him as if he were an invalid or a king or both. He chuckles as I pop the pieces of food into his mouth and our eyes lock fleetingly. I live for that eye contact, of which there is little. He does see me, I think. Then his smile drops like a stone and he wanders off.

His sunny moments are beautiful – he sways on his feet, smiling into the air, his hands in his pockets or in front of his face. He delights in sweet foods and comforting stodge like rice and toast. But he becomes easily frustrated – at invisible things and my suffocating attention. I just want us to be together. My older brother and sister have each other after all. We are a pair too.

One day my mum brings him back from the doctor's. She places him on the kitchen worktop and gives him a biscuit to cheer him up, his little legs dangling above the red and yellow chequered lino floor. My brother and sister crowd round him, gasping and laughing and pointing. I edge over.

'What are you looking at?'

They ignore me. I can't see anything unusual.

'Mum? Can I see what they were looking at?'

'It's nothing, don't worry.'

I can see from my big brother's face that it is not nothing.

'Why can they see but not me? That's not fair!'

My mum sighs, comes over, unzips my brother's shorts and I see a little white bandage over his willy, with a tiny dot of blood on it.

'Oooyah! What's . . . happened?' I gasp.

'He's been circumcised,' she says. I have no idea what that means. It's a big word for such a small spot. But it looks sore. My brother who had been distracted by the

Chocolate Digestive, looks down, sees the little red spot and starts to wail again.

＊

That ugly house is special. My parents love its new-ness, the smell of fresh paint and new floors rising to meet their nostrils. Doors and windows close precisely without sticking or squeaking or revealing huge gaps. In the last house Mum had laid the carpets herself and had the blisters to prove it. She bought a roll of rough brown carpet from a basement on Argyle Street, hacked at it with blunt scissors then nailed it to the floor with a hammer, its rough fraying edges rising stubbornly along the skirting boards. Outside, triumphant weeds lined the edges of each grey slab of the footpath that led to the front door. My dad worked for days ripping out the parched stony grass, levelling and hoeing the claggy soil, then sowing new grass seed. A man passing by wearing a hat and smoking a pipe slowed down and stood behind the low garden wall.

'WEED. ALL.'

My dad stopped to wipe the sweat that had gathered in his generous eyebrows and looked at him.

'WEED. ALL.'

'A doll?'

'NO,' the man kept shouting, despite being just two metres away, 'YOU. NEED. WEED. ALL. DO. YOU. UNDERSTAND?'

'I will weed it all, aye,' my dad replied, perplexed.

'NO. YOU. NEED. TO. USE. WEEDOL.'

'Aye OK, I will. Thank you.'

'RIGHT YOU ARE.'

And with that he walked off.

But nothing needs to be weeded here nor painted. My mum gets the professionals in to lay thick furry carpets this time. The house has a garage, its lawn is newly laid, the flower beds full of fresh topsoil as soft and dark as muscovado sugar. There is a cloakroom and two bathrooms, one suite is sky blue, the other the colour of overboiled peas. My older brother and sister have a small room each at the back and I share a room with my little brother next to my parents. The walls in our room are orange and a small electric organ stands there with one key inexplicably missing revealing the plastic innards of the machine. There is a blackboard in there too, and I once put a piece of chalk up each nostril and lost one, despite my mum trying to locate it with one of her hairpins. I wept inconsolably when my older brother told me that I would probably die slowly and painfully of chalk poisoning. An MFI wardrobe holds my little brother's clothes and mine, his tiny shorts and tank tops folded next to my dresses. This is where I often hid stolen biscuits too, sometimes forgetting them for days after, when my mum would pull out clothes for me and a squashed Trio or Breakaway would spring on to the carpet and lie there accusingly. My brother's collection of trucks and cars lie on the floor and I trip over them every day, after which he cries until his face is even more red, then meticulously re-parks them in razor-sharp lines while humming to himself.

There is one square window which opens outwards on to the street. I sit on the ledge, my legs dangling out, nothing to stop me from falling headfirst into the flower beds. In that crow's nest I enjoy a full view of the vivid city to my right, hazy in sunshine. To my left the street spreads out before me leading up the hill to the path that runs through the whole estate, past my beloved uncle and aunt's house and finishing at the low brown buildings of my school. The lawns are small and neat, the cars parked in driveways primary-coloured and new. The house directly opposite lay empty for a year until a family of four arrived, their two girls smirking at me in the sunshine. We become friends the next day. Their mum is petite and beautiful and wears peasant blouses and crinkly skirts. Their dad is handsome; he owns many sweaters with deep V-necks and diamond patterns and his eyes leak when he laughs. The girls come to all my birthday parties in velvet maxi dresses, clutching huge presents. And yet I have never seen the inside of their house. Whenever I go to see if they are coming out to play I climb the four steps to their front door and press the bell. Their mum or dad open it and beam at me.

'Oh, hullo pet – JULIE! JANET! I'll just go and see where they are. Hold on.'

They push the door to and I wait, listening to the voices inside. I can see warm lights and shapes on the other side of the glass. But I'm dying to see their house, to see what toys they have in their bedrooms. The door opens and out they come, with their mum and dad throwing hats and scarves after them. This happens every time until I ask my mum why I can't go inside their house when they can come in to mine. She tells me that some people are very 'houseproud' which means they don't want kids making a mess. This makes little sense but it does stop me wondering what is behind their front door. One day as I sit on my window ledge I see a girl who lives a few streets away. She climbs the steps of Julie and Janet's house, presses the bell and I watch as the door opens and she hops over the magic threshold. The door slams shut heavily and I feel the vibration across the road. I fold up this memory and put it away.

*

It feels as if we have been looking for my little brother for an hour but we find him after fifteen minutes. He is five hundred yards away at the bottom of the steep hill that takes you out of the estate. He has crossed one road to get here and is pushing his buggy along, his little arms stretching up high to grip the handles. He looks too small and vulnerable to be alone in this landscape, the huge apple-green hills rising behind him, the busy dangerous town in front. All the effort has made him hot

– his fat cheeks are red and shiny, he is sweating under his navy-blue dungarees and red polo-neck jumper, his curls plastered to his wet forehead. My mother lets out a strange sound when she spots him and leaps out of the car before it has completely come to a stop. He looks surprised and annoyed to be plucked from his great adventure and starts crying. She scoops him up, sits him on her knee and we drive back up the hill in silence. I look at my brother, relieved, not knowing what this calamitous feeling is rising in my throat. I reach between the seats and rub his doughy fingers. He doesn't even look at me; he just keeps staring out of the window.

Gujranwala, Pakistan, 1958

My mother lies on the charpai, her face turned away, her right forearm hooked over her eyes, shielding them from the amber lamplight. She looks like a broken bird; her arms and legs are thin, her body slight. I gently push my thumbs into the smooth flesh of her shins noticing anew how her skin changes from the colour of thick cream to cinnamon as I reach her tired feet.

I have been massaging my mother's legs and feet for about half an hour now mostly in silence. She is a small narrow woman but carries on her shoulders the weight of one thousand moustachioed wrestlers and has to lie down several times during the day. In these moments she rarely speaks and if she does it's a random thought about something that happened last week or last year, a slight that has festered, a wrong that has returned to pluck away at her insides. She often appears to be muttering to herself, chastising someone, whispering indignantly. All day her sighs gather and tumble like an autumn breeze.

As I knead away at her legs the sounds of the house rise and fall around me. The squeak and bang of doors, the thump of rubber flip flops on hard unsympathetic floors, a metal spoon scraping the inside of a pot, the constant instructions issued to the servants and their indignant replies.

'There are too many people in this house,' my mother often tells me.

I lose myself in this opportunity to touch my mother; the last time she hugged me may have been when I was an infant. She has the same hairless vitreous skin as me, the same thin face, the same small alert eyes. We share the same short flat eyelashes and eyebrows that will not lie straight. The only difference is our hair. Mine is inexplicably tight and wiry but when I oil it, wash it and brush it a hundred times it is soft and thick and fluffy. My mother's is thin and defeated and only reaches her shoulders. She has to use a paranda to weave it into an acceptable plait.

A massage is my mother's only indulgence in her physical health or appearance. She doesn't own any kajal or lipstick; she never changes her hairstyle. The only jewellery she wears are two thick gold bangles, one on each arm. Hameeda Begum is just forty-seven years old but appears twenty years older. Something has sucked the life out of her.

I will do anything for my mother. I am the one whom she asks to massage her feet or to walk up and down on her back, smoothing out the knots and bumps that plague her. She appears at my bedside in the black of night touching my arm and whispering: 'Baby, baby,

I am so thirsty, please can you come with me to get some water?' I am perhaps eight or nine and in darkness I walk down four flights of stairs with her, shrinking from the shadows that gather in dark corners. I work the hand pump for ten minutes until the water runs cold and clear then I fill two metal cups and hand them to her. I watch as she gulps them down, her throat bulging monstrously, enjoying every last drop and wiping her mouth with the corner of her dupatta. Then she places the cups down and touches my head giving me a thousand sweet blessings.

'Allah will look after you, may he give you good fortune, many cars, a beautiful house. May he make sure that your handbag is always filled with money . . .'

No servants are allowed to sleep in the house overnight so when my brother returns late, banging on the gate to be let in, she wakes me again and we go and open it. She scolds him for being late but she does it quietly so that my father doesn't hear.

In that house we are many. Samina the eldest, strong and straight-backed; Khalid, his cheeks low-hanging and fat with the privilege of his sex; Naz – fiery and inconsistent; then me; then Neelam – gentle and quiet; and finally Kaukab the baby. We argue and laugh and conspire; we fuss over clothes and hair and embroidery. My brother seems vexed by our occasional feuds and the heat and light we produce; along with my father he is one of just two men in the house. He is often gruff and spoilt but I know that he loves us unconditionally. A heavy weight hangs on his shoulders: five whole sisters, each to be kept safe, educated, and then married well.

But it is not just the eight of our family that fill the house. Hookum Deen works in our small aluminium factory, pressing the pots and pans, the ladles and trays. He is an efficient, kindly man with dark eyes, a nose like the side of a mountain and a moustache the colour of midnight. He does all sorts of odd jobs too – bringing our hot lunches in tiffin boxes to school every day: a couple of soft chapatis, bhindi gosht or tarka daal and a salad of translucent mouli and carrots as red as bricks. Our friends enviously eye the steaming contents until we share with them.

I am just ten when I am given an unsolicited gift. A long thin rectangle of material to be gathered up, slung over your shoulders and draped over your chest. I soon conclude that the dupatta is the most annoying and impractical thing ever created. It becomes wrapped too tightly round my neck, it trails in the dust or gets caught in the spokes of bicycles. It is so cumbersome and infuriating that I often screw it up into a ball or tie it somewhere while I play my games. I return from school and my mother's eyes clamp on to me.

'Where is your *dupatta*?'

I clutch my neck where it should be.

'Oh, no!'

Her face is screwed up in despair and anger. She slaps her forehead theatrically.

'I don't believe this. Again? How many times now?'

This is a question that on no account should be answered.

'You'll have to find it. Think! Where did you leave it?'

I try to remember the point at which I finally lost patience with it.

But my mother is already summoning a servant to go and find Hookum Deen. He appears, wiping his hands on a rag.

'*Jee, Begum saab*?'

But when he sees me standing there, he immediately gets on his bicycle. He has had to do this many times. I hop on the back sheepishly, sitting sideways clutching on to the little seat on the rear wheel as he launches us out of the gates and back into the dusty city and the rising afternoon heat. I anxiously scan the side of the road for the white dupatta in case it has flown off and settled in a ditch. I have lost three already; carelessly dropped in the road or left in a tonga, no doubt taken by a girl whose delighted eyes settled upon it. My only hope is that I have left it at school, somewhere safe. We stop outside the gates and I leap off. I run to the backyard and search everywhere for it – checking all the places I have discarded it before: spread on top of a bush, tied to a pole – nothing. I am just about to give up and yield to the wrath of my mother when I see a tiny white dot dancing behind a tree. I run towards it and there it is: my abandoned dupatta tied tightly to a low branch, flapping sternly at me in the afternoon breeze. I clutch it to my chest and run out, waving it at Hookum Deen triumphantly. He says a few words of prayer as I climb back on the bicycle. As we gather speed I raise my hand victoriously and the thin white veil trails behind us in the perfect sky.

Mistri-Jee fixes everything – including the machinery in our aluminium factory where he is the manager. And it is he who drives our black car, my father's pride and joy. My father calls three of us – me, Naz and Neelam – and we race down the stairs and jump in the back. Mistri-Jee stands in front of the car in a clean, crisp white shalwar turning a handle at the front to make it start, my father in the front passenger seat with his walking stick by his legs. We drive to Nandipur Canal and stare at the murky water, preferring it to the stagnant atmosphere of home.

The money collector is Sharoo, although his reluctant moustache suggests that he is much too young for such an important job. He gathers money from the shopkeepers who have bought pots and pans from us. He always has his shiny black book and pen with him, nervously chewing the top of the pen as he arrives to account for everything to my father. He cycles the two and a half miles into the centre of Gujranwala and back to settle debts, pay our electricity bills and bring back books and stationery for us.

One day he appears before we have even had our breakfast. He rings the bell on his bicycle a few times and we look at each other in surprise. He bundles in noisily, covered in sweat and dust.

'*Bhaji*! I've seen the results! You have both passed, *Masha'allah*! And – so have I!'

He does a little dance in the hall and we stare, taking in what he has said.

Like my sister Naz and I, Sharoo has passed his matriculation exams. It's his third attempt. Because he works every day, he hasn't been able to study the way we have and has fallen short a few times. He is elated, the first person in his family to pass his matric. For my sister Naz it is also a huge relief. She had been trailing behind and had performed poorly in her preliminary exam. We shared a room and at night when I was studying she would beg me to turn out the light so she could sleep.

'We'll study in the morning!' she would moan. 'Enough now. Put that light out!'

But I didn't trust myself to wake up early so I kept going. She would turn dramatically on her side and go to sleep. When her results came out, my father had a sharp word with her and told her she had to do better. So she had reluctantly stayed up with me and it had worked. She got 624 out of 1000.

Meanwhile I had one of the best results in the school and won a scholarship to college but when my father wrote down my marks, he looked at them inscrutably and then leaned back in his chair.

'780 out of 1000. A decent mark.'

There was a silence; something else was coming.

'But you know you could have done even better, don't you?'

I wasn't sure that I could have but I noticed the ghost of a smile on his face. That was his way of saying well done.

Sharoo's father Mamma Deena wipes the tears from his eyes as he takes in the news. He is in his sixties and has seven other children. He wears a small turban and dhoti and his white moustache sits more confidently on his face than his son's does. He walks to the market every day to collect the lamb and chicken. In summer he brings okra, turnip, gourd and long green beans; in winter we have potato, carrots, spinach, peas and cauliflower. When the sun is high we sweeten our mouths with mangoes, melons and plums; as the temperature drops we sprinkle salt and pepper on orange and guava halves. Bananas are scarce. Once my brother went to East Pakistan to play in a football tournament and brought back two dozen. We ate one a day, slowly, silently, savouring the mild sweetness and the strange sticky texture.

On the open fire in the kitchen my mother makes every kind of food – frying the onions to just the right deep colour, getting the balance of ginger, garlic and coriander just right, simmering it and reducing it to the perfect caramel texture. She can make a delicious meal from the blandest vegetable – potatoes, peas, beans – and daal so soft yet intense that you could cry. She marries meat and vegetables together expertly: cauliflower and lamb, chicken and spinach, lamb and okra. Her koftas and eggs are sublime, her mince and gourd indescribable.

The only meal I cannot enjoy fully is murgh shorba.

There is no better flavour than that of a fat chicken bred outside and fed on corn. I slurp up the intense soup and do not waste a drop. But I never get a leg; one goes to my father and one to my brother. I make do with a thigh or breast piece. I ask my mother if I will ever be able to have the leg piece and she shakes her head. She tries to convince me to eat the wing but it tastes dry. So I watch and wait for years, wondering if I will ever find out how it tastes. And just when I have given up, my brother goes away on a short trip and the chicken leg appears on my plate. My mum glances at me, her face blank. It is everything I hoped it would be: the meat is light and dark and falls away from the bone when you prod it with your roti. I eat every drop slowly – sinking my teeth into the chicken, sucking up all the smoky and intensely flavoured soup, stripping the bones and crunching them like sugar cane.

Apart from my father, we all eat together sitting on the low wooden stools in the kitchen. It is a quiet and quick interlude. I always feel as if I have eaten something sweet and beautiful; my mother looks as though something bitter has lodged in her throat. I make approving noises but she never looks up; she just continues chewing away at the invisible thing that can never be swallowed. When she makes the chapatis she keeps hers wrapped in a separate cloth. Before she sits down to eat she washes her plate and glass again – both are kept separate from everyone else's. My mother is never at ease.

*

'Baby!'

A voice travels up the stairs summoning me and I snap out of my thoughts. My mother motions that I should go and I respectfully smooth my hands over her shins, rub my hands together to signal that I have finished, adjust my dupatta over my chest and in a low voice I say to her: 'Ummi, come downstairs. Let's eat.'

She turns her head to me slowly as if it is made of the thinnest china and fixes me with her small dark eyes. When it emerges, her voice is as flat and dry as the Kharan Desert.

'No. Today I will not breathe the same air as that woman.'

*

My father's house was built in 1928. It took a year and a half to construct, with labourers transporting materials on the backs of buffaloes and laden in carts. Twenty years later we complain that the house is in the middle of nowhere, is too old-fashioned and doesn't even have flushing toilets. But my father won't hear a word of criticism. He tells us that when this house was completed people from all over Gujranwala came to stand outside and gawp. Many squatted in the street, their arms folded over their knees, their chins lifting slowly to take in the top floor. So many people assembled that two tea stalls arrived on wheels to take advantage of the crowd.

The house is three storeys tall, with high walls surrounding the roof space. It is set around twenty metres back from the main road which heads into the city centre in one direction and to Hafsabad in the other. A mosque stands on one side; on the other our aluminium factory. Shop owners come from all over the city to inspect and order all sorts of pots and metal implements from us. In the courtyard we tether two buffaloes and the women of the house use the milk to make yoghurt and lassi, tipping it into large earthenware pots. We aren't that keen on the lassi and the excess is distributed to poor people in the town who come to the house with children strapped to their backs. Palm trees are placed in front of the house to break up the red of the brick. Every window has mesh attached to it to keep the mosquitos out and grey wooden shutters help to reduce the catastrophic heat of summer.

The men's living quarters take up the ground floor. There are two formal living rooms and a large internal corridor which we call the cold room. When it is too hot we close all the doors, douse the floors with water, put on the ceiling fan and sleep on charpais. For six months of the year we are engaged in an impossible battle with the heat, moving around the house to outwit it.

In my father's office stands an imposing desk where he signs papers, tots up columns of numbers and plays chess; local people place their money and jewellery in his tall grey safes. The panchayat gathers in the courtyard to settle disputes and my father presides there. Forty chairs are stacked in piles, the woven seats worn out by men who shift uncomfortably as their reparations are decided. They are periodically renewed by the man who comes to repair them, unravelling the thick waxy strips and re-knotting them underneath. Five hookahs stand fat and silver, ready for smoking and sharing. Every day the mashki sprays water on the ground to keep the dust from rising.

Our main living space is on the first floor – the sitting room for visitors, our bedrooms and the kitchen. This floor is also where my father comes to distribute our pocket money on Mondays – an eight-anna piece for all the children – which he plucks from the pockets of his freshly pressed waistcoat.

But it is up on the roof that we really come alive. Here my brother illicitly flies thin kites of acid yellow and powder blue that swoop and climb in the bright skies; he ruthlessly cuts other kites with his string and celebrates as they fall to their dusty end. He clenches his teeth and tries to hang on to his own kite until a superior craft looms over his and chops down his honour, his beloved kite spinning and plummeting into oblivion. Then he yelps and swears and we widen our eyes and cover our ears.

This is also where my sisters and I gather ostensibly to study or shell nuts or work on our embroidery. But we have discovered that on the roof you can hear the music from a stall on the street at the back of our house that sells paan and soft drinks. This is the only place we can listen to music. My father believes that music and gossip magazines will rot our brains and distract us from our studies. But we soon learn about the secret place from where the music travels to us on an east wind. The weaving and dipping film soundtracks on Radio Ceylon make our eyes water and our hearts burst. The tragedy and hopelessness of love makes us yearn for it and fear it. While we creep around secretly listening to music, my father sits glued to the huge radiogram in his sitting room all day. He takes in the cricket commentary, the news and satirical programmes on Radio Pakistan, moving closer and closer, pressing his ear against it as the reception waxes and wanes.

Going to the cinema is also out of the question. But on a college trip to the mountain city of Murree we gorge on three films a day, shocked at our disobedience and greed. When I am eighteen I sneak to the cinema in my burqa with my married sister Naz to see *Zehr-e-Ishq*. We get a horse and cart home and as we climb in, gathering our skirts and veils around us, the driver confirms casually 'Babu Allah Ditta Butt's house?'

Grateful for our burqas to conceal our identities, we tell him that he is mistaken and divert him to my sister's address. This most scandalous news must never make it back to our father.

*

My father is not easy to love; he is intimidating and unsmiling. But I do. By the time I know him properly he is in his seventies and has lived many lives – a childhood in Gujranwala, years working in Kenya for British bosses, and now a patriarch and elder in his home city. Tall and upright, his white shalwar kameez and waist-coat are always immaculately starched and pressed. His eyes are dark like bullets, he has a large square nose, thin lips and few expressions. But the most arresting thing about my father is his skin, the true colour of which has been eaten away by the vitiligo that consumed his father too. His face and hands are swirled with patches of deep brown and white, the skin on his legs the first to go.

He is strict, aloof, distant, the head of a complicated and huge household that is rarely harmonious. He appears to inhabit another world, one he escapes to. He hardly ever joins us as a family, preferring to stay in his own part of the house and seek the uncomplicated company of men. My mother and siblings find him too daunting to talk to and often nominate me to do the negotiating. His standards are high and he demands the best of you at all times. But while he insists that you stick to the rules and follow principles, he does too. He refuses to abandon his responsibilities and always keeps his promises, even if that means my mother has to live only half a life.

A man of strict routine, he wakes at 7 a.m. and drinks a glass of warm water and a cup of tea. Then he slowly climbs the stairs to the third floor and performs circuits of the large room there, sticking close to the walls as his balance deteriorates, until nature takes its course. Then he descends to the second floor to eat his break-fast – always the same: two slices of toast, one fried egg and a cup of tea – while listening to news and cricket commentary on his beloved radio.

His mother had always massaged his tired legs; when he married that task fell to his wife. But soon it passed to his children and again, just like fetching water for my mother in the middle of the night, I find that I am the only one willing to do it. My heart sinks when he summons me as this is not a quick job. Sometimes after half an hour, he appears to have dozed off and I slowly stop, eyeing the door for my escape. Suddenly his voice fills the air.

'Baby, have you fallen asleep?'

'No, father, I–'

'Well come on then.'

He quizzes me about my studies; he is obsessed by my marks. I never really understand why as I know that after college I will have to get married. Nevertheless, we continue in this strange but not unpleasant charade for years.

THREE

Gujranwala, India, 1943

I was supposed to be a boy. The pattern was already set. A girl Samina; a boy Khalid; a girl Naz; and then me. But I was so stubbornly female that my mother turned her face to the wall and cried a thousand tears. The frowning midwife tried to console her by saying that at least I was fat and fair; that I looked like the beautiful white baby on the tins of Glaxo powdered milk. So for the first twenty years of my life I was called 'Baby' instead of my given name Almas.

My mother's tears did not stop. Not only were there now more daughters than sons, but she now had four children – two of them under two years old. She was struggling with the workload and the disappointment. And that is how I lost my older sister before I even knew I had one. My aunt – who hadn't been able to have children – offered to unofficially adopt one-year-old Naz. My mother agreed and so Naz was taken to Lahore to start her new life.

My sister had the full attention of two parents and all the privileges of a sturdy middle-class Lahore upbringing. My uncle made a good living selling fine carpets of silk and wool to local people and rich foreigners; and he could speak English. Naz only wore clothes of silk and georgette and ate the best food. In the summer while the rest of us stewed in the aggressive dry heat of the city, she escaped with her family to cooler hideaways in the hills. They boated on the lake shaped like an eye in Nanital; they sipped lemon water in Mussoorie; they counted the seven hills of Shimla where the air was fresher and thinner and the temperature rarely climbed beyond twenty-five degrees.

But when Naz was six, my uncle died suddenly and without a salary to support them my aunt and sister had to return to Gujranwala to live with us. And so I had my sister back. But what a creature she was. She cried if she had to wear cotton, saying that it irritated her skin. She was picky with her food and refused to eat most of the vegetables that my mother cooked. Accustomed to being the sole child in the family, she struggled to adjust to a large house with many children. She was spoilt and impatient, prone to tantrums and sulks. I eyed her with envy and wonder, this sister born in the same month as me, just one year apart. And yet so dissimilar. She spoke differently, carried herself differently. I felt ungainly and gauche beside her. I coveted her grand clothes and felt dowdy in my cotton shalwars. I became obsessed by a pink silk gharara she owned, dreaming about it most nights. I had never seen such a brightly coloured garment. I longed to run my fingers over it, to see if it felt cold or hot, whether its shocking colour would stain my hands. But my sister forbade me from even touching it.

One day in Spring Naz left the house with my aunt. I watched from a high window as they climbed into a tonga and drove off. The temptation was too much for me and I raced down the corridor to our room, straight to the wardrobe and there at the back in a wooden box I found it, wrapped in tissue paper. I plucked it out and put it on, twirling about in the old spotted mirror, watching the jewelled hem of the skirt dance around my ankles. I kept out of sight of my mother for hours, swishing about in the gharara, feeling like a Mughal princess or a famous actress. I was so intoxicated by the skirt, by the feel of the silk against my legs that I lost track of time. Suddenly I heard the gate squeak open and bang shut. Panicked, I ran back to the room, struggling to get it off and stuff it back into the box but the zip had jammed. My fingers became slick with sweat and kept slipping off the fastening. I heard a cry of pain and looked up to see my sister already standing in the doorway, her eyes wide in horror and anger.

'What are you doing!' she screamed, as I finally got free of the material. 'I told you! You can't touch that. It's mine!'

I pulled my shalwar on and faced her.

'I'm so sorry! I only tried it on for a minute . . .'

Seeing the look in her eyes, I tailed off.

She clenched her teeth in anger and flew to a drawer to extract a pair of scissors.

'No!' I screamed grabbing the skirt to protect it. But she was pulling it from me, her strength phenomenal, the scissors looking grotesque in her tiny hands.

'Don't! If you don't want it, give it to me! Please give it to me!' I wept.

But my sister was set on destruction.

'It's dirty now! You've ruined it! No one can wear it now! I hate you!'

She plunged the scissors into the garment and I heard a sickening ripping sound. I couldn't watch such a beautiful thing being needlessly destroyed so I turned and ran, my tears hot on my face, my bare feet thudding on the floor. Why was I surprised that such a horrible thing could happen in such an unhappy house?

*

For years I felt that what happened next was because I was being punished for taking something that was not mine. I felt inadequate and unimportant beside my sister. She wasn't just better dressed and better spoken than me, she was cleverer at school too. She found everything easy whereas I struggled. The further ahead she went, the further behind I fell. It was pointless. My confidence had disappeared. Inevitably I was summoned to my father's study where he sat looking grave. He clicked off the radio.

'Baby.'

Only he could say an innocent word like 'baby' in such a serious tone. He looked at me levelly. 'What . . . is going on with your studies?'

I searched for the words but they died in my throat. At the age of just six I knew that he would not be able to understand my feelings of jealousy and inadequacy.

'I don't want to go to school' I said weakly. 'I don't like it.'

His expression didn't change, his mouth frozen in a thin straight line.

'Don't want to go to school? Are you mad? You must get your education. I don't want to hear you say that again. Now get on with it and work hard. Understood?'

I nodded, knowing that I couldn't suddenly change how I felt. The gap between me and my sister was too wide and I was about to topple headfirst into it. He turned and switched the radio back on. The conversation was over.

When there was no improvement, my mother said that she couldn't take it any more, that I was making her ill and stressed. She spoke to her sister-in-law, a widow who was a private tutor in Lahore. She agreed to take me in. I was to go and live with her forty-five miles away in Lahore until I improved. I didn't want to go but I had no choice.

Auntie Nafeesa was incredibly strict. She was short and stout, her teeth black from eating too much paan.

She made me study all day and I had to do lots of house-work too. But the worst thing was the other occupants of the house. She had two sons, neither of whom I liked. She told me that Adil who was thirteen was a sahen-jee – one of God's people. But his expressionless face and huge hulking body frightened me. He could not walk or talk and he mostly sat on a charpai all day, waving his arms, making baying noises. Often he rocked the bed so violently that I feared it might topple over. His mother was constantly wiping the dribble from the corners of his mouth. I had to feed him chopped and mushed up food and I felt faint with fear every time; I was terrified that he would bite my fingers off. The older son Ayub was twenty-five and had a foul temper. He appeared to hate his mother and one day after they had argued and she had left the room, he threw a plate after her. I ducked just in time and it span over my head and shattered against the wall. I stood rooted to the spot, confused by the violence around me, wondering how I had ended up in this terrible household.

I began to realise that although my home had not been the happiest, virtually anything would be better than this. And I became desperate to return there. Three months into my stay there was a banging at the gate and in strode my brother Khalid. I rubbed my eyes but it was him. He had arrived unannounced, holding a yellow balloon on a string which he handed to me. I wanted to leap into his arms but he looked blank and uninterested.

I stared up into his face hopefully. Had he come to take me back home?

'I just came to see how you were doing. All OK? Studies good?'

I nodded non-commitally even though I wanted so much to tell him that he must take me back, that this house was full of bad-tempered people who never smiled. He drank his tea, made enquiries of everyone's health and then he was gone, humming a tune, without even a backwards glance towards me. Tears gathered in my eyes. I ran to my room and tied the yellow balloon outside my window where it fluttered in the dust and wind for days.

That day I had a glimpse of the sun in that balloon, of home. I started to study even harder. Eight months after I left, I was back in Gujranwala, ready to take my place in the same year as my sister, much to her annoyance. I crept back into the house where my mother was kneading some atta for the chapatis. She stood back using her forearm to push the hair out of her blank face.

'So, you're back, eh? Straightened yourself out?'

'Yes, Ummi,' I replied, trying to keep my voice level.

She looked to her sister-in-law who nodded.

'Well, thank goodness. Now I have one less thing to worry about.'

I headed to my room, trying not to run.

Baljaffray, Scotland, 1976

From the top of the hill far, far in the distance I can see my three markers: a narrow sandstone castle, a clump of ancient trees as thin as dandelion stalks and beyond that the tower blocks of Glasgow pointing straight into the sky like stalled rockets.

My feet are planted on the ground on either side of my sky blue and silver tricycle. The street is quiet, the sky is indecently blue, holding the promise of another fizzing late summer's day. I have completed my fourteenth circuit of the street – huffing and puffing up the incline, a tight half-circle of the cul-de-sac, and back down again, past the busy lizzies of No. 11 and the crazy paving of No. 3. We are No. 1, the first house on the drive, on the brow of yet another hill that rises to meet us.

There's a scratch on my new black patent shoes so I lift my foot to rest it on the front wheel and try to rub it off with a wet finger. I rock impatiently back and forth, glancing at the front windows of my house, the curtains still stubbornly drawn, nothing stirring. Where is everyone? This is a big day. This is my first day at school.

I have been up since 6 a.m. That is when I went into the next room to wake my sleeping parents, tugging at the quilt covering my mum saying I didn't want to be late. One eye peeked out of a mass of curly black hair and she shooed me back to my room and deposited me in the top bunk, above my sleeping three-year-old brother. But it is no use. I creep back in at 7 a.m. and pester her until she gives up and helps me dress, a finger on her lips to warn me not to wake Imran. I pull on a tiny grey pleated skirt, a white shirt, a white, orange and brown tie and a brown blazer. My brand new socks are box-fresh white against my brown skin and my mum ties a polka-dot ribbon in my curly hair. The uniform has hung in the wardrobe I share with my brother for weeks and I inhale its newness, its promise. My older brother and sister have been in school for years and often come back with tales of bruises and homework and playtime and school dinners and I cannot wait to do the same. So I am awake, dressed and fed by about 7:30 a.m.

Here on my tricycle, I pedal furiously up and down the hill, my white socks skimming perilously near the oily bicycle chain. It is so sunny that I am squinting; my expression is made even more pronounced by the injury I acquired a few days ago to my right eye by walking into a rose bush. It has crusted over but resulted in my eye stretching up at the corner making me look lopsided. My dad makes me pose for far too many Polaroids and Super 8s with my little brother who looks hot and

bothered and starts to cry. Then my mum takes me to
school. We stand at the end of a queue in the playground
and wait to go in. Mum is wearing a white broderie
blouse with puffy short sleeves and white trousers, her
thick hair tied back in a ponytail. I spy a girl with a
polka-dot ribbon in her hair too and show her all my
teeth. Her mum clocks me smiling at her.

'Och look, Carol, why don't you go and play with
the nice Chinky girl?'

Carol and I lace fingers and head inside.

*

School is everything I want it to be and more. I am
first in and last out, lingering at the end of the day to
precisely pack my brown satchel. There isn't anything I
don't like about school: the lessons, the lunch, the queu-
ing, the teachers, the rules. I suck it all up and still want
more. I make friends easily, whooping and screeching at
playtime and kicking footballs with and sometimes at
the boys. I am a relentless show off. I want to be at or
near the centre of attention at all times. I am so desperate
to be in the school magazine that I copy a poem about
a stickleback out of a book then shove it behind the
bookcase and enjoy the admiration of my teachers and
friends until someone cleans behind the furniture and
my lie is exposed.

At one point there is a short period when me, my
older brother and my sister are at the same school. A

talent show is held in the gym. A freckly boy tap-dances along a narrow bench singing the song from the Topic advert – 'What has a haz-el-nut in ev'ry bite? Thick milk choc-o-late for your dee-light . . . ?' then he lobs a Topic bar into the crowd and there is a frantic scramble. A bored-looking girl does silent cartwheels. Another plays 'Three Blind Mice' on her recorder after two false starts. Then it's my sister's turn. I hold my breath. She does two impressions – David Bellamy and Magnus Pike. Everyone erupts into applause and I nod proudly as they nudge me and ask: 'Is thaaaat your sisturrrrr?'

*

I am busy at school, busy with my friends, with my fibs, with writing stories and with looking after my little brother. When the playtime bell rings I sprint out of my classroom into the playground, round the corner to find him standing on his own as usual, his school jumper covered in crumbs, already eating the remnants of the single Chocolate Digestive my mum gives us as a playpiece. He looks at me blankly, dropping the cling film wrapper to the ground and eyeing my biscuit and I give it to him. After he has eaten that, there is not much else to do but trudge around the playground. He never plays with anyone in his class. He just keeps looking at the ground or into the distance, laughing and talking to himself or concentrating on something on his hand or in the air. When the bell rings I deliver him back to his class queue and wait until he is safely in the care of the teacher, then I run back to my own classroom, always the last one, my tummy rumbling.

One day I see a teacher trying to get him to put his blazer on before he goes outside.

'Put this on please.'

He looks through her and keeps walking.

'Blazer. Please. It's chilly,' she says, raising her voice.

I bridle, not understanding why she is talking to him as if he can't hear.

'He's not deaf, miss, he can hear you,' I interject.

'Well, what is he then?' she asks, slightly exasperated.

I don't really know the answer to that.

'Does he speak English?'

'Yes of course!' I snort.

She looks expectantly, still holding the blazer.

I search for the word my mother uses.

'Special! He's just . . . special.'

'Right,' she says. 'Well, special or not, he has to wear his blazer.'

She thrusts it into my hands and I go to find him.

Every day we walk the perimeter of the playground together. Sometimes I ask him about his class or teacher. He rarely answers, stuck in the glue of his thoughts; if I persist too much, he starts to cry. I look around at the other children in his class and wonder if any of them could be friends with him. I ask a little blonde girl if she will play with my brother for a Chocolate Digestive but she shakes her head. I'm desperate to go and play with my friends but the sight of him walking about on his own at the edge of everyone else breaks my heart and I cannot leave him.

One day I give my biscuit to him and tell him that I am just going to play with my friends, but that I can see him from where I am. Everything is fine until I see an older boy approach and say something to him. The boy laughs but there is no reaction from my brother. This happens for a few days and then finally my brother starts to cry. I am there in seconds.

'What's wrong?'

He lifts his little curly head.

'Bad boy. Calling . . . me DanDan. Every. Day.'

'DanDan?' I repeat, confused. But my brother has said enough. He is staring at his hands again, lost in his own world, humming gently. He is smiling at something now but his face is still wet with tears.

I run after the boy who is older than me but around the same size.

'Oi you – leave my wee brother alone.'

He wheels round.

'I didnae dae nothin'.'

'He says you keep calling him DanDan. Why d'ya call him that?'

I am inches from his face. His eyes widen and then he folds himself over, laughing.

'Whaaaa? Hahahahaa. Naw. Not DanDan. RAMJAM,' he says triumphantly.

'What's a Ramjam?' I demand.

The boy is still laughing.

'Wha'? You've no' heard of a Ramjam? But you're wan too.'

He draws closer, like he is explaining something very complex.

'A Ramjam! A Paki. A sambo. A w–'

Bang.

He doesn't get his final word out because I have shoved him in the face.

'Don't call my brother that! I'll fight you!'

The boy has lost his balance and is sitting on the ground, looking surprised. I stand above him, furious and shocked at my strength. A tiny thread of blood appears under one of his nostrils.

I can hear a commotion behind me. It is my little brother leaping around, rocking on his heels, laughing his head off and clapping wildly.

'Hahahahahahaaaaaa do it again! AGAIN!'

Other children are looking aghast. A teacher comes running out and pulls me away by the elbow.

'WHAT are you doing? We do not fight in this school!'

'He called my brother a bad word!'

'Miss, she just hit me for nothing!' comes the whiny voice.

The teacher looks at me.

'That's not true!'

'Well WHY did you hit him?'

'He called my little brother a Ramjam.'

The teacher blinks.

'A what?'

'A Ramjam. It's like a P– . . . a P- ' I trailed off, not able to say the word. I am only six and I already know its power.

'Well?'

'It's a naughty word.'

'Well it doesn't sound very naughty to me. Inside, now. You're going to be in big trouble for this.'

Her grip on the flesh of my arm is hurting me.

'But . . . I need to look after my brother, my mum says I can't leave–'

'Inside. Now. Shocking behaviour. We. Are. Not. Savages.'

As I am pulled inside, I glance back at my brother who is staring at his right hand again, on to his next dream or mania, unprotected, vulnerable. The boy has got up and is wiping his nose. He walks off. I have to write out fifty lines; but he never bothers my little brother again. Largely because, a month later, the headteacher asks my parents to take Imran out of the school because they can't cope with him. I get to keep my playtime snack but I miss him.

*

That house on the hill had the best of us; we were happy there.

Mum and Dad, four kids, growing and elbowing, shouting and crying, leaping from sofas, banging heads, scratching faces and bickering. Our house became even fuller with a constant stream of visitors and guests: the posh cousins we hosted from London, the relatives from Pakistan in flares and wide-collared shirts, the huge birthday parties and endless friends knocking on the door to see if we wanted to come out and play.

Childhood suited me. I was constantly bloodied or dirty, always being hoisted into and out of hot bubble baths. An inner motor was propelling me to live at one hundred miles an hour. I bundled into rooms and interrupted conversations; I spoke to strangers in super-market queues and on ferries; I wriggled my bottom into the centre of long lines of aunties on sofas. A huge head of curls announced me before I even spoke. I existed. No one could ignore me.

And I loved that house. The little dining room at the rear of the house bridged the living room and the kitchen. In there stood a white Formica table that was always being extended for parties and guests with six revolving matching chairs; a central ceiling lamp with a cable made of what looked like curly telephone cord could be pulled down to illuminate our meals. On this table I mixed and shaped plates of white rice and brown masoor daal into a delicious glutinous mountain and devoured the lot. Here I watched my dad eat everything at lightning pace, his jaw clicking as he chomped on meat, rice, bones and salad. When the rice pot was empty he would ask my mum for it and spend ten minutes bashing at the fried-on crispy remnants at the bottom with a metal spoon, telling us all over the din for the one hundredth time that the poori was the most delicious bit. Often everyone would leave and I would have to stay until I had finished my pint glass of lukewarm full-cream milk. My mother, who had imported her nutritional beliefs from Pakistan, would park a spiteful-looking green broom in the corner of the room as an incentive. On this table we fought over puddings and portion sizes; we spent ages measuring exactly the same levels of Coca Cola into glasses. My big brother polished off an entire Sara Lee strawberry gateau after my sister foolishly bet him that he couldn't. After school we ate Mr Kipling cakes, corned beef sandwiches and hissing glasses of lemonade or Irn Bru. We were always hungry.

At the weekends we hauled a single mattress from one of our beds, placed it over the stairs and slid down it. It was mayhem and there was often blood and bruises as we collided with the bannister or the wall. On Sunday mornings we all piled into our parents' bed. If you were lucky you got to lie next to an adult and not a sharp-el-bowed or farting sibling. Dad was loud, his laugh could burst your eardrums and he always smelt reassuringly of Birds Eye beef burgers and stale Brylcreem. If you ended up next to Mum, it was like lying next to a marble statue. Her skin was cold, pale and glass smooth – she had no hair on her arms and legs unlike us. And she always smelt of Oil of Ulay or Vaseline which she rubbed into her face and hands every night. If she had just woken up her densely curly hair was all over the place – and she was always slapping at it and smoothing it down.

The phone rang early one Sunday – too early - before we had even dived under their duvet. I climbed down from my bunk bed past my sleeping brother and went next door. Dad was on the phone, listening quietly. There was a stillness and attentiveness to him that I had never seen. My mum had her forearm drawn across her eyes which seemed odd. Both my parents were doing things they didn't normally do. I stared, as other siblings appeared rubbing their eyes.

'What's happening?' we asked.

'What's wrong with Mummy?'

She let out a gulp and a sob.

I realised that my mum was crying – something I had never seen her do. Thankfully she was shielding her eyes – I don't think I could have borne to see her tears, this Fairy Queen who always blotted away mine and made me feel better.

My dad put his hand over the phone, his face flat and grey and whispered to us: 'Mummy is upset because Uncle Javed has died.'

My mum let out another sob and I dissolved into tears too.

Glasgow, Scotland, 1973

I don't see the lorry until it is too late. A grey and orange metal box, it swings in front of me and I slam on my brakes to avoid hitting it. The force makes the whole car skid and swing round and for a moment I think I am going to die. My hands are in the air, not on the steering wheel: I am no longer in control of the car or where it is heading. I screw my eyes tightly shut and as the car comes to a halt my head plunges forwards and then back against the headrest. I open my eyes. I am alive. But something is wrong. I move my arms and legs. My head is spinning, I feel nauseous. Then I realise that I am not moving but everyone else is. Cars are racing past. I hear them beeping their horns at me and as the vomit rises in my throat I finally understand that my car has spun round on the outside lane of the M8 and is now pointing in the wrong direction. I need to turn the car round but how do you do a three-point turn when cars are whizzing past you? I start to edge forward, my hand shaking as I struggle with the gears. Some cars slow down, I presume to help. But they are just full of men with hard faces, sneering and telling me I'm going the wrong way and that I'm a stupid cow. One van passes and the young men inside just stare open-mouthed and burst into laughter, whacking each other on the shoulders in disbelief. I eventually get the car facing the right way. I drive slowly off the motorway, my back slick with sweat, pick up my son from nursery and go home. Then I phone my husband, the shock finally leaking from my body as I weep into the receiver.

'Almas, are you OK? My God!' Arif asks. 'I'm coming home right now!'

'No, there's no need. You'll be home in a few hours.'

My little son is playing happily with his cars, the sight of his huge hair and big teeth giving me much needed comfort.

'Is . . . is the baby OK?' asks my husband.

I rub my huge stomach. The baby is still kicking.

'Yes. Of course. Everything is fine, Insha'allah.'

Baljaffray, Scotland, 1980

I wish I had a granny. A real one I can cuddle when I'm sad or run away from when she tries to kiss me. One who will sometimes pick me up from school and take me home for my tea; who will buy me extra birthday presents and feed me too many sweets; one who puts too much butter on my sandwiches and winks at me from the kitchen counter. That's what my friends' grannies are like. A specific breed of Scottish woman – quick to laugh and judge, rich in hankies and Pan Drops. A daunting army of cardigans and handbags, always in the hairdressers or the bingo.

I have two grandmothers but see them rarely; they live thousands of miles away in a magical land of smoke and dust and marigolds. My father's mother, my Daddi-Ummi, decided on our names – issuing them over crackly phone lines from Lahore. My mother's mother is my Nano-Jaan. She lives with my Aunt Samina in Lahore. But I cannot recall either of their faces. I keep secret from my parents the treacherous thought that the nearest I have to a grandmother is Helen, whom I see every day, who has looked after me from birth, who wears a cardigan and looks like a proper Scottish granny.

On the day I forget my P.E. kit I see her at the school fence waving at me with my little gym bag. I run to her, my face open and happy, with a wide grin.

'Thanks Lelly!'

'Och ye'd forget yer ain heid if it wisnae screwed on!' she laughs.

I walk back into the playground, waving at her.

'Who's that lady?' ask my friends.

I look over at her. She is still standing there, smiling in the sun, with kindness on her face, sweeping back little bits of hair that are blowing into her eyes.

'Oh that's my gran,' I say slackly, caught up in the moment.

'No it's not!'

I bristle.

'Yes it is, it's my gran . . .'

'But she's got white skin!'

'So?' I say aggressively.

My friends decide to leave it and we go back to playing hopscotch.

Later the teacher shows us how to write a letter. She asks us to write one to our grannies.

I decide to write one to my Nano. I have met her in Pakistan but all I can remember is her crinkly eyes, her soft voice and low laugh on the end of a phone line. I know nothing about her life; I can't even speak the same language. So I opt to write a letter like everyone else. No-one will ever know that the two don't match up.

> *Dear Gran,*
>
> *How are you! I am sorry to hear that you broke your ankle. I will bring you some Chocolate Limes because I know they are your favourites. Can you still go bowling? It sounds lots of fun! I like pancakes the best with Stork on them, do you? They are yummy. What are you watching on TV? Oh well, I must be going now. I'll come and see you soon.*
>
> *Love, Aasmah.*

I sit back and contemplate my work, wondering if it will be good enough to be put up on the wall. But to my horror the teacher says that we are to take them home in the envelopes and get the addresses from our parents because we are going to post them tomorrow. My face falls. I now have a made-up letter to a granny who doesn't exist, who certainly doesn't live in Glasgow or like Chocolate Limes.

All day and evening, the letter burns a hole in my school bag. I am too embarrassed to admit to my mum that I haven't written a letter to my real grandmother. The next day the teacher tells us all to put our envelopes on the table and she will bring us a stamp each. The girl next to me keeps staring at my blank envelope then shoots her hand up.

'Yes, Wendy?'

'Aasmah hasn't written her granny's address, miss!'
I glare at her.
'Aasmah, hurry up, please. We're going to post them.'
I look at her. I don't know my granny's address and I am pretty sure that a fourteen pence stamp won't be enough for a letter to Pakistan. My mum has special thin blue folded letters that she fills with her distinctive writing and posts to her family in places with names like Lahore, Gujranwala, Rawalpindi and Karachi. The teacher is still looking at me expectantly; other kids have spun round in their chairs to gawp. So I pick up my pencil and write what I hope is a fictitious address in Glasgow:

Granny Mrs Mir
53 Cherry Drive
Glasgow
G61 G61

*

My Nano comes to visit us the following year. She is small but mighty, grabbing us for a cuddle as we pass by, showering us with kisses that are too wet and words we do not understand but which sound like ancient poetry and magic spells. She smells of another world – unfamiliar, unperfumed, neutral; of material bought from Lahore and stitched in tailor's sunless rooms; of clothes stored next to peppercorns to discourage moths. She wears a shalwar kameez and keeps her dupatta on her head, constantly pulling it over her hair, smoothing it over her temples and looping it behind her tiny ears. She doesn't have many teeth and her voice is low, her tongue clicking on her bare gums. When she laughs she keeps it within her body, her eyes crinkling as she chuckles away, sending the laughter back into her stomach. My mother calls her 'Ummi' and I fully understand that this is not just my grandmother, this is my mother's mother. I stare hard at her, gobsmacked that my mum – so young and energetic – will ever look like my grandmother. And that I will look like my mother does now – with a husband and children and a car and a dressing table full of gold barrels of lipstick and bottles of Oil of Ulay.

My grandmother prays five times a day, folding and unfolding her prayer mat and standing with her hands on top of each other, looking to Mecca and back, muttering words that sound grave and comforting. I have never seen anyone pray; it is like she is in a trance. My mother tries to get us to say short verses from the Qu'ran at bedtime but they are more comforting bookends to the day than anything of any religious significance.

La ilaha illallah muhummadur Rasulullah
Bismillah ir-Rahman ir-Rahim

I hear my grandmother say these words as she stands and kneels in a corner of the room and I feel connected to her. My little brother, who is six or seven, creeps up on her while she is praying and whips off her dupatta, then runs away with it. I regularly see her chasing him up the street, sometimes ducking under the little railings between ours and the next house. Helen often joins in the pursuit too. Before she prays, Nano spends ages washing her hands and then she bends her legs and puts her feet into the sink and scrubs them clean too. Helen marvels at her athleticism; Nano is just ten years older than her.

I watch my Nano closely. She loves us all but she saves a particular love for my little brother – constantly hugging him and speaking lovingly into his face and smoothing his hair as he protests or tries to pull away. She knows he is special and her love for him becomes special too. When she is around us or busy doing something she seems happy and connected. At other times, I observe her sitting on her own in the lounge on the edge of the sofa, plucking at her sleeves and constantly rearranging her dupatta. She talks to herself in a low voice. I wish I could understand what she is saying – it sounds plaintive and anguished but it is so soft, so secret. Her face is often collapsed into sadness, the air around her is devastated with her sighs.

'Why does Nano talk to herself?' I ask my mum.

My mother considers this for a while and replies:

'Because she has a lot of things in her head to think about.'

'Is she sad?'

'Not any more.'

'Why was she sad?'

'I'll explain to you one day.'

I watch how she eats – the exact opposite of my dad who loves food. He piles his plate high and laughs and talks as he eats; my Nano eats little and slowly. My eyes nearly fall out of my head when I see her scoop up her rice with her fingers not a spoon like the rest of us. When she drinks from a bottle of Coke she doesn't put it into a glass, or drink it with a straw or press it against her lips; she lifts it up, sticks her tongue out and pours it down her throat, making sure the bottle doesn't touch her lips. She drinks half the bottle in one draught, rests and then has the other half. I never tire of watching it.

She likes fish and chips too but her biggest pleasure is a Bounty. She eats it slowly, chewing it over and over with her few remaining teeth, making it last a ridiculously long time – at least twenty minutes – where I would have hoovered it up in three. She then smooths the wrapper for about five minutes until it is perfectly flat before putting it in her pocket.

One day after school we are eating biscuits, drinking Coke, and doing our homework. Helen is looking after us and suddenly Nano starts flapping her arms and protesting in Urdu, getting up from the dining table. My little brother looks up momentarily at the fuss then goes back to his colouring. He never stays in the lines. Helen and I try to get to the bottom of what is wrong but neither of us speak Urdu. Nano leaves the room. When my mum comes home later we tell her what happened. She then tells us that there was a picture of a mouse in our colouring book and Nano has a phobia of mice – she can't even hear the word or look at one in a book.

'But why Mum?'

'She hates dirty things – haven't you noticed?'

It is true that my Nano is always washing her hands, soaping furiously up to her elbows, scooping water from the tap over her forearms and hands, then closing the taps with her elbows, never touching them. She doesn't like door handles or buttons and is always standing at the sink, scrubbing away at something or some part of her.

*

We are the joke-shop generation. We amuse ourselves with whoopee cushions, mousetrap chewing gum, itching powder and stink bombs. Hardly a day passes when a boy doesn't lob one of those ampoules of yellow liquid into the playground and fill it with the unmistakable stench of rotten eggs. Whoopee cushions are placed on the chairs of teachers and no one owns up. I notice it's only boys who do it and who often find themselves at the end of the deputy headmaster's belt. But I am intoxicated by the hilarity and infamy of a successful practical joke, so I beg my mum to let me buy some itching powder. She relents but tells me I'm not to actually use it on anyone. I keep it hidden for days, desperate to deploy it, looking for a victim. It would of course be more fun to use it on a smelly, annoying boy, but I only have access to the girls' clothes in the gym changing rooms. I hatch my plan for one afternoon's P.E. lesson but I make a fatal mistake. Not able to keep my clever idea to myself I tell my friend Shona who looks scandalised but promises to keep it secret. I empty a little bit of the weird fluffy mixture into Janet Regan's tights and rejoin the netball lesson. Janet doesn't appear in the lesson after lunch but the head teacher's secretary does. She comes in, speaks to the teacher who takes her spectacles off and nods. When the bell goes for break she shouts: 'All the girls stay behind, please.'

I start to panic. The boys take ages to shuffle out, intrigued by what's happening. Girls are never in trouble. The teacher comes to stand in front of her desk then perches on it.

'Someone in this room put itching powder in Janet Regan's tights. Would anyone like to own up?'

Absolute silence. I feel myself turning red and look at Shona. She looks like she is going to cry.

The silence grows. I can hear the boys screeching outside and suddenly I long to be out there, running on the grass verges, whooping and thundering in the playground, breathing the cold clear air in, instead of being in this oppressive classroom with everyone sitting like statues. I am nine and I am a coward. I don't own up. But I don't have to. Shona bursts into tears, bowing under the weight of the terrible secret I thrust upon her. The teacher's eyes settle on her in surprise.

'Right all of you can go. Shona, stay behind.'

She looks at me in horror, her cheeks red, her bottom lip wobbling. I wait until all the girls have left and then the teacher looks at me irritably. The door closes.

'I didn't ask you to stay behind.'

'It was me. Not Shona.'

The teacher's face clears. This makes much more sense. The noisy, attention-seeking girl rather than the one who blushes if you even speak to her.

'You can go Shona.'

She hobbles out.

'Aasmah, go and wait outside the deputy head's office.'

I get up and walk to Mr Baird's office. I have never spoken to him and have only seen him at assemblies and occasionally stamping through the playground in a black cape like a demented bat. He is a furious-looking man with a thin face and horn-rimmed glasses. I sit heavily on the hard chair outside the office as pupils walk past, staring and whistling and muttering under their breath.

'Haha, you're in the shite.'

'Ye're gonnae get belted.'

I sit up. I hadn't even thought about that. Suddenly I am terrified. I don't want to get the belt. Will my hand hurt? How many times will he hit me? Do they belt girls? My dad will go crazy; my mum will be so upset, embarrassed. I sit there for ages, feeling seasick, my thighs sticking painfully to the plastic chair. The bell goes for the end of playtime and I watch the other kids trudging to lessons. I envy their freedom to get on with the school day – I am suspended outside the deputy headmaster's office, waiting for the unknown. The door opens suddenly and I jump. A boy I recognise from Primary 7 comes out, nursing his hand, his face thick with tears. I look at him in horror, taking it all in.

'Don't do that again!' comes the voice from inside. He slopes off. I wait, glued to the chair.

'Right Irene, I'm away for my lunch–'

He reaches the door and sees me.

'Another one? For goodness sake. In here, now!'

I stumble in, past Irene, who is putting her lipstick on.

He sits behind his desk, consults a piece of yellow paper and looks at me over the top of his vile glasses.

'Which one are you?'

I can't even speak.

'Ah, itching powder.' He takes his glasses off. 'Like practical jokes do you?'

I shake my head in shame, all the while scanning his desk for the legendary belt. Where is it?

'Would you like it if someone put itching powder in your clothes?'

I shake my head again. I think I might cry soon. When is he going to tell me if I am getting the belt and will he give me some time to mentally prepare myself for it? He considers me for a minute. His stomach rumbles loudly.

'Stupid behaviour. Appalling. Don't do it again. You'll have to write one hundred lines: "I must not play practical jokes on my classmates." Got it? On my desk by tomorrow. Off you go.'

I stare at him in shock. That's it?

'Well off you go then! Show's over.'

I tiptoe out of the door into the corridor and back to the classroom. Everyone stares at me as I find my way to my desk; they've all worked out what I have done. Janet Regan is back and is glaring at me with a red face. Her tights are off and she has a wet towel wrapped round her ankles. The teacher gives me a disappointed look and hands me a letter for my parents. At the end of the day I pack my bag and leave the building, most of my friends giving me a silent and wide berth. But as soon as we are out of the school gates, they crowd round me, wanting to know what happened in Mr Baird's office.

'Oh my God – what happened?' asks one.

'You can't say God!' shouts another.

'Tell us – did you get the belt?'

'I have to write a hundred lines . . .' I offer.

'Aye, but did ye get the belt?' they insist.

I consider this for a moment, see the excitement in their eyes, and understand how famous I will be.

'Yes. Yes I did,' I lie.

'WOW!'

They throng around me all the way home, asking loads of questions. I love the attention. Did it hurt? Did I cry? I am a hero, a rebel. I've joined the upper echelons of cool kids. It was easy. I am so capricious: one moment ready to wet my pants in fear, the next lying barefacedly to be more popular.

My mum reads the letter. She tells me off but she isn't as angry as I thought she would be. She and my dad are too distracted by talk of a new house. I ignore this. Why would they want to live anywhere but here?

*

Sadly, my parents do want to live somewhere else. They've found a bigger house about a mile away which might as well be in another country. We don't get a say. I am heartbroken to be leaving my school, the estate, all my friends, the burn, everything.

'But you'll have your own bedroom!' says my mum, her eyes shining with excitement.

I don't really want my own bedroom. I like sharing with my little brother. This house is fine.

After we leave the house on the hill, everything falls away. I pine for it for twenty years. As we follow the removal van down the hill in our car, I feel like I have left something behind. I turn to look and see that my bedroom window has been left open.

'Mum, we haven't closed the window!' I yell, convinced that she will stop, that I will be able to run up those stripey stairs one more time.

My mother stretches her tiny body to peer at me in the rear-view mirror but keeps driving.

'It doesn't matter. The new people will close it.'

The New People. Who were they? I hate them already. Was there a lucky girl my age who would find all my secret hiding places; who would slither around on that carpet with her Sindy dolls and felt tip pens; who would spend almost every day at the burn at the bottom of the hill as I had; who would sit on the window ledge at the front and become the new Queen of Baljaffray? I feel dizzy and wind down the window to gulp some air. I must have known that things would never be the same again; that by gaining a new house we would have to lose something.

I watch the house grow smaller as we slip down the hill. Too late I turn to look for my three markers – the castle, the clump of trees, the tower blocks – but they have already disappeared.

FOUR

Lahore, Pakistan, January, 1966

The woman snips the end of a thin paper cone. A smell of bitter smoke and herbs fills the air. She squeezes it and a brown-green paste appears. She works briskly and silently, gripping my hand with one of hers and weaving the cone in and out and around my palms. I dare not move; I do not want to break her concentration. She paints on exquisite loops and flowers. When it dries and cakes she scrapes it off, sponges it with a clean cloth and applies oil, pushing it deep into my palms with her strong thumbs, making the colour more intense.

'You have proper ladies' hands,' she pronounces, breaking the silence at last, and I raise my eyebrows and look at them afresh. I had always thought my hands too petite, my nails too small, impossible to grow or paint. She starts to push at my cuticles with a soft stick. The whole process is strange and new and not entirely unpleasant, but it is taking quite some time. I ask her how much longer and she shrugs and starts to file the ends of my tiny crescent nails.

Now I sit beside my new husband as relatives mill around us. We are quiet. I look down at my hands again

– the nails freshly painted, the thin gold panj ungla span-ning my fingers. My crimson silk gharara bunches on the floor next to Arif's feet. I note that they are long and narrow, his shoes black and well-polished. The huge rug is awash with patterns, flowers, vines and arches. I have counted the flowers on the border many times and find the symmetry pleasing. There is a cup of tea and some laddoos on an elaborate plate in front of me but I dare not reach for them. My spine is curved like the side of the moon; I am too weighted down by heavy material, jewelled borders and numerous necklaces and earrings. My husband in his three-piece suit is unhindered and picks up his tea. He slurps loudly as he swallows it because it is hot and I see his mouth stretch and his eyes narrow in discomfort as he does.

Our relatives are discussing how cold it will be in Scotland, Arif's job and where we will be living. After about an hour we still haven't spoken to each other. But I can sense that he wants to. Here we are, married, but like two Sphinxes. He seems lost for words, a strange thing in a man who always has so many. Then I see him motion to his five-year-old nephew Bobby.

'Hey, come here, little man!'

Bobby approaches with the swagger of a boy three times his age.

'Yeah?'

'Look at your new auntie's hands. Aren't they beau-tiful?'

The little boy peers at them suspiciously then looks unimpressed. He shrugs and wipes his nose on the sleeve of his cardigan; something on the other side of the room has caught his eye. I can see my husband is getting desperate.

'They're so beautiful. Why don't you kiss them?' he urges.

Bobby looks confused and disgusted at the same time. He expels his answer like a bullet.

'Kiss them yourself!'

I snort and collapse into giggles, my many necklaces and bangles jingling in applause. Bobby looks pleased with himself but no one is more pleased than my husband who has made me, the silent hillock of jewels, laugh and in doing so has broken the ice.

*

My sisters-in-law, Bilquis and Parveen, are tall handsome women. Their hair is cut short, their lipstick is dark, their shoulders broad. They are efficient and direct; no wonder they found me.

They had been given an impossible task with a ridiculous deadline. Their brother was coming over from Scotland for six weeks. Before he landed, they had to find him a bride. The marriage would take place within a week and then we would fly back. They spent many afternoons visiting families and speaking to matchmakers. Some of the families weren't right; some of the women were unsuitable; other families baulked at the distance they would have to send their precious daughters. A wedding brought them to Gujranwala where they got talking to a well-connected woman. She listened to their frazzled story and directed them to Allah Ditta's big house on the outskirts of the city. They pitched up unannounced, climbing out of the car in their best clothes. They banged on the gate and the chowkidar opened it with a question mark on his face. I came down to see what all the noise was; and with sunflower oil in my hair and unwashed clothes I came face-to-face with my future in-laws.

The marriage was agreed swiftly and a few days later my brother delivered my sleepy photo to my future husband's family so that they could get my passport made. Then my future mother-in-law and sister-in-law took me shopping for wedding jewellery on Mall Road in Lahore. As we pulled up outside the jewellers in a car, they exclaimed that there he was, their son, their brother. Under cover of our niqabs, my sister and I turned to look and saw a man coming out of a bookshop. He looked incongruous. Tall and slim, wearing a dark European suit, with skinny trouser legs and a thin tie. His complexion was so fair it was practically red and he had a large nose, ears and a full head of glossy black hair, parted deep at the side. He walked confidently with long jerky strides. People stared after him as they would a foreigner. Then he was gone. My sister pinched my arm approvingly as we got out of the car to go into the jewellers; I realised I had been holding my breath.

But we almost didn't get there. My father was bursting to tell me that, as I had wished, my prospective husband was not a businessman who sold carpets or pots; he was a salaried employee. And even better in my father's eyes that he lived abroad, in the UK of all places. As he had to return to the UK in four weeks, the wedding was set for 18 January. I was pleased, marginally more thrilled at the chance to go abroad than to get married.

At college the news spread quickly. Almas is marrying a man who lives in the UK. She is leaving Pakistan in January. Girls regard me enviously, they see the walls and borders around me melting away. But some want to destroy it. They start to spread a rumour that the man I am marrying in two weeks is not in fact an auditor, but a bus driver; that I will live in rags in a cold, inhospitable country while my husband does a job they think beneath them. The whispers reach my father who brushes them off but when they become more persistent he starts to feel the eyes of the city fix pityingly on him, something he cannot bear. The wedding is in danger of being called off until copies of pay slips from Glasgow are hurriedly despatched to Gujranwala and everything is resolved to his satisfaction. I decide to take nothing for granted again and pray for the wedding day to arrive quickly.

Bearsden, Scotland, 1982

Mrs Harris wears blue eyeshadow and her ankles are as thin as twigs. A belt cinches her tiny waist and I wonder if she has the same number of ribs as me and how exactly she breathes. She wears high thin strappy shoes because she is not much taller than the white metre stick she uses to explain distance to us. She makes maths, which I regard with growing suspicion, almost bearable. She instructs us to draw friezes of Scottish kings and medieval villagers and tells us off for not giving the women 'any bosoms'. She holds books as if they are precious boxes, peering into them as if the subjects might leap from within them. She turns pages with care and smooths down covers. She throws herself into the voices and lives of the characters and encourages us to be loud and expressive. Leaving my old primary school had been a wrench but a couple of weeks into the new one and I have almost forgotten it.

It is a pretty, faded Georgian building; the words 'Boys' and 'Girls' are etched into the sandstone arches above the two separate entrances. The picture windows are long and narrow; gargoyles spring from the top;

a curtain of seventy-year-old trees stands in the play-ground between us and the furious traffic on the main road. Inside on either flank of the main hall are two staircases with iron bannisters. The upper level is galler-ied, with an open corridor running all the way round the building. A large cupola sits in the centre of the ceiling. The younger classes on the lower level; the older on the upper. In the north corner stands the music room where the teacher sits unsmiling behind his red beard, always clad in brown corduroy and Harris Tweed. We eat our lunch in a different building – the small gym on the bottom level, the dining room above. It isn't a modern school; the paint peels, the radiators don't always work and a section of ceiling once fell in – but it still feels special.

Apart from in the music room, all the teachers are women. Mrs McDonald has short grey hair and silver glasses and twitches her nose like a rabbit when she is deep in thought; I am transfixed by her beautifully precise copperplate writing on the blackboard. Miss Jackson is a choleric woman with warts on her face who insists on teaching us half an hour of Bible class every morning and has a degree in sarcasm.

There are many new friends but hanging out with them after school proves difficult. Our new house, as beautiful and spacious as it is, is far away – about a thirty-minute walk, and few children are prepared to trudge out there, wandering down dark lanes and twisty roads, huge gaps between houses. We are isolated, down a long cul-de-sac, at the bottom of a hill, behind a huge gate. In our old house we lived on a street next to other families and kids. But here friends can't just cross a road and ask us to come out to play. Now it has to be pre-arranged and they usually have to get a lift from their mum or dad. In my last house, a friend would knock on our door almost every day; here the bell is ostentatiously eight notes long and I rarely hear it.

The rest of my family is captivated with the new house. It is huge, we can all stretch out. There is so much space – too much. We scatter to our rooms and close our doors. My room is at the front of the house with a dormer window set into the eaves and two sloping ceilings. From my window I can see Glasgow, its rooftops still catching the sun. The garden is magical, many lawns and rockeries and secret steps and passageways, a field of daffodils at the bottom, archways cut into the towering hedges. We are fortunate. But we have lost something by not living on top of each other anymore. We all drift; ties are slowly cut as our limbs stretch into adolescence and away from each other, not to return for decades.

I spend a lot of time on my own – reading, writing stories and waiting for school on Monday when I am with people my own age all day. I have my first crush too. A boy called Andrew. All the girls like him – they write their names and add his surname and draw a love heart around it. At the beginning of a new school year the teacher puts us together; we sit centimetres apart every day. I watch him write – his brown hair falling into his blue eyes, his writing so intense and heavy that it makes the pages in his jotter curl. He is left-handed and sits on the right: I am right-handed and sit on the left. He also has a habit of folding one leg under himself as he sits so we end up even closer. As we write, our elbows bump together all day; behind me the other girls fold their arms, bite their pencils and glare.

*

We are getting changed for P.E. For once no one has forgotten their kit so none of us will have to wear anything ill-fitting or stained from the lost property box. All the girls are crowding round Wendy Christie; I sidle up to listen. She is telling everyone about a blonde princess who has been killed in a car accident. She heard it on the news. Her name was Grace. She died on a mountain somewhere abroad. Our mouths drop open; some of us look sceptical. Beautiful princesses don't die horrible deaths crushed beneath the metal of cars on perilous mountain roads. It's all too much.

'Was . . . was she a real princess?' asks a girl.

'Yes of course she was!' says Wendy huffily, shaking her perfect blonde bob.

'Well I've never heard of her,' says another girl, chewing her lip.

'It was on the radio this morning. I heard it.'

'Well, where was she a princess?'

'I don't know . . . America or something.'

'What was her actual name? All of it?'

'Oh gosh I don't know . . . Grace Something . . . Kennedy! That's it!'

Silence. Some girls nod.

'Hang on. Grace Kennedy's not a princess! She's black!' exclaims Susan McCord.

They shoot me a look and start to snigger. I'm not sure why. I am neither a princess nor called Grace. But I know it has something to do with the word 'black'. I curl my toes and feel a space opening up between me and them. They all start arguing again and then the teacher comes in and asks why we aren't dressed yet and if we aren't in our kit in two minutes, we'll have to do twenty press-ups.

I have a lot of friends at school. Perfect Wendy Christie is not one of them. She hangs out with the other flawless girls with smooth hair and pencil cases full of raspberry and grape scented rubbers. She is always immaculate, the top of her white ankle socks perfectly level. I never noticed this stuff before; now I see it everywhere. I'd give anything, absolutely anything, to have straight hair. But my hair is a mess: my childlike curls have fallen out and now it is just frizzy and wavy and doesn't respond to hairdryers or gel or mousse. It can't be coaxed into any of the hairstyles that are popular: a shiny bob; a spiky mullet; feathered layers. It just gathers around my face like a halo of black candyfloss.

School is still fun though, largely because of all my friends. I get on with my schoolwork, throwing myself into everything – the English, the netball, the hundred metres.

The only thing that spoils it is strange moments that occur randomly, just as I am lost in the lesson. We can be reading a book about world history and the teacher will say the word 'African' or 'Indian' or there is a picture in a textbook of a tribe of people somewhere hot and far away, and the entire class will turn and look at me, some laughing and pointing, others looking sheepish. No one ever articulates it but it becomes a dead certainty that if we are discussing people who are not white, I begin to feel a creeping jeopardy. I start to consider my skin colour for the first time at length, often staring at the sharp contrast of the white of the cuff of my school shirt and the brown of my skin. I look around the class. I am the only one. I try to forget about it. Outside it's sunny and I have netball practice later.

*

We are built for rain. Our faces are torn to shreds by the cold but we never wear big coats or deploy umbrellas efficiently. The tough boys roam about in December in shirt-sleeves and full scowls; the same boys strip off their shirts and tuck them into their belts in April when a few weak rays of sun pierce the grey sky. We bow our heads and push into the horizontal rain, reaching our homes or classrooms with water dripping down our necks and pooling on our backs in a damp oval. A fusty smell rises from our soaked blazers; our socks are always wet. Sometimes the rain falls for days – a downpour that bounces off the pavements or a sticky hissing drizzle.

We eat for the climate, for comfort. We pile into bakeries and chippies, thawing our bones, warming our insides with sausage rolls and bridies and chips. We are petticoat tails and a pan loaf, bottles of ginger and a double nugget from the ice-cream van. We are cold and hot, sweet and sour, bland and spicy. We are Scottish.

I love being Scottish. I wouldn't want to be anything else. Forty minutes' drive north and we are in the amber beauty of the Trossachs. Twenty minutes the other way, we are in the concrete heart of Glasgow – tall and grey, sandstone and glass. I am only eleven but I would defend this country with my life. I would send them homeward to think again. It's in our blood. I never question that it isn't in mine.

When I am old enough, I suck up the story of why we are here and not in Bradford or London or Birmingham. It is because of my Aunt Bilquis – who studied for her PhD in Pharmacology at Glasgow University in the

1950s. My dad and some of his brothers followed her here, to a place they had never heard of. They stayed and squabbled in the same dingy flat in Finnieston. They never left.

*

I am obsessed by netball. I am goal defender, never an attacker. I get no glory but I know my worth and so does our coach who regularly pats me on the back. But then my parents make us go to Pakistan for six weeks one Christmas and when I come back someone has taken my place and I am demoted to goal keeper. I take this badly. I sulk as I get ready for netball practice, with little enthusiasm for my new position.

'Ooooh, nice bra!' says Angela McManus, trying to lighten the atmosphere.

Everyone turns to look, some impressed, some jealous. I have started wearing a bra which is both exciting and cumbersome. I still don't quite know when you keep it on and when you take it off. Nevertheless I've joined an elite of girls who have started wearing bras and become more grown up and interesting than the others who are still wearing babyish vests. But I'm not keen on undressing in front of other girls. I have never seen any of my mother's flesh, apart from her arms – she keeps it well-covered in trousers and has never worn a skirt. But here at school things are different. All the girls strip off down to their underwear and I've clocked that they all have pink nipples whereas mine are brown. Another inexplicable thing I must keep secret.

'Yeah I think I've got that one. Is it from Markies?' Angela continues.

'Yes,' I mumble. All my underwear is from Marks & Spencer. I didn't know there was anywhere else.

'And it really shows off your tan!' says Lesley.

The sniggering starts again. My face is burning. I used to love being the centre of attention, but not any more. The giggling gives way to an awkward silence. I feel weary. It's an effort to lift my arms to hang my clothes on the pegs.

'Shuttit, Lesley, that's not a tan. That's her skin. Stop being ignorant.' says Angela.

My eyes feel prickly.

'S'ok, don't worry,' I croak.

But I do worry. Something I never really noticed before is becoming an issue almost every day. I am starting to realise that life would be much simpler if I looked like everyone else.

*

So much of our childhood is spent playing in or near shallow water. It takes me a few years to realise that the burn I played in as a small child near my old house is the same water I am standing in right now. It flows from there and reaches behind the local library that I visit practically every day. I stand in the shallow water and chuck leaves and twigs into the fast-flowing stream that disappears under a bridge; I pick my way through the crackly leaves and thin branches of the wood that border the burn. I feel connected to my old house, which lies just a mile west from here. I like my new school but something is shifting and I often yearn for what I left behind.

The library is another blonde sandstone Georgian beauty – inside it is full of nasty office blinds, strip lights and officious people. But I crouch in corners poring over books before I select three, take them to the lady to get them stamped, and cycle home to consume them. I read through the day and often the night by torchlight, my eyesight already starting to deteriorate. The next day I am back to choose another three; the lady at the desk raises her nacreous green eyelids and says I'm a wee bookworm.

The truth is that books are filling a gap that has opened up at home. When I'm not at school, I feel at a loose end. A family of six and yet I am mostly on my own. I turn to my printed friends. I love everything about them – the reassuring feel of them in my hands – the soft plumpness of a paperback; the flat smooth opulence of a hardback; the writing on the back, the sleeve, the typeset, the sigh and creak when I open and close them.

And I am losing my little brother. Once we were put together – the same room, the same fold-down seat at the back of the car, just two years apart. Now we have different rooms and so much space between us. We used to go exploring together, he trailing a few steps behind in his own world. Now we are rarely together. He sometimes got irritated, losing his temper over small things when he became frustrated, but it never felt personal. Now he has taken to talking to himself, turning his back on us and occasionally scowling so darkly that we are baffled. I take it badly. I feel as if he hates me. He mutters and scowls at me and I go crying to my mum who reassures me that my little brother still loves me; it's just getting harder for him to show it. He is also getting more physical. In addition to the scowling, he's starting to throw things – a glass, a plate, a toy car, LEGO. He is obsessed with all cars – Volvos and Mercedes are the best he tells me, but he nurses an unexplained anger for Minis. Unfortunately our neighbour has a Mini and he sneaks into their driveway and smashes every window of their car. It seems like every week something bad happens.

*

Winter is coming because we start doing Scottish country dancing practice in P.E. in preparation for the school dance. The group dances are huge fun. Lines and lines of uncoordinated children bashing into each other and falling over. An energy I didn't know I possessed is unleashed as we whirl and dash around our groups of eight. We are drunk on air and bagpipes. But when it's a couple's dance, instead of pairing us up, the teacher asks the boys to pick their partners. I watch in increasing horror as it gets down to the last five girls, then three, then two. The last boy looks miserably at both of us and then points at Susie McCann, aka the Nose Picker. I am left on my own. The music starts up suddenly and I go to sit down at the side, wobbling on my legs like a newborn calf, desperate for the solidness of the bench beneath me. But the teacher blows his whistle and summons me over like a sheepdog.

'You'll have to dance with me Aasmir!' he shouts.

The class erupts into laughter. I look at him in shock. What does he mean?

'Right, watch!' he says.

Everyone stops. Thirty pairs of eyes are on me. He holds me tight like a rag doll and spins me around the gym, my legs like jelly, my shoes squeaking on the floor.

Step we gaily on we go, heel for heel and toe for toe . . .

It is so awful – the laughing children, the inappropriate closeness of a male teacher holding you by the waist and hand. My legs are buckling and my face feels like it is on fire but I understand that if I fall over, I'll never live it down.

Arm in arm and on we go, all for Mairi's wedding . . .

I grit my teeth and try to ignore the very adult male smell drifting from his armpits as they loom over me. I feel as if I might vomit and decide to hold my breath instead.

'Right – now you lot try!'

For the next thirty minutes I try to stay on my feet, returning to my friends for the group dances. They are still laughing.

'Hahaha, is that your boyfriend?'

'You make a lovely couple.'

I glare at the boys. I thought they were my friends, but they wouldn't even pick me for a dance. This is a hot and poisonous anger I have never felt before.

'Aasmah and Smithy up a tree . . . K-I-S-S-I-N-G.'

The same thing happens the following week but even the teacher has had enough of me this time and tells me to go and share the last boy who chose. I trudge over. The boy and the girl stare at me and then turn their backs. The teacher blows his whistle again. He loves that whistle. Thinks he's at Hampden.

'Ho! You two lovebirds – you need to share so everyone gets a turn, got it?'

The boy growls at me:

'Fine. But I'm no' touching yer hands. OK?'

I'm taken aback. Tears stab my eyes. The question 'why?' fades in my throat. While they do the first couples' dance, I sit on a bench and try to make sense of what he said. I watch him twirl the girl around, touching her hands. My hands are clean; there are no pen marks. I think he must be getting me mixed up with the Nose Picker. Or maybe I misheard him. But, no, when it's my turn, I get wearily to my feet and he springs backwards and hisses: 'Mind? Nae hands.'

So we dance a dance that requires you to hold hands and spin round, to link arms. We do it all at a distance as if there is an electrical current between us. The anger in his eyes, the way he won't look at me, his flushed face, the insistent drunken music. I am relieved when it's my turn to sit it out. I watch again as he grips the hands of his partner. Elsewhere in the hall, Andrew swirls round Perfect Wendy Christie, the flippy ends of her hair dancing in time to the music, her face flushed with the effort and the attention. I lift up my hands and examine them again.

*

Spring is coming and excitement is building in my chest. I'm on the relay team after beating all the girls in a race in the playground. We'll be representing our school at the Highland Games. And I have discovered I am good at spelling, probably because I am always reading. I win every spelling competition in class. Everyone lines up at the front and the teacher asks us to spell a word. I am always the last one standing. It becomes more and more important for me to win each time; I don't know why. Maths is sometimes a struggle, but words are easy. The boys look at me in admiration when I win for the seventh time.

'You're a bloody genius, man! That's EPIC! How d'ye know all those wurrrrds?'

Renfrew Airport, near Glasgow, February, 1966

The aeroplane door resists for a moment or so then opens with a clunk and a hiss. Within moments a finger of chilly air has made its way down the aisle of this jet and coiled itself around my neck. I am gathering my belongings together when I feel a cold that I have never felt before. I look up to see where it has come from, expecting to see an ice monster grinning before me. But there is nothing to explain it – just a mêlée of people all trying to uncoil themselves from their seats and empty lockers at the same time, brushing off the crumbs of the last few hours and smoothing down their clothes.

The last leg of this epic journey is finally done. It was a farewell in stages; I shed my old life and stepped into a new one somewhere between the dusty beauty of Baghdad and the parallel lines of Geneva, a journey that originated in Lahore and ended in Glasgow. I am tired and groggy, the cold has colonised my body, my kajal has gathered under my eyes like soot. But an elation I have harboured for months is now propelling me up out of my seat, along the aisle and out of the door into I am not exactly sure what.

The only bruise on my heart is the memory of how I said goodbye to my parents. My father – a strict, emotionless man whom no one had ever seen cry – had dumbfounded us all by wailing like a child in the days preceding my departure and at the airport. In that harshly lit chaotic place, with relatives crying and shouting and men in uniforms and moustaches watching on, I gulped back huge tears as I confronted the enormity of what was happening. I could not wait to get away, start my new life, do all the things I had always wanted to do. But here standing before me was my father – unrecognisable in tears and pain. It was as if the sky were falling in. I felt wretched.

My mother was so intertwined with me that she had begun the process of disconnection early on out of necessity. She still wept but once she knew that I was marrying a good man and going abroad, she cried for herself too – the mother left behind and the young bride she had once been. She smoothed my hair, whispered the same sweet blessings she had whispered to me as a child and let me go.

And now here I am on a plane with a man I barely know but with whom I will live for the rest of my life. How many years will that be? Fifty? Sixty? And how many children? We have been married just a week and there have been few private moments so I haven't had many opportunities to really look at him. I am still discovering his face, the proportions, the symmetry, the dips and inclines of his nose and cheekbones. When he dozes off I wait until I hear him snore and then take the chance to study him. A tall man, crammed into a tiny aeroplane seat, the drinks trolley bashes into his elbows and knees constantly. He is as usual wearing a three-piece suit, the legs and lapels cut thin according to the fashion, making him appear even taller and skinnier.

At least he looks warm. Just one hour into my journey I am regretting my choice of clothes. For some reason I opted to wear a thin green silk shalwar kameez, on my feet a pair of black patent-leather slingbacks, my pale bare heels exposed to the draughts and air conditioning of the plane. The shoes are one of three pairs that I had made for me by the Chinese shoemaker on Mall Road in Lahore. Just twenty-three and already troubled by squashed feet, the idea of getting made-to-measure shoes had beguiled me for years. Mr Chan's workshop was small and it looked as if the ceilings were held up by pillars of shoeboxes. Strips of leather hung from nails, little hammers, scissors and pins were strewn everywhere. It smelt of glue and leather and smoke. He invited me to place my foot on a sheet of paper, traced an outline, drew a line from the heel to the tip of my big toe, then he measured my arch with the yellow tape he looped around his neck. Three weeks later, my shoes were ready – three identical pairs of slingbacks – black, cream and pale pink, lined with the softest buttery leather. It was like sinking my feet into a cushion. But now on a draughty flight to a cold country, the sling-backs are feeling like a ridiculous vanity.

The journey takes more than twenty-four hours. We start in Karachi, with stops in Tehran, Beirut, Baghdad, Rome, Geneva, London, then Glasgow. My sadness fades with each stop, my old life drains away. I know that I will have to forget it – the smells, the sounds, the beauty of my life in a small city in Pakistan – and embrace something huge and unknown. How would the air smell in the new place? How would the blankets feel? What would people make of my English?

Over twenty-four hours we are offered many different types of food, most of which I have never eaten before, all of which I gobble up. The first snack is a samosa – which sits flaky and golden beneath a clear plastic dome like a diamond ring in a jewellers. I am captivated by the presentation rather than the flavour. I have tasted better samosas in the dabba near my college. The next is a slice of sponge cake which comes with a tiny fork. I eye it for several minutes watching how my husband, who has now lived in the UK for six whole years, tackles it. He uses the side of the fork to cut it, spears the tiny piece with the prongs and drops it in his mouth. I try too, letting the sponge land on my tongue and dissolve deliciously. When it is all finished, I spend a few minutes chasing the remaining crumbs round the plate with my spindly fork before abandoning it and using my fingers to squash them together in a pleasing soft, oily ball and depositing it in my mouth.

Dinner is chapli kebabs and rice, with two triangles of soft naan. I marvel at how an entire Pakistani meal has been contained so neatly on one tray. A perfect display of culinary geometry; a collection of squares and circles and rectangles somehow fits together within the tray and contains everything I need – kebabs, rice, yoghurt, salad, salt and pepper, cutlery, a napkin. I stare for a good few minutes, not wanting to spoil the perfection. Then I gingerly start to remove the plastic lids. I like my food hot, but I spend a long time eating that meal, scraping the last remnants of each container until it is white again, emptying every last onion and cucumber from the salad pot, licking the spoons and then putting all the lids back on, completing the puzzle once again. Early on I spy the perfectly ironed thick cloth napkin with the letters P, I and A embroidered upon it and avoid using it. I re-fold it along the lines and place it in my handbag. Then I curl up as best as I can, leaning on my coat against the cold window and I tumble into my dreams.

*

My mother stands before me. But she is unrecognisable. She is neither timid nor bowed, her face is not hollow nor defeated. Instead she is tall and straight, her voice is steady, she does not sigh. She beckons to me and I approach.

'Come, let's go up on the roof and take our embroidery with us.'

I stare.

'Come on then!'

I can't speak, my tongue lies thick and obsolete in my mouth.

She laughs at me and motions that I should follow. Scooping up a basket containing our embroidery frames and threads, she makes for the stairs. I stumble after her, my legs heavy and light at the same time. Everything is upside down. I have never seen my mother walk like this: so quick on her feet. She pushes the door to the roof open and the sunlight floods in. Without taking my eyes off her, I sit on the charpai next to her as she folds her legs underneath her body. She looks around, one eye closed against the brightness. I feel no heat from the sun; it's like I'm not really here. The noises of the neighbourhood are loud but muffled – pots clanging, servants shouting, dogs barking.

'I hope the music man comes today, eh?' she grins at me.

All I can do is stare. She has never listened to the music or sat up here for more than five minutes.

'Cat got your tongue?'

I nod. I want to speak but my dreams have taken my voice. I look at her ageless open face, her pink cheeks, her chin high, not buried in her chest, her back straight.

'Well, we'll just have to make our own music.'

And she launches into a song that I have never heard:

'*A thousand years will pass, my love,*
I yearn to tell you what it is
This thing that coils around my heart
But this bird cannot sing, cannot sing . . .'

*

I fall out of my dreams in the morning, my eyes crusty with dried tears. I think of my mother and father, their faces receding as the grey miles hiss by. How far was I from them now?

A tray is placed on my table. I can't quite work out what the smell is, but it is not entirely unfamiliar. I lift the cover which is opaque this time and there before me lies a golden bun. I carefully lift the top half to reveal a perfect circle of omelette, enticingly thick and studded with onions, mushrooms and coriander. I bend my head, close my eyes and inhale the vague smell of home. Again I watch as my husband squirts ketchup on his, replaces the top, cuts it in half with his knife and starts eating it. My husband eats fast. I learn later that food was scarce in his family and you had to be quick.

As we leave Asia and enter Europe the cuisine changes. Between Geneva and London, we are served chicken sandwiches on thin white bread which are sophisticated and delicious but lack spice so we smother them again with ketchup. Our dessert is two petite fairy cakes, with thin wobbly lines of yellow and pink icing.

Everything I eat is an unusual treat, presented immaculately and eaten entirely.

As the food changes, so does the scenery. Rome and Geneva Airports are like nothing I have ever seen before. Clean and ordered, the planes standing in parallel lines. I am restless and I want to write down how I am feeling – a strange mixture of excitement, fear and guilt. But I have no paper and no pen with me. I take out the menu card – stiff, heavy and cream; and when the air hostess comes by I get my husband to ask her for a pen. She takes it out of her top pocket, clicks the top of it and hands it to me.

This is the first plane I have ever been on. The houses look tiny and I finally understand how big the world is and how small we are in it.

The plane goes high, through clouds and sun. And so it is with life and with this decision I have made to follow a man I did not know three weeks ago to a country thousands of miles away.

Sometimes I feel infused with the sun – excited at the prospect of a new home, a new adventure. Other times I feel overwhelmed by dark clouds – guilty at abandoning my parents and unsure that I will be able to cope with so much change all at once. The only thing that calms me is that I have known my husband for just three weeks and he transmits so much warmth and affection that he lessens my anxiety by half.

And yet I don't think I will ever forget the sight of my weeping father, my mother's sad grey face, the tears of my sisters and brother at the airport. Especially my brother. He has always been stubborn and mean with his love. But in those last minutes together, his usually loud voice was reduced to a whisper and he kept wiping his eyes. I couldn't bear to look at him; it was too much.

Everything will be OK, what's done is done.

*

By the time we leave Geneva I feel my gloom lift. We have been well fed and my husband has taken to holding my hand which I find simultaneously scandalous and pleasing. If anyone passes I withdraw my hand immediately. Three weeks ago I was still wearing a niqab in public and had never touched a man. Arif told my father that he didn't like niqabs and I received the message joyfully.

There is a real sense of anticipation now; we are only a few hours from the United Kingdom. I want the plane to slow down; I'm not ready. But I also want to be there now, unfolding myself out of this seat, unpacking my life on to a bed I have never slept in before, lining up my toothpaste and toothbrush in an unfamiliar bathroom.

Once we have landed, we gather all our luggage together. My black leather bag, my coat, my magazines. Lastly, a small straw-coloured rigid suitcase that will rest on the top of successive wardrobes in a lifetime of houses. My children will commandeer it and use it as a dressing-up box. My older daughter will search through it to stage amateur plays in the garage of a house on a hill. My younger daughter will fill it with books and photos and precocious teenage poems that only hint at her troubles. My older son will fill it with credit card slips as he pretends he is running a business. My youngest son will use it to right himself as he tries to walk, two years later than most children.

But I do not know any of this yet. As I make my way to the door of the plane, all I know is that I have married a tall man with a strong jaw, a steady job and thick dark hair; and that he has brought me to a place called Glass-go.

FIVE

Gujranwala, Pakistan, 1955

I never understood why my mother's family agreed she could marry my father. After all, he was twenty-five years older than her. And he already had a wife.

A stranger brought the answer to our house twenty years later but by then it was too late. My mother was stuck. My father and his wife were first cousins, barely years between them, but had only managed to produce two daughters. The failure hung over them for years, perplexing, unfixable. There was even a long discussion about my father adopting one of his brother's sons. But his wife was insistent: take another wife and have your own son, your own blood.

Into this ambush wandered my mother. It wasn't uncommon for men to have two wives – some were determined to produce a male heir, some married widows so they wouldn't be destitute, others did it just because they could. My mother had presumed that the first wife would step back; that she would be free to be a spouse, a mother, the keeper of a house. Instead she acquired an unwelcome shadow overnight that never receded even in the daylight.

There was the briefest of honeymoon periods in which both eyed each other quietly and coolly. But something about my mother irritated my stepmother. Maybe it was her youth, maybe it was the thought that this was the woman who would give my father what he desperately wanted – a son.

But a son didn't come. The first child was a girl – Samina. The shock rang around the house. No mithai was handed out, the child was barely looked at. My mother tasted the disappointment in the air. During her pregnancy, the barbed comments had begun. A critical commentary commenced of her: her habits, her tastes and finally her childbearing skills. My stepmother was after all the incumbent, the original, the matriarch, so she dug her heels in and wouldn't budge. My mother felt intimidated by this tall well-dressed woman almost twenty years her senior, who would wait until she had spent hours cooking dinner and then serve it as if she had made it herself.

My stepmother was from a tiny village near Gujranwala; my mother came from a big city, Lahore. This irked my stepmother and she often complained that my mother was too modern and affected; that she talked differently and sat differently and often mimicked her.

'*Hai*, what is the Lahoran saying now?'

'You might do that in Lahore, but not here.'

My mother was already a quiet woman and she was further diminished by the impossible situation that existed in the house. But even she couldn't bear it and after two years, she told my father that she couldn't live like this and when was his first wife leaving. Never, he said. I have a duty to her too.

Thankfully the next baby was a boy, Khalid – the prize. The gloom lifted in the house for a while and sweets were distributed to friends and neighbours. But after the birth my mother became sick, losing weight and coughing blood until she was diagnosed with tuberculosis. She was sent to a sanitorium in Nanital where she stayed for two years. My aunt looked after Samina and Khalid and brought them to visit their mother, at a distance.

When she resumed her married life in Gujranwala, she was yet more weakened. All the progress she had made trying to assert any authority had been lost in the interim. My stepmother was re-energised, ready to defend the territory she had regained. She hardly ate, often crying and plucking at her clothes and hair. She became obsessive about hygiene, constantly washing her hands and elaborately avoiding touching the tap by turning it off with her elbows. She wouldn't touch door handles either, using her feet or elbows instead. She kept her plate and cup away from ours and wrapped her rotis separately too.

Naz arrived, then me a year later. So broken was she by the weight of disapproval of giving birth to another two girls that she finally fought back. She found

another room in the back of the house and made it into
her kitchen. From now on she would cook her own
food and get the credit for it. But still, if my mother
had cooked a vegetable dish, my stepmother would
entice my prized brother into her kitchen by preparing
meat and making him eat with her family. My mother
would look winded and desolate. By this point they had
stopped speaking to each other directly. If they wanted
to communicate, they would say something to someone
else while the other was in earshot or send a message via
a child or a servant.

My stepmother spent decades trying to undermine
my mother. And yet I did not dislike her as much as
I should have. She was a confident, talkative, direct
woman who had little time for any of us, apart from my
brother and occasionally me. I was in awe of her physi-
cality, so different was it to my mother's. She was tall and
fair with good straight hair. She always wore beautiful
fashionable clothes and plenty of gold jewellery. She had
one thick gold bangle on each arm and the large gold
discs she wore in her ears were so heavy that the holes
in her ear lobes had stretched into long vertical lines. I
stared at those earrings for years – the intricate pattern on
the front and the plain smoothness of the back. I spent a
lot of time observing her unseen, trying to work out why
she was so hostile to my mother, and how life would be if
she were not here. I often fantasised about coming home
from school one day to find her gone. Then we could

have a normal life. But my stepmother had sunk her iron hooks into the concrete of our home and would never leave. It was a strained and ridiculous set-up. We grew up with her two daughters who, although much older, were pleasant to us. The only friction in the house was between the two wives – and occasionally my father when he was drawn into it. For some reason he had not anticipated that two wives might not get on. His stubbornness meant they had to live together in that simmering house, constant tiny sparks of fire making everyone tread carefully around them.

'If you want to know what hell is, have two wives!' my father would say when it all got too much and the enmity between my mother and stepmother boiled over. Demands were made and rejected. Chests were beaten and rivers of tears were shed. But nothing changed. For thirty years, two families lived in that house, together but apart. Two women, wives, mothers battled each other. There was no peace, only war.

But my mother had one trump card. She had produced the only boy among my father's eight children. When Khalid was born, special prayers were said to ward off the 'nazar' or evil eye. He was simultaneously cosseted by my mother and scrutinised and held to a higher standard than the rest of us by my strict father. He was obsessed by football – which my father thought a waste of time; they constantly locked horns over education and leisure. But my mother adored him and watched him closely, all the time fearing that her precious and solitary son would come to some harm or disclose some imperfection. It was not until he was eighteen that this happened.

My mother is sitting with us at lunch when she suddenly stops chewing and grabs my brother's shirt.

'Hey, Ummi, what are you doing? Leave me.' He tries to shrug her off.

But my mother is clawing at his shirt buttons. We look on in shock. Then she picks him up by his elbow and pulls him out into the sunlit yard, the pots clattering around their feet. We look at each other. What has Khalid done? Then we hear the wail.

'Noooo. Nooooo. Hai hai!'

We run out to see what is happening. My mother is beating her chest, her mouth open, her eyebrows slanted in despair. She is so upset she can't speak. Her hair is askew, her cheeks flushed. My brother is looking confused, his hands by his side, his palms upturned in surrender. And then I see it. In among my brother's chest hairs on a smooth patch of brown skin lies a tiny white dot. We all know what it is.

The condition that had colonised the bodies of my father and grandfather had lain dormant in her only son for eighteen years. She had prayed and checked him constantly. But now it was here. My mother cries for weeks. By the time he is forty-five my brother's bronze skin has turned completely white.

Glasgow, Scotland, 1979

'WHERE ARE MY BEAUTIFUL PIECES?'

My dad is back and as usual he is very loud. My dad cannot cough or laugh quietly. He cannot open a door or leave or enter a room without a huge bang and crash. His burps are legendary – several notes long: 'Dah-errr-oooo'. His yawns sound like the descending notes in a scale: 'Arr-arr-arr-ahhhhh'. His sneezes are sudden and catastrophic and make small children cry. He is six foot three inches tall and fills every space he inhabits with his bulk and his voice. He scoops us up, demands and deposits kisses, pinches our cheeks – he is made for this. A handsome giant, a Bollywood Cary Grant, every bit of my dad is big: his palatial nose, his frequently hairy ears, the unsolicited moustache he grew and got rid of when we all refused to kiss him, the gold crown in one of his bulbous teeth. His shoes are vast and lie like shipwrecks all over the house; his shirts as big as sails lie soaking in the bathtub. He is as man-sized as the tissues he uses. You cannot ignore my dad.

We realise early on that while my mum is conservative with treats and rewards, my dad believes there should be virtually no limits. Double it, triple it, eat, eat, eat. He hates denial, abhors the word 'no'. We swarm round him whenever we need or have been refused something. We climb on to his knee and cry into his huge face. He melts and we are victorious. Just give them the chocolate, darling. No daughter of mine will go hungry. My mum shakes her head in frustration.

When we are out with Dad he is free with his money. He enjoys peeling a big note from his brown leather wallet and handing it to the man in the ice-cream van. The biggest ice creams for everyone with all the extras, he demands. And when we eat out, there is always more food that we need. We'll have six fish suppers, please; eight donner kebabs; twenty-four shish kebabs and fourteen naan. My mum quietly beckons the waiter and cuts the order in half. At home my dad encourages her to put more food on our plates in case we starve to death between lunch and dinner.

Years later my dad tells me that when he was growing up in Kasur – a family of four boys and two girls – there wasn't a huge amount of food to go around. They were all over six foot tall and always hungry. My dad cycled thirty miles a day to get to and from college in Lahore. When my dad arrived in Glasgow in 1960 money was so tight that he would nurse a single cup of tea in a café on Gibson Street for two hours, then scold himself for spending the money in the first place. He wasn't poor but there wasn't anything to spare.

Some people continue to be frugal with their money after such an experience. Not my dad; as soon as he has money he sprays it everywhere. He buys a nice car, the best shirts and shoes and ties; perfume and cashmere sweaters for my mother; a new TV and VCR; treats for us; a big house.

And the latest camera. My dad is the family photographer. He snaps every new bike, every family birthday, every lopsided sandcastle. What he lacks in skill, he makes up for with consistency. He takes hundreds of photos of us. We inherit a legacy of overexposed slides, juddering Super 8 films and blurred Polaroids. But it is only when I am born that my dad finally finds his muse. There is a disproportionate amount of film of me, mainly because I love to perform and my dad loves to take photos. I toddle about in mini-skirts, my nappy hanging out at the back; I peek from behind walls and blow kisses at him; I wheel around on my tricycle whooping and waving to him over my shoulder. We have found each other.

My dad delights in us. When I cry into his face he turns my sadness into laughter by saying that my tears have dripped into his mouth and he is going to die of salt poisoning. When I yawn within reach of him, he pokes his finger in my mouth and spoils my yawn. When I sleep he comes in and stares at me for five minutes because he loves the way that I still lie like a baby, with my hands by my ears. When I am six months old, my parents take me to Pakistan. They leave me in the plane with the air hostesses while they walk around Doha Airport to stretch their legs.

'What should we do if she cries?' they ask.

'She won't,' says my dad authoritatively. 'My daughter doesn't cry.' And he was right.

When we get to Lahore, my three-year-old cousin takes a dislike to me and in the middle of the night, my dad wakes to see him pressing his foot on my stomach in the cot on the floor by the side of the bed. He shoos him away and stays awake guarding me for as long as he can. He drifts in and out of sleep all night waving his arm over me to protect me from nefarious toddlers.

But while my dad can be soft, he can be inflexible too. He is obsessed with the news. He reads the *Daily Telegraph* from cover to cover every day. Over the years, we have to fit our TV watching around his. When we get back from school, we dive straight in front of the TV to watch our programmes before the huge news takeover begins. My dad sometimes arrives home at 5:30 p.m. – just in time for the ITN *News* at 5:40 p.m., then straight on to the *Six o'Clock News*, then the Scottish news at 6:30 p.m., then Channel 4 *News* at 7 until 7:50 p.m. Then thankfully there was nothing until 9 p.m. – a whole hour and ten minutes when we could plead for *Dallas* – then it was back to the 9 o'clock news, then the 10 o'clock news. By the time it was *Newsnight*, we had all given up and gone to bed.

But nothing is as bad as the cricket. When Test matches are on, the TV is locked on to it for what seems like weeks. If Pakistan are playing there is hysteria, the world stops. My dad and my brother sit there gripped. Sometimes my dad is snoring away as the match plays out, and my brother suddenly screams: 'He's out!!' At which point my dad wakes, drops the remote control and his paper, sits upright and wide-eyed and shouts:

'Eh? Ohhhh . . . He's bowel'd him!'

*

My parents are Muslim. I have seen my mum disappear to pray in times of real suffering but never my dad. I've not seen either of them go to the mosque. They are not devout Muslims, but one thing that is not negotiable is the forbidding of alcohol and pork. We are told very early on that we are not to eat any pig.

If only this were simple but I soon discover that there are approximately fifty-three words for pork. Every day at school is a guessing game. Is gammon ham? Is ham the same as pork? What are chipolatas? What was a loin chop? What's in a sausage roll? Can I eat stuffing? If I couldn't work it out I would just ask for the vegetarian option, which was usually a scoop of grated cheese instead of a burger or chop. I eat a lot of grated cheese. Grated cheese and cabbage. Grated cheese and chips. Grated cheese and coleslaw. I compile and keep adding

to a list of all the words for pig or things that had pig
in them:

Pork
Ham
Bacon
Gammon
Dripping
Luncheon meat
Scratchings
Stuffing
Salami
Spam
Sausages
Sausage rolls
Square sausage or Lorne sausage
Crackling
Chipolatas
Steak and kidney pie
Scotch Egg
Pepperami

We tend to eat a lot of things with 'beef' or 'lamb' in
the name although beef sausages were apparently tipped
into pork casings. We thought 'steak' always meant beef
until we realised that steak-and-kidney pie contained
beef steak but pork kidneys. I found out that roast
potatoes were cooked in pork dripping. Captain Birds

Eye was our friend. We ate a lot of beef burgers and fish fingers and eggs but everything else was a stressful tightrope. What exactly was Hungarian Goulash? What kind of mince made up mince and tatties? Food came with a side order of questions.

Thankfully there was no pig in our puddings – just sugar. The desserts were scrawled on the tiny blackboard in the gym – and set our mood for the rest of the day. Heaven was caramel fudge tart, baked apple sponge, chocolate cake, iced gingerbread – or the king of puddings: jam and coconut flan. Someone invariably rubbed the 's' and 'e' out of the word sponge. But no one could erase the two most dreaded words: currant tart – more commonly known as flies graveyard – was a particularly nasty concoction that reeked of a post-war sacrifice that was no longer required. Even saturated in custard it was foul – the nasty little currants floating like dead insects above a very short, dry pastry.

On a good pudding day the queue heaves and swells. We wolf down our meat or grated cheese and veg then wait to be called for pudding, sitting on the edge of our stools. Then it is a mad scramble in case it runs out. Legs are chopped and elbows deployed. Sometimes you don't get portion justice – your pre-cut piece in the large metal tray is unusually small; sometimes you get a thick corner piece with extra buttery pastry. There is one dinner lady who always notices that I have to have a ladle of grated cheese instead of the ham or pork chop and she gives me a slightly bigger portion of pudding. Of course this is not a good thing on flies graveyard day. And sometimes when she isn't in, or is in the back washing the trays, I end up with grated cheese, boiled cabbage and carrots, followed by a slab of flies graveyard capsizing slowly in gluey custard.

*

I am at my friend Linda's house for tea. We walked home together, turning into an unfamiliar street, excitedly talking over each other about all the fun things we would do when we got home. I couldn't wait to see her house, her room, her toys, to play with her wee baby sister.

We hang up our coats, wash our hands and eat our snacks. When we are shouted down for dinner, we slowly drag ourselves to the table. There on my plate, to my horror, lies something that looks wrong.

'Wow – gammon!' squeals Linda, wriggling on to her chair.

I stare at the gammon steak with a triumphant slice of pineapple fizzing on it. My face falls. I had told Linda to tell her mum that I couldn't eat pork. Isn't gammon pork? I am not a hundred percent sure. Heat rises in my face.

Everyone is wolfing down their food.

'Are you OK, dear?' her mum said. 'Not hungry?'

'I– I–, it's just that . . .'

She looks encouragingly at me, blinking.

'. . . I'm not allowed . . . to eat pork. Is this pork?'

Silence.

'Oh. Not allowed? How come?'

It was the 70s. Everyone ate everything. There were no fussy eaters. Food was fuel. But I had a reason. I just didn't fully understand it.

'Because . . . I'm Mu– Muslim?'

The word feels thick and unfamiliar on my tongue. Everyone is staring.

'I did . . . tell Linda . . .'

My voice has shrunk to nothing now.

Linda's mum considers this for a while, then her face brightens.

'Ahh, Linda didn't tell me. Wee madam. Shall I make you a cheese sandwich?'

The clouds part. I am to be saved by cheese again, possibly grated.

'Oh yes please, thank you!'

She gets up to make it. I shoot a look at Linda, who is in gammon heaven; her dad keeps his eyes on me. It is absolutely mortifying. I eat my cheese sandwich gratefully then Linda's mum brings a Bird's trifle out and we all pile in.

*

Home is a safe haven; there are no booby traps there. Married at twenty-three, my mum applies herself to cooking just as she did to her studies – and her food is exceptional. Even if I crave burgers and chips and all the things everyone else eats, I am intoxicated by this particular alchemy of garlic, ginger and onions dancing in oil; of coriander, cumin and chilli mixing and melting to form the scaffolding of every meal. Her tarka daal is heartbreaking – gingery, studded with tiny emeralds of fresh coriander and crescents of crispy fried onions. It is piled on top of a mountain of fluffy rice or scooped up with a soft grateful roti. Her perfectly round lamb koftas floating in a pot of bubbling sauce and surrounded by boiled egg halves melt in your mouth and make you weep. She makes a lamb and spinach curry that is ambrosial. The lamb is tender, the spinach perfectly spiced, just the right proportion of vegetable to meat. You eat one mouthful and surrender completely. Occasionally she makes us eat some oily mushy vegetable like turnip but that always goes down badly with my dad who expects meat every day.

My mum may be a magician in the kitchen but it doesn't look effortless. Cooking this kind of food is a chaotic and smelly endeavour. Big slabs of meat arrive from the halal butchers in Glasgow and mum sets about chopping them all up and cutting off bits of fat. There is a terrifying stainless steel mincing machine in our kitchen where hunks of meat are forced in the top and pushed down with a plastic plunger. The mince appears out of the other side like wriggling meaty red caterpillars and drops into a waiting bowl. Trays upon trays of raw kebabs and koftas wait in line to be fried or frozen. It is a massive production line. The windows steam up and the extractor fan is always on. The smell of coriander and diced onion is overpowering – filling my lungs and making me feel nauseous and worried about smelling of curry at school. Then there is the making of the ghee which is a peculiar and greasy job. A plastic carrier bag full of Echo margarine arrives. We have to peel off the orange waxy wrappers and drop the blocks into a massive steel pot on the cooker until it melts into a viscous liquid. My mum skims something off the top, cools it, pours it into a large plastic container, waits for it to set and uses it to fry everything for the next month. I never understand why we fuss around melting and boiling butter for hours just to end up with more . . . butter.

But the best food times are the weekends. Mum makes parathas – and puts a spicy potato stuffing in them which we eat with yoghurt. Sometimes we restrict ourselves to a plain one but have it with fried eggs. We stab at the yolky middle with the fried bread, scooping it up messily and dropping it into our mouths.

I find the food production line in our house overwhelming. The hiss and squeal of the pressure cooker, the stubborn smell of cumin and fenugreek, the yellow stain of turmeric on surfaces and fingernails. The only time I get involved in any preparation is when my mum is making chapatis. She expertly kneads and pinches and rolls and flours and pats. When I am seven I insist on making a chapati for my dad every dinner time. He comes in ravenous from a full day at work and has to eat a nasty little disc the size of a cookie and the thickness of a sponge. I stand over him proudly and watch him chew and chew, trying to swallow the hellish pellet, almost burned on the outside, borderline raw on the inside.

Occasionally my dad takes charge. He makes eggy toast – French toast, in other words – and we sprinkle it with too much sugar and wolf it down. Our dad conspires with us in our innocent greed. He never says we have had enough. He is a good-time guy.

One of our safe foods is eggs. Fried in ghee with a yolky middle; whisked up with onions and spices and coriander and fried into a delicious omelette then clamped between two slices of buttery toasted Mother's Pride; scrambled with full-fat milk so it was creamy but not wet with plenty of salt and pepper. It was one of my favourite meals. So when Wendy's mum asks me what I would like for tea – my choice – I say:

'Scrambled eggs?'

'Oooooh, great idea. Breakfast for tea!'

She heads off to the kitchen. I hug myself; this is going to be great. And I have already spied a Cadbury's Swiss Gateau on the kitchen worktop. When the scrambled eggs arrive I can hardly contain myself. I sprinkle lots of salt and pepper on the eggs, then start buttering my toast, watching it melt satisfyingly into the bread. Everyone is digging in. My first mouthful is amazing – she made them just like mum! The second is yummy too. I lift my eyes up to approvingly share in the meal and notice that they are all staring at me. I freeze. What's wrong? Maybe I have spilled something on my top? Or burped loudly? I gulp down my mouthful and look at Wendy.

'Why . . . are you eating with . . . your hands?'

She sounds both disgusted and embarrassed. I look down at my hands and then at everyone else's which are holding forks and knives, albeit hovering in mid-air. In our house we eat any kind of bread with our hands – rotis, naan, pizzas, parathas, sandwiches, toast. I am completely flummoxed. I've been caught out again by the rules. Maybe they eat their morning toast and jam with a knife and fork too.

'Wendy . . . don't be unkind,' says her mum, 'People do different things . . .'

She pats my elbow.

But I don't want to be different. I pick up my fork and knife and start sawing at the toast. How am I supposed to cut it? In squares? Triangles? And how can I keep the eggs on there? When you wrap the soft toast round the eggs like a roti, they don't fall out. This is a tricky balancing act. I try to look at what everyone else is doing. In the end, I just eat the toast and then the eggs separately. They don't taste as good; they stick in my anxious throat and are slightly too salty from the single tear that gathers on my chin and falls into them unseen.

Wendy's mum is kind and the cake which I make sure to eat with a fork is delicious, but I do wonder when I am going to get it right.

*

We look like our parents. My older brother and I have my mother's curly hair. We all have a bespoke version of our dad's substantial nose and some of his height. And yet there are mountains between us. They pronounce English words differently to us. My mother cannot say the 'jzhhh' sound in 'pleasure' or 'measure'. My dad says 'nounsense' instead of 'nonsense', 'loin' instead of 'lion'. My mum always spells 'John' as 'Jhon' when she writes a letter to John Paul & Sons Dairies for our milk deliveries and it cracks us up. Dad manages petrol stations so we talk about cars a lot. My parents pick their own pronunciations. Peugeots are PYOO-joes; a Mercedes is a Murr-suh-DEEZ. And their sweet tooths are just not Scottish enough.

My parents never had chocolate or sweets as children; bananas were a special treat. Big occasions might call for the teeth-withering sugar of gulab jamun and laddoo, but by the time they moved to Scotland their internal sugar blueprint was set – and it was fruit. They obsess about and hunt down the right sort of mangoes and delight in endlessly gutting and slicing fussy fruits like pineapples and melons and foisting them upon us while we are just trying to watch *Dallas* in peace.

But fruit isn't sweet enough for us. We have already moved on to the hard stuff – a quarter of Kola Kubes with an Irn Bru chaser, five Highland Toffees and a Drumstick, burning off the enamel on our teeth. Every child I know is obsessed by fizzy sweets and chocolate bars. We cry and argue over them. Kids eat chocolate bars on their way to school, at break time and on their way home. And so I become addicted. I demand more but my parents are unequivocal. So I do the next best thing. I steal other people's. In primary school I sneak back in after playtime has started and crawl under the communal desks. I go through other kids' schoolbags to see if they have any extra chocolate. The first day I swipe a Texan bar; the next a Penguin biscuit. After that the teachers realise something is going on and make everyone put their playpiece on their desk every morning. I stop; but my buzzing greed doesn't.

I soon understand that I will have to buy my own chocolate. My parents are really strict about pocket money though. They don't really understand why I need it; I am fed enough at home. But I am still hungry for sugar, always unsatisfied. So if I can't swipe other kids' chocolate and I am not given money for sweets like everyone else, I will just have to find the money. I start to slip change that is lying around or down the sofa in my pocket, I rifle through my dad's suit pockets which are always reassuringly full of change. I take a fifty pence, careful not to swipe everything. My dad is so relaxed about money that he never notices. I never try this with my mum – she would catch on within a day. I hide the change in my inside blazer pocket, walking slowly past my mum and dad in case I jingle. Then after school I head to the newsagents and stand in front of the plastic jars of sweets, wondering what I will pick a quarter pound of today. Chocolate Limes, Pineapple Chunks, Pear Drops, Strawberry or Lemon bon bons, Midget Gems, Sherbet Drops, chocolate mice – all delicious, all to be cracked open on my poor teeth and the evidence destroyed well before I got home. My mum has a sixth sense for these things though and one day she hides in the doorway of a shop next to R. S. McColls and catches me coming out with a bag of sweets, marches me home and makes me empty my pockets.

As the years pass tiny things change. My dad occasionally eats a purple-wrapped Fry's Turkish Delight or little boxes of sugared almonds which look pretty but taste of soap. At a push, my mum will eat half a Bounty – slowly and purposefully – because she says that her mother, my Nano, likes it too. My dad develops a thing for Cadbury's Fruit and Nut, no doubt from all the shifts he does in our petrol stations sitting on a wobbly stool in front of all the chocolate bars handling filthy ten pound notes and dealing with occasionally hostile customers who refuse to believe he can possibly be the manager until he uncoils himself to stand a full six foot three inches from the floor.

'Awrite, big man, keep yer hair on!'

We love going to the petrol station, mainly because we are surrounded by chocolate. When my mum isn't looking my dad slips us a treat. We poke our noses into the stockroom. Boxes and boxes are piled high with ridiculous numbers of chocolate bars inside them. Forty-eight Kit Kats, one hundred and twenty-eight Twixes, fifty-four Mars Bars. And when my mum takes us to Pakistan for the Christmas holidays, the suitcases are full of comfortable M&S bras for her sisters and boxes of Cadbury's chocolate for all my cousins. They put their hands out and I combust with jealousy as they take their share.

The only place we can eat as much sugar as we want is at birthday parties, four of which follow in quick succession every year in August, October, November and December. The cake is ordered from a bakers and is always pink or blue – it looks like a castle and tastes as light as a feather. We eat Mini Rolls, French Fancies, jam tarts, Mr Kipling apple pies, YoYo and Penguin biscuits, Wagon Wheels, cheesy footballs, Chocolate Digestives, cheese and pineapple on cocktail sticks stuck into an orange, egg sandwiches, corned-beef sandwiches. Loads of kids come, loads of cousins come – it is a sugary and vomitous free-for-all. My dad takes the photos and the Super 8 movies. My mum presides and looks beautiful in an impractical sari or super cool polo neck and flares, brandishing a knife to cut the cake, wearing winged eyeliner and with her hair pinned up like an Asian Joan Collins. A former teacher, she is in her element, marshalling children into circles and games. She loves a round of Ring-a-Ring-of-Roses; my friends watch her in awe. During musical bumps, we throw ourselves down on the carpeted floor so hard that pictures and photos rattle on the walls. Someone is always sick.

Gujranwala, Pakistan, 1953

Auntie Sarfraz is my mother's only friend. She lives on a street off the road that runs behind us. Her house is our only social outlet and I am so glad of it. It is small but immaculate. I love how particular she is about her furniture – it is all symmetrical and tidy, her chairs are always covered in clean sheets and her cushions are always plump and lined up perfectly. I crave this kind of tidiness and order. Auntie Sarfraz has the face of an angel – full and round, not gaunt and sad like my poor mother's. She is very fair and short and plump; her clothes are always bright. In my house I feel starved of colour and joy. But not here. She talks to me for hours about everything; she gives me weak tea and brings a plate of the most delicious biscuits I have ever tasted – pale brown, round, and filled with flakes of coconut. I feel calm here.

In her house I see my first pedestal fan. It is long and pale green and I love to sit in its stream and feel its coolness. We have ceiling fans in our house but I have never seen a portable one. She even takes it out into the courtyard one day and I bask in the decadence of it all. Sometimes my sister Naz comes with me; but I like it best when I have Auntie Sarfraz all to myself. I begin to wonder if other mothers are calm and happy like her. The only spoiler of my enjoyment is her husband. When he comes home, he scowls at me and asks his wife when I am leaving. Which is pretty much as soon as he arrives. All I know about him is that he owns an electrical store in the centre of the city. He is short and thin, with small eyes trapped behind thick glasses and a mouth full of misery. I gather up my dupatta and skip home.

Gujranwala, Pakistan, 1958

In my penultimate year at college I secure one of the principal roles in the end-of-term play. It is a romance called *Ziddi*. The bride and groom were cast; I was the sister-in-law. Everything was going well until, on the third performance, the teacher told us that a photographer was coming to take a picture for the college magazine. It was a girls' school with a female audience, so I didn't have to wear a burqa. But if a photographer was coming, anyone who read the magazine would see my face. I couldn't abandon the role so when the photographer arrived I turned my head away from him. And then I prayed that my brother wouldn't see the picture. But of course he did.

'Baby! What the hell is going on? Your photo is being sold in the market place!'

He stands before us in the living room, red in the face.

'What?'

'Your photo. Your school play. Some bastard is selling it in the market. Why the hell did you let them take your photo?'

'It was just for the school magazine. I didn't know he would try and sell them outside, did I?'

'Well, he did! They're all looking at your photo in the market. It's disgusting, shameful. What were you thinking?'

'Oh come on . . .' I say. 'I bet you can't even tell it's me. I turned my face!'

'Well, I can see it's you! What the hell were you thinking?'

'I knew you would react like this – that's why I turned my face. No one else did. Give me some credit.'

'You shouldn't be in a play if everyone can see you.'

'Well, I'm in it now, aren't I? I can't just abandon it.'

'Yes, you can.'

'What?'

'You can't be in the play any more. Tell them you're out.'

I am furious, battling to keep my voice level. I have always played by the rules, keeping myself covered in front of strangers, even turning my face away when no one else bothered. And still – still I am to be penalised. Not for the first time I envy my brother his gender – his ability to do anything, go anywhere at any time. He is free to be the college Romeo that everyone says he is. Nothing bad will happen to him. And me? It's not like I want to dance through the market at midnight with bells round my ankles. I just want to act in a college play.

'I can't tell them that. I must do the play. Be reasonable.'

He stares at me, his eyes angry. But he sees in my face that for once I am not going to back down.

'OK. You can do the play. But you have to promise that you won't act in any more plays at college. This is the last one.'

I nod with gritted teeth.

'Wait.'

He leaves the room, while my sisters look sheepishly at me. When he returns he has a sheet of paper and a pen with him.

'Write it down.'

'Write what down?'

I am beginning to feel exasperated.

'Write down that you give your word not to act in any more plays while you are at college.'

I consider him for a while and, just to defuse the highly charged situation, I bend my head and write out the promise. He takes the paper from me and heads out of the room, blowing ostentatiously on the ink to dry it. The next year, my final year at college, the teacher decides to put on my most favourite play of all time – *Anarkali*. I am inconsolable, but I keep my promise. I have learned this from my father.

Glasgow, Scotland, 1986

I don't see much of Imran any more. Sometimes I pass him in the hall, where he stands staring out of the window, muttering to himself, playing out both sides of a conversation, adopting different pitches and characters. Then he will either scowl at me or look through me. His head is low, studying a pattern on the floor or a shape dancing near his feet; or his chin is raised as he tries to defeat whatever is tormenting him, pulling him in large exhausting circles all day every day.

But my little brother loves music. Not just the ghazals of Ghulam Ali, but pop music too. He is so precise about the Urdu of ghazals, despite not speaking the language. But when it comes to pop music in English, he hears what he wants to hear. If I am playing a song he likes, he barges into my room.

'Hey, Aasmah! I like this song!'

He is smiling and starts singing along to Janet Jackson, closing his eyes and hamming it up.

'*Smell I think of you . . . baby . . .*'

'Haha, it's 'when' I think of you . . .' I laugh.

He frowns: 'No. No, it's not.'

He repeats his line and I let it go.

Another day I am playing on repeat 'Tender Love' by The Force MDs, which he loves.

'*Shminder love . . .*'

'It's 'tender' love . . .'

A cloud passes over his face. He looks furious.

'It's NOT!'

He gives me a filthy look and turns his back on me so he can continue singing. I let it go. Again.

But my brother's main obsession – apart from cars – is the weather. He watches the forecast very closely every evening. Sometimes I can hear him outside my door, muttering to himself for half an hour. Then, all of a sudden, after he has turned it round in his head five hundred times, he pushes the door open:

'Is London always hotter than Glasgow?'

The correct answer is: not always but more often. The answer for a peaceful life is: no, of course not. But even if you lie, he still needs confirmation four or five times. Then he might leave. But doubts remain. Was she lying? The forecast in the paper says it's hotter down there. Then he will go and ask someone else; if they lose their patience, he will flip – shouting and spitting or increasingly throwing something to the ground, like a plate or a vase. These are edgy times. Most of my mum's ornaments are missing wings or legs or are in the bin; increasingly we feel as if we are tip-toeing barefoot across those pieces of glass.

SIX

Glasgow, Scotland, 1983

We are always in the car; driving makes things better.

It calms my brother after an explosive episode; it makes us feel special when we can sit in the front with a parent and choose the radio station; it centres us after a trying day when we have not found our place. Cocooned in a car, the wet thud of the door, the clicking of the indicator, our parents' watchful eyes in the rear-view mirror. Glasgow spins past us and we sink into the seats and into our thoughts.

The red-brick tenements of Maryhill shoot by, men in football scarves gathered outside pubs, the bare spaces and flat puddles of Woodside, old women in plastic headscarves dragging tartan shoppers over crumbling pavements. We reach the outskirts of the city centre, the road rising up and snaking round to meet Cowcaddens, the M8 thundering over our heads. And then we are into the centre – sinking into the grand greyness of this tidy city, its cupolas and gargoyles, its arches and pillars, its pedestrian precincts and buskers.

When we are very young, all six of us pile into the car and dad drives us to the airport. We emerge from the

Clyde Tunnel, leaving the motorway behind us and find the road that loops around the perimeter of the airport. We park up in a dusty layby and jump out of the car, pressing our noses up against the wire fence, squinting at planes as they plunge towards the tarmac or shoot into the sky. My dad is enthralled by these planes and stares at them a little bit longer than the rest of us as they melt away.

The drive to the petrol station takes us from just north of the city to the gateway to the mythical east end. We descend from the motorway and loop round to sit at traffic lights in front of the Victorian blackness of the Royal Infirmary – looming tall and hideous over us. Soon we are rising and falling on the grand-sounding Alexandra Parade, before turning left opposite the old Wills cigarette factory. Thousands of these trips, with the same start point and destination.

We make these journeys so often that the routes become etched in our minds; any deviation is unsettling. We take comfort in the routine, staring at the shops, the houses, the roads, always in the same order. Pistons and Components. The Chip Chik Inn. Blockbuster Video.

Young and untroubled, I study the toy shops and newsagents. I cheer as my mum speeds and skips over the steep hill on the Switchback Road. I drink it all in – my city, my world. Later, I watch as it recedes from me. I stare deeply into the faces of the people outside. It takes me years to understand something that was always true.

These people are old and young, straight and hunched, kind and choleric. But they are not the same as us. And we are not the same as them.

Maryhill, Glasgow, Scotland, 1969

I step out into the street, my black shoes peeping out from beneath the skirt of my green sari. I am wearing my black coat – the same coat I brought with me on the plane three years ago – and I grip my large black bag in my right hand. I assess the journey ahead. I have to take two buses to get to school, so I allow extra time in case either is delayed. Ten minutes into my journey, the sky has turned from a neutral white to an elephant grey. I watch in dismay as large thick raindrops cling to the windows of the bus. One change, one bus and a walk until I get to work. By the time I reach the gates of the primary school, I am soaked. I hurry into the toilets and try to dry my hair on the industrial towel roll. My thick coat has taken most of the rain, but the water has soaked through to my sari underneath. I rearrange my embroidered palloo and wonder how it can be both cold and rainy in August.

Another teacher comes in and stops in her tracks.

'Oh, Mrs Myre! Och no, you're drenched!'

The woman whom I recognise from the staff room yesterday is wearing fewer clothes than me – a corduroy mini skirt and a thin shirt – but looks smart and dry.

She bolts into a toilet stall and comes out with a few sheets of Izal toilet paper – and hands them to me.

'Gie yerself a wee rub! You'll soon dry out.'

She smiles again sympathetically and disappears into the cubicle.

I pat myself with the paper then let out a groan. My outfit is ruined; I feel scruffy and creased. I have lived here for three years and still cannot fathom the weather. It is nearly 8:30 a.m. and I need to get into the classroom. I lift my dripping hem and my black shoes give a sad sigh as I squelch down the corridor, my curls already reinvigorated by the water and starting to frizz around my head. That day I resolve to travel to work in more practical clothes – trousers and a jumper – and change into my sari before lessons. You are not allowed to wear trousers in school and I have no intention of wearing a skirt.

I love everything about my job – the structure, the lessons, the uniforms, the teachers – but not the chalk dust. It makes me cough and splutter and I have to get my sinuses drained regularly by my GP. But I love having a job, I love working with children. I even like the school dinners. They don't taste of much, but they keep you warm. I have developed quite a thing for mashed potato and apple crumble.

Just two months into the job and there is already a pupil I look out for. His name is John and he sits on the end of the second row. He is thin and pale, with curly brown hair. His eyes are always bloodshot, but they are mostly closed because John falls asleep in my class every day. He buries his face into his folded arms and I watch as his little head and chest rise together. He is by no means the only one. Many of the kids look exhausted, as if they haven't slept. But John is so slight that I feel protective towards him. He has never handed in any homework; when I ask him where it is, he says he has lost it on the bus. After class, I ask him why he is always sleeping. He shrugs.

'Well, what time did you go to bed last night?'

He considers the question, perhaps never having been asked it before.

'Dunno, miss – after twelve mibbe . . .'

'Why so late?'

'Ah wis waitin' fur ma maw tae come in.'

I try to keep my eyebrows level.

'And when she does come in . . . ?'

'She picks me up aff the settee and puts me tae bed.'

He looks pleased with his answer. His love for his mother is painted all over his face.

I speak to the head teacher, who looks pained.

'We can't solve problems at home, Mrs Mir. It's unfortunate. But this is the case with lots of children here.'

I think of my own children, who are with Helen. How things have changed from that day in August when

I sent my husband to the launderette with the nappies and he came back with a tiny, shy woman with an enormous beehive.

'This is Helen,' he announced half triumphantly, half nervous about my reaction. 'She can look after the children!'

I didn't know what to say. She wasn't quite what I was expecting. Her shoes and clothes seemed worn and old, her jet-black hair was all over the place. And she seemed nervous and spent a lot of time looking at the floor and rubbing her hands on the sides of her legs. I looked from her to my two-year-old daughter and my newborn son.

'Have you . . . looked after children before?' I ask tentatively.

'Only my own, Mrs Mir. Two boys, all grown up now. But I've always wanted to look after kids.'

Her voice is so kind. I hand her my son and watch her face melt as she receives him.

'Oh, you are a good boy,' she croons, and my son wrinkles his nose and shows her his gums. My eldest child, who has been watching sagely, approaches, looks up into her face, then clambers on to her knee. I have never seen anything like it.

A few weeks later, I notice that John isn't asleep but is in fact staring intently at me. When I catch his gaze, he blushes furiously and looks away. This goes on for a few days until I summon him and ask him if everything is OK. He shrugs, his hands deep in his pockets, his chin on his chest and says 'Aye'.

Such a little thing with so many grown up mannerisms. He turns to go, but at the door he stops and looks back.

'Miss?'

'Yes, John.'

He looks troubled and I worry that something bad has happened.

'Is everything OK at home?'

'Aye, miss.'

'Then what is it?'

He bites his lip and blushes again.

'Ah canny say. It's . . . bad.'

'Well, if you don't say then I can't help, can I?'

He considers this and nods, his chin dipping into his chest again.

'Colin says . . . says . . .'

I wait.

'Colin telt a lie.'

'Oh right.'

'And ye shouldnae tell lies, right?'

'That's right.'

Silence.

'What was the lie?'

'It's a really bad yin. He says . . . he says you're . . . you're . . .'

A door slams in the corridor. He jumps.

'. . . a P-Paki.'

He puts his hands on both of his hot red cheeks, scandalised.

'And yur no', are ye, miss? Ye . . . yur nice.'

I try to stifle a smile.

'Well, the thing is, John, I am actually from Pakistan.'

His eyes widen.

'The word is Pakistani. You're Scottish and I'm Pakistani. It's a long word, isn't it? Pak-i-stan-i. Four syllables.'

He just stares.

'And I hope I'm still nice?'

'Aye, but ma maw says Pakis ur dirty an 'at.'

'Well, am I dirty?'

I bring my hands up into view and turn them over so my palms are visible.

'Naw.'

He looks confused.

'Well, then maybe your mum got it wrong. It happens.'

'OK, miss.'

'Anything else, John?'

'Well, whit should ah say tae Colin?'

'Tell him that, yes, I am a Pakistani, and if he has any questions to come and see me.'

His brow is less knitted than it was when he arrived and now he walks easily to the door, picking up speed as he goes and disappearing out into the playground. Colin never comes to ask me anything and John resumes his sleeping sessions in lessons, but I bring in my wedding photos to show the class and they ooh and ahhh over the photos of me in a red silk sari and jewellery and my husband as slim as a reed in a black three-piece suit.

'Ye look like a princess, miss! Jings! Look at thaim bloody jewels!'

The rest of the year passes uneventfully and when June arrives I tell them they will have a different teacher next year. When they ask why, I say it is because I am going to have another baby.

Glasgow, Scotland, December, 1979

At school we are reaching the first stages of hysteria over Christmas. The classroom is heavy with tinsel and holly. The tree sits fat and lopsided in the main hall, loaded with inexpert decorations and lumps of inedible gingerbread. The teachers tunelessly hum Christmas songs; even the grumpy janitor wears a Santa hat atop his furious face. Every day brings another activity: we make Christmas decorations with old Christmas cards; we produce Advent calendars; we fashion clumsy gift boxes out of cereal packets and coloured foil paper for home-made tablet or shortbread. Cans of snow spray and plastic tubes of glitter stand to attention on our desks. Cotton wool clings to our school jumpers; we have glitter in our ears. We buy bumper boxes of cards from R. S. McColls and give the jolly fat Santa ones to the friends we like and the austere Victorian ones to those we don't. Every day, the school Christmas post appears – red envelopes thrown on to our desks in an unscientific popularity test. We whoop with delight at everything – even the appearance of a roll of sticky tape or a tube of wrapping paper.

We practice our hymns for the Christmas concert and, if we are lucky, our lines for the Nativity. I am never chosen but don't mind, as there are only really a few main parts. But I take my hymns very seriously, belting them out so loudly and word perfectly that the teacher selects me to sing one of three solo parts. At the concert in a beautiful cold church, I sing my part loudly; the words mean nothing to me but I love singing. My parents should be here, like those of the other soloists are, but of course they are not because I haven't told them. I finish my part and the next soloist picks up. The wide eyes of the congregation linger on me long after I have finished. I must have been really good, I think.

I love walking home on the crunchy snow and seeing all the decorations and trees in people's windows. My favourites are not the oversize Santas but the fairy lights threaded through trees that twinkle intermittently, extending their Christmas cheer out into the street and making me feel part of it. I linger at snow-capped low garden walls staring into people's homes, their living rooms lit by a special warm fuzz, mums and dads in fluffy sweaters and socks, the TV on, a huge Christmas tree dwarfing everyone, a beautiful inviting tableau.

I can still hear Slade's 'Merry Christmas' and jingling bells when I close my eyes at night. It is all we talk about. It's like we have lost our minds. At school I can go along with the mania, I can talk about turkey and mince pies and Brussels sprouts, although I have never eaten them;

I can speculate about presents, although I never give or receive any; and I can make decorations with skill and enthusiasm, but I will throw them in the bin on the way home because we have no tree to put them on.

Because in our house Christmas doesn't just not happen; it is banned. I must be about seven or eight when I realise this. Walking in the door of my house is like walking through the wardrobe into a reverse Narnia. There is no magic here. No decorations, no production line of parsnips in the kitchen, no wrapping paper poking out of drawers, no big plan for the big day. Nothing. Christmas Day is like any other day. When I ask why we don't have a Christmas tree or why we aren't having a special meal, my mum tells me in hushed tones that it's because we don't celebrate Christmas; because we are Muslim. This befuddles me, as the only Muslim thing I do is not eat pork. I don't go to the mosque, I don't pray, my parents haven't insisted that I speak Urdu or Arabic, I've never been taught the Qu'ran, although I see it on the highest shelf of our bookcase. We hardly celebrate Eid either. I don't mind being a Muslim, but it seems to involve not celebrating Christmas, not being like everyone else and not doing anything in its place either.

Every year I ask more and more questions. Every year I hope my parents will see sense; that Christmas isn't really about Jesus; that I won't be seduced by Christianity; that trees and selection boxes and tinsel are harmless, secular fun. But every year I am told – no.

I am too young to really get to the bottom of why my parents have such a strong reaction to Christmas, but as the years march by I realise it has more to do with my dad than my mum. The more trenchant my questions become, the more she hushes me in case someone hears me. Who? Then I realise it must be my dad. My larger-than-life, pinch-your-cheeks, squeeze-the-life-out-of-you-when-he-hugs-you dad. He works every day at the garage – weekends, bank holidays. He never has a day off. Except for Christmas Day and Boxing Day. On those days my loud, affectionate, well-groomed dad becomes unrecognisable. He sits in his chair in his dressing gown, stubbly and strangely dishevelled and watches TV, studiously avoiding any mention of Christmas. If a Christmas programme or advert comes on, he shakes his head and changes the channel. He seems annoyed, angry, but I don't know what about. There isn't a whiff of Christmas in the house, he has two days off – so why?

One year I try to intervene. It is early December and Christmas is already in full swing. I wait until my dad is in a good mood and slide on to his knee. He pinches my cheeks and cuddles me, his comforting Brylcreem-and-beefburgers-smell meeting my nostrils as he tries to read a cricket report in the paper.

'Dad?' I venture

'Yes, my princess?'

'Can I ask you a question?'

'Of course. Anything.' He kisses my fingers, his huge nose bumping against my tiny knuckles.

'I was just wondering if maybe this year . . .'

He turns the page and I almost fall off his knee. He giggles.

'. . . if we could have a . . . Christmas tree . . . you know, for Christmas. Just a tiny one. And I could get you a present, Dad, maybe a–'

'A what?' he sounds incredulous and irritated, all his good humour has drained away.

'A tree . . . ?' My voice was drying up in my throat.

'No.' He shifts.

'Can you get up, you're hurting my legs.' He sounds annoyed.

I stand up.

'Oh. Why not, Dad?'

'Absolutely not.'

'But why?'

'We're not Christian. We don't have trees. Christmas is stupid anyway. It's a lot of rubbish. Absolute rubbish. I don't want to hear the word.'

I stare at his face. His mouth is tight, his eyes on his paper. God how I hate the huge paper he always wraps around him when he doesn't want to talk. I wish I could punch it, rip it to shreds, set fire to it. I stand there for a while until I feel the stab of tears and then the liquid pooling in my eyes. I don't want him to see me cry, so I turn and walk away.

In the kitchen, my mum is cooking as usual. The pressure cooker hisses menacingly, the air is thick with coriander, the windows are steamed up. The smell, the noise, the light – the absolute antithesis of Christmas. It's stifling and suddenly I feel trapped in my alternate anti-Christmas reality. She sees my tears and her shoulders dip.

'What's wrong?'

'Dad hates Christmas!' I cry 'So no Christmas for us. Ever. It's so unfair!'

'I told you we don't do it.'

'But you said it was because we're Muslim. He says it's because he hates it. Why does he hate it?'

My mum looks fed up.

'It's just the way it is. Stop going on and on about it. It's the same every damn year. Round and round in circles. It's exhausting. Just leave it, please?'

I have no option but to leave it. What my dad says, goes. If he hates something or someone, there is no going back on it. He loves or he hates. His emotions are huge, like him. He wants to buy everyone an ice cream or he never wants to talk to them again.

So Christmas is banned. It is the same every year, although I notice, as my face gets harder and my tears more profuse, my mum tries to make tiny changes. She buys us selection boxes from Safeway, she starts leaving little presents outside my door, one year she even lets me decorate my bedroom with tinsel. But the miserable essence of our Christmases never really varies. I wake with absolute dread on Christmas morning at the barrenness of the day ahead. I stay in my pyjamas all day feeling miserable, watch the Top of the Pops Christmas Special with my siblings in a different room to my dad, eat a normal meal of boiled white rice and curry – not even pilau – then scoff my selection box and go to bed sugar-charged and tear-stained, glad the whole awful pantomime is over for another year.

Sometimes we spend Christmas in Pakistan. There it is easier to ignore. The trees are green, the days hazy and sunny, the nights surprisingly cold. I find it less awful but I still feel a wrench when it gets to midnight on Christmas Day. My thoughts turn back to the world I have left behind, the world I cannot bear to be excluded from. Drunk people in Santa hats, special films on TV and illicit Christmas parties at school.

Strangely my dad likes Hogmanay. Maybe because it is just a moment, not a month. And not too Christian. Maybe because he feels guilty about the Great Christmas Shutdown. Who knows? We are all allowed to stay up, watch the bells ring out on the TV, drink glasses of Coke and eat peanuts. We have to say Happy New Year to unknown relatives who phone specially from London and America and Pakistan. We are glad we can share in something that everyone else is doing too. We can say Happy New Year to people for days after, a simple shared midwinter exchange. It reconnects us to others after the traumatic fracture of Christmas Day – at least until next year.

But I nurse the hurt of no Christmas for years, decades, more so than my siblings, although I note they never go big on Christmas for the rest of their lives. As I get older and the ban ossifies, I give up the fight and take to staying in my room all day, reading, listening to records and crying angrily but silently. The Christmas experience is an annual reminder that I am not like everyone else and I never will be.

When I finally leave home at twenty-four, I take control of Christmas. I go to buy a tinsel tree for my flat – but then, at the last minute, realise I don't have the energy or will. Twenty-four years of nothing has set the precedent. I also know that Christmas is for ever ruined; that it relies on family to make it work – a family that I keep a distance from at Christmas, not wanting to ever taste that self-imposed misery again. All my friends spend Christmas with their families – so I am on my own. For the next fifteen years, as I live in Glasgow, the Midlands and London, my dad asks me why I am not coming home for the holidays. The irony is not lost on me. What for? So we can ignore Christmas all over again? I always opt to work Christmas Day, much to the delight of my employers. I walk the entire festive floors of department stores, touching baubles and trying to figure out what mince pies are. Christmas is utterly lost on me and to me, but at least I can rest my hand on it now without being scolded. I am forty-seven when I have my first Christmas. I am fifty when I buy my first proper Christmas tree. My unexpected daughter looks at me expectantly and I do not hesitate to give her the Christmas I never had. We taste it together. It is sickly sweet and gravy-rich. It is glitter in our shoes and sticky tape on our clothes. It is the soft breath of twinkling fairy lights wound round a bannister or a picture and icing sugar dusted on to Christmas tree-shaped biscuits. It is seeing her face, her smile, lit by candles and finally making peace with what eluded me all those decades ago.

Bearsden, Scotland, 1983

There are certain things that mean it is going to be a peaceful day in our house. If the numbers and words align in my little brother's head; if he gets all the answers he wants; and if Philip Hayton is reading the BBC News.

Over the years we learn his preferences and obsessions. He loves cars and any TV shows to do with cars. *The Dukes of Hazzard, The A-Team, Knight Rider.* We tape every episode – or 'corder' it, as he calls it – and he watches them all the time, memorising dialogue, facial tics and tiny technical details, like number plates and colours. He is obsessed by the weather forecast and only likes it when Philip Hayton is reading the news, 'because he is very smart, you know, Aasmah?'

He loves sweet things and has no boundaries. Where I could eat a chocolate bar, he could eat forty-eight, and he once did. Forty-eight Kit Kats from a box from the Cash 'n' Carry, telling my mum that he 'felt a little bit sick'. Another time he ate too many guavas from a tree in Lahore and expelled pale yellow vomit everywhere.

My brother displays obsessive traits and fixates on one thing for decades. His favourite cars are Volvos; he is obsessed by the weather in Glasgow and how it compares to the weather in London or Pakistan. He has the same conversations with us for thirty years and we learn what to say. You must agree with him; if you don't, no matter how subtly or reasonably, he becomes furious, either immediately or later that evening when a crashing glass or a screaming noise indicates that he has been stewing over your incorrect or inauthentic response for hours and it has finally boiled over. The script becomes predictable. His eyes flicker, his jaw moves, he whispers, berating someone, rocking on his heels, dancing about. His anger never subsides, it has to come out. And when it does, he screams, kicking out and balling his fists, occasionally lunging at you. The only people who can calm him down are my parents; the rest of us seem to make him worse.

But my brother also gives us moments of pure pleasure. Because he spends so much time in the company of adults, he apes their way of talking. At the age of eight or nine he sounds like a man who has been propping up a Trongate bar for thirty years. 'Aye, you wouldn't believe it to look at him. Absolute gem of a guy.'

'Have you seen the traffic? Bloody terrible. It's the council's fault, you know, Aasmah? Roadworks ev-er-y-where.'

Sometimes he will see or think something funny and giggle away for ages, tossing the funny image around in his head, the shadows and bogeymen chased away for one delicious hour.

He switches from wise phrases and clichés to secret gibberish. 'Back of the hossies. Some nice goats. Man of the TV.' We hear these phrases for thirty years and never really know what they mean.

He goes through a phase of memorising calendars. We ask him what day 5 September 1976 was and he can tell us. This is our favourite trick. We are impressed and he feels clever. We connect over something useful and understandable. But after some years of this, he grows tired of being the performing seal and stops doing it. My parents ran petrol stations then expanded into garages and car hire. He meticulously remembers the number plates of cars long since scrapped.

He has affectionate names for us. I am Meal, no idea why; my mum is Nicky – apparently after a book she once read him about Naughty Nicky the monkey; my sister is Corned Beef Nose. This nonsense is preferable to when he loses his temper or becomes frustrated with the shadows dancing in his head and starts to kick at the car or at us, or swears in public.

These meltdowns are the worst. What happens at home – the screaming, kicking, throwing – we keep to ourselves. Living in such an isolated place makes my parents relax; my brother can scream into the air and no one hears or calls the police. My dad is a sociable man who loves to take us all out, but it is becoming more difficult and stressful.

'We're going out! Get ready, everyone,' Dad shouts up the stairs, and we all hop about in joy. All six of us pile into the car, elbows digging into each other, little punches being dispensed. My parents have already extracted promises from my little brother that he will behave. In the restaurant he always sits beside my dad because he can calm him down, apparently. But this is prevention rather than cure, not that there is a cure. I don't think we ever really enjoy a meal out when he is there because we are waiting for the explosion. When it comes it is almost a relief. Someone says something wrong or something flashes in his head and he starts staring at his hand or into the distance and rocking. At this point, our food starts to stick in our throats and we wait for the inevitable.

'You're a bloody bitch!' he screams at no one, banging the table.

'Aaaghhhhhhhhhhh!'

He stands up with such force that his chair falls over.

'God is a bastard!'

The colour drains from our faces; the restaurant falls silent. My dad looks angry and embarrassed, my mum crestfallen. Sometimes my dad takes him outside for some fresh air and bear hugs. But, when they come back, we have bolted our food and are ready to leave. We drive home in silence; our trips to restaurants grow rarer.

*

It didn't work out for my brother at the primary school – they couldn't do much for him. And so he started a long list of special schools with even longer names in places further and further away from our house.

When I am ten years old, he is attending a school that requires him to be picked up by a special minibus from outside the town hall, which is near my school. My parents drop both of us off there at 8:30 a.m., then I am to wait with him until the bus comes and walk to school. I sit on the steps of the town hall, he stands nearby staring at his hand as usual, and we wait. People passing slow down as they notice something different about us. My little brother is still cute at eight, but there is something about the way that he stands, the weight on his toes, leaning forward, that always makes people look again. That plus the whispering to himself and the hand movements. I will do anything for my brother, but I am getting to the age where I realise this is something else that sets me apart from everyone else. Most of my friends are sweet about my brother – they love playing with him and always say hi; but some cower, afraid, and never come back. And as he gets bigger and louder, he becomes less cute and more frightening. My heart flips every time he gets on that bus, two feet on each step as he always does, his little bag on his shoulder. He is unruly at home, but when given rules and regulations by external people, he is pretty quick to fall in line. I don't really understand what his school is like. Does he like it there? Are they kind to him? Does he have any friends? I dismiss this immediately. Of course not. He has never had a single friend. All he has is us.

Our conversations as we wait for the bus are minimal. He obsesses as usual about the weather or Pakistan or cars or *The A-Team*. But if I ask him if he likes school or is it fun or what does he do there, he looks distant or starts talking to someone imaginary. He can't really carry on a conversation; he only knows how to tell me things – opinions, facts. I always wonder if he is lonely; years later I realise that it was me who was lonely.

*

One morning we arrive in the car park at 8:30 a.m. and wait. And wait. It gets to 8:45 a.m. and there is no bus. I start to worry that I might be late for school. It gets to 9 o'clock and I am beside myself. My brother is pacing around, shaking his head and muttering, upset by the change in routine. I have never been late to school and am terrified. Will the door be locked? What should I do with my brother? I can't take him with me. I take him by the hand and go to the phone box. I reverse the charges and luckily Helen, who is at home, answers and agrees to walk to meet us. Because we live in the middle of nowhere and Helen is in her sixties, this takes half an hour. I deliver my brother to Helen and then run to school. It is 9:40 a.m. – the first lesson is almost over.

I knock on the door of the classroom and go in. My teacher looks unimpressed. She opens her mouth but I blurt out:

'I'm sorry Mrs Jordan. The bus didn't come for my wee brother and I had to phone home!'

The class bursts into laughter and I have no idea why.

'Sit down, Aasmah. It's quite the pantomime with you, isn't it?' she says.

I take my place, sweaty and puzzled. What have I said that was funny? Am I not in trouble? Is everyone laughing because they know my wee brother takes a special bus?

Robert McKendrick pokes me in the back with a thirty centimetre ruler.

'Oi! Are you an alien?'

'Eh?'

Stuart McConnell grins next to him.

'E.T. Phone. Home'

They all burst out laughing again. I haven't seen *E.T.*, but I am just relieved that they haven't rumbled me.

*

I don't remember the moment that my parents tell us that something is wrong with my brother. They use different words. He is special, his development is slow, something happened when he was born. He is 'hand-icapped'. All these urban myths and half-explanations do nothing to clarify, they just cloud things. My dad is particularly reluctant to accept that something isn't right. It will work out in the end, he says.

I do remember the day he finally stands up and the day he walks. With his tongue poking out, he pulls himself up on to the sideboard where the large radio sits. He looks like he has climbed Everest, his chubby cheeks red from the effort, matching his polo-neck jumper. The day he walks is, of course, captured on Super 8. He is standing at the top of the hill that leads down to the burn. We are there en masse. In the foreground is my little brother, like an inverted V, his feet on the ground and his little hands, his bottom in the air. He pushes himself up, waits to balance, then starts to motor his tiny legs forward until he falls and picks himself up again. My mother is in front of him, her hair in a high bun, in flares and a polo neck, with a glass from the petrol station promotion half full of Coca Cola and a McVities Chocolate Digestive as an incentive. She keeps moving backwards every time he gets near and soon his little legs tire and he falls over on to the grass and starts to cry. In the background we are performing for the camera as usual. All three of us are horsing about, dancing. For some reason my sister has a cricket ball, which she throws up to catch, but instead it lands on my head and she sweeps me into a delicious hug to comfort me. It is chaos. We are six. We are complete. That day our hearts are bursting with hope because my brother has finally walked and it's surely now only a matter of time before he catches up with everyone else.

Glasgow, Scotland, November, 1973

My fourth child is born in unusual circumstances. Imran arrives with none of the drama that accompanied the others. He appears quickly at 5:02 a.m. on his exact due date, unlike my previous three. They all looked a bit overcooked or underdone. But this one looks like a doll – a good healthy colour, shallow brown curls and eyelashes, a perfectly round face and a rosebud mouth. A golden child. A perfect baby who feeds well and sleeps well, like clockwork, who only cries if there is something fixable wrong – like a wet nappy or hunger. He is docile and placid. Even when he is a bit slow to sit up in his pram, I put it down to his placidity. When we play with him, he doesn't really interact. If I put him next to another baby or child, he shows no interest. Again I think he is just very independent. When he still isn't walking at two, I take him to the GP, who says that it is nothing to worry about, that some children walk late and that because he is quite big that might be putting him off. This all sounds feasible. He starts to walk finally when he is three, although it takes a huge effort by me. He seems to inhabit his own world; if he can't do something or reach something, he gets frustrated and cries easily. The doctors say he is just a late developer. I notice that when he is lying in his cot, he places his hand in front of his face and moves it from side to side, his eyes and head moving with it. At first I find it cute, then I realise it might be unique to him. I feel that something is not right but I have no idea what it is. All my children walked and talked at the correct intervals – but he is late to walk, talk and come out of nappies. When the time comes for school, he starts at the same primary school that all of my children attend. But he doesn't last long there. He doesn't really engage with the teachers or pupils, and just stares into space or at the wall; often he cries and screams for me. After a few meetings, the head teacher says that we will have to take him out; that he is disruptive; that they don't have specialist staff to teach him; and that he would be better suited to a special school.

At home he loves to play with cars. He lies on his side, his ear to the floor, his arm extended, and moves his cars around the carpet for hours with huge precision. He is ritualistic about many things. If I have to change his clothes, he wants all his clothes off before he even thinks about putting the new clothes on. And it always has to be trousers first. If I try to put pants on then a top, this causes a huge meltdown. Many times I try to teach him at home, using flashcards, but he loses interest quickly. He is my most challenging pupil. Did something happen at birth? Did my accident contribute to anything? Why did this happen? For years we thrash around in the dark, going round in circles, becoming frustrated. It is not until 1994, when he is twenty-one, that we finally get the answer.

Mum at twenty.

My Uncle Khalid on his wedding day
with my grandfather, 1964.

Mum receiving yet another prize at college.

My mum, far right, turns her head to avoid the photographer
at her college play.

Winning the badminton doubles cup
at college.

Three sisters – Auntie Naz,
Auntie Samina and Mum, 1963.

My Auntie Neelam and
cousin Asmi.

Is this the most romantic photo ever? The Campsie Hills behind them,
Mum and Dad, matinee idols, 1966 – the year they married.

Me, still not much hair
at seven months,
with Mum.

Imran, starting to stand at two.

A unique hairstyle and not many teeth
at primary school.

Hanging out
with my cousins
in Rawalpindi,
Pakistan.

Dimples and
Toothless –
me and my
wee brother.

Deep in the
gloom of my
teenage years.

A rare trip after school with my friend Felicity.

Dad, Mum, me and my huge glasses at Prizegiving, around 1987.

The kindest face – Helen in her seventies.

My Nano's only visit to Glasgow, mid-1970s.

SEVEN

Bearsden, Scotland, 1984

Things falls apart one Friday. I should have known. Fridays are always strange. In that seething secondary school, it is like a grenade pin is pulled and children behave differently, appallingly to each other. Violence is meted out during the week in a piecemeal way, but as we approach the end of the week, the beatings become more vicious and regular. It feels like we live on the edge on Fridays.

This school is like something from the pages of a science-fiction novel; a factory, an experiment. It is huge but it still cannot accommodate the growing numbers of children as the catchment area expands, so portable cabins and annexes are constantly added. It is a mess, overloaded and ungovernable. In my year alone, there are seven classes of thirty. I am not entirely sure why I have ended up here. I was supposed to go to the same secondary school as my sister – but something changed at the last minute as always, something to do with Pakistan or my brother that I didn't completely understand. What I do know is that I do not like this school; it feels edgy and unpredictable and, for the first time ever, I do not feel safe.

Even worse on Fridays is the double dread of Religious Education followed by Science, the two most unpopular subjects. I find Science baffling, but nothing is as bad as R.E. Religion confuses me. It seems both important and unimportant at the same time. People are always arguing about Catholics and Protestants, but I have no idea who is who and why it matters. A paradox exists of the importance of and total disrespect for religion. At birthday parties, parents glare at me thunderously if I say 'Oh God!' or 'For God's sake!'; school assemblies are steeped in Christianity, which I find unfathomable but unproblematic. Yet many children are openly hostile about religion. They sit on gravestones with cans of beer and cigarettes; they boast about having sex in churchyards. I also realise that religion is something else that can potentially divide me from my friends; so I pretend it does not exist.

We sit in that classroom on a Friday afternoon, furious and bored, learning about world faiths that we don't care about and will never retain in any meaningful way. As the teacher, a young man whom many of the girls have a huge crush on, reads from a book about faith and belief, the atmosphere is sharp and tense, the clock ticking slowly towards the release and mayhem of 3:30 p.m.

We have worked our way through Buddhism, Christianity and Hinduism. Today it is Islam. So disconnected am I from my religion – apart from dodging pork in the canteen and crying at Christmas – that I haven't fully grasped that I am in fact a Muslim.

So when Mr Lang asks if there are any Muslims in the class, I look to see if there are. There is a lot of turning round and shifting and shrugging before he fixes his eyes on me.

'Aasmah?'

'Uh-huh?'

'You're a Muslim. Can you tell us about Islam, please?'

I feel mortified. Everyone is staring at me, curious, surprised.

'I don't know much about . . . it.'

'Come on, don't be shy.' Mr Lang is growing impatient. 'We all want to know. You're a Pakistani, aren't you?'

The air changes. Some kids giggle at the word.

'No . . . I'm Scottish. I . . .'

'What do Muslims do?'

I think hard.

'Well . . . they pray . . . and don't eat pig . . . ?'

My voice trails off.

'That's so stoopit . . . why would ye no' eat bacon? It's delicious!' says Grant McHugh. Everyone laughs. He looks at me with contempt.

'Yes, Aasmah, they pray and they do not eat pig. And do you know why?'

He is looking expectantly at me again, urging me on with his thick eyebrows. I don't know how I have stumbled into this test, for which I am fully unprepared.

'Because it's . . . dirty . . . ?'

Howls of derision from a class raised solely on gammon and Lorne sausage.

'How's it durty?' says Stuart McBride. 'YOU'RE the wans that are durty!' He gets ready to spit then thinks better of it, swallowing the ball of saliva, and instead moves his index finger slowly across his throat at me.

'Right – enough!' says the teacher, who can see he isn't going to get anywhere fast with me. 'Open your books at page three. NOW!'

The children turn back to their books, but there is a fizz of discontentment in the air. I look at the book. It is called 'Ayesha's World', and on the cover is a picture of a young girl in a black headscarf, her skin the colour of toffee. My heart sinks.

'Sandra. Can you start reading, please?'

My friend Sandra, who is sitting across from me and has been staring out of the window, sighs loudly and in a bored voice starts to read.

'Ayesha lives with her mum, dad, brother, two sisters and her gran and grandad. She is a Muslim.'

I look at the picture of Ayesha, a timid looking girl who keeps her eyes down and looks sad. I am annoyed that Sandra is pronouncing it 'Aye-ee-sha' – adding a whole syllable where it is not needed. I have two cousins called Ayesha. The extra 'e' hangs over me in the air like a huge bubble of poison. Sandra continues, as if she is reading a shopping list.

'Ayesha loves going to school. But she is not allowed. To eat pork or have a boyfriend.'

Gasps.

'Whaaaaat?' says Susan McCritchlow. 'Why no'? Are they durty too? Jeez!'

She's glaring at me. I am frozen, but my face is burning at the same time. Mr Lang raises his eyebrows.

'Do not blaspheme, Susan!'

'Absolute nutters,' she mutters, rolling her eyes in disgust at me.

'Are YOU no' allowed a boyfriend?' she demands of me. 'Who'd want to go out with YOU anyway?'

Boys near me are nodding and fanning the air under their noses, suddenly complaining of the smell of curry.

I look up at the teacher for support. He seems bored of the conversation now and is turning pages. Tears prick my eyes and I feel an anger building inside me.

When the bell goes, I can't wait to get out of this room. I feel like a layer of my skin has been peeled away, one that I must keep stuck down at all costs. It is a dangerous environment to be flagged as something different and potentially despicable.

At this school any weakness or distinction is ruthlessly exposed and punished. A boy with epilepsy is harassed until he has a fit; an Asian boy is kicked in the back regularly until he punches one of his attackers square in the teeth, knocking four of them out; a girl who is deemed to have stolen someone's boyfriend is dragged by the hair along the concrete by three other girls, and stamped on, black footprints left all over her white shirt. Justice or punishment is delivered in a millisecond, a swift cruelty that no one ever appears to question. It seems hideous to me. I decide to keep my head down and hope that this passes me by. Primary school had been a place of fun and friends and netball and custard. There were fallouts and feuds but none were nuclear and none ended in blood or bruises. Here there is a fine line between an embattled peace and all hell breaking loose. Crowds of boys suddenly run from one end of the playground to another, shouting 'fight, fight, fight!' and 'fucking kill him!' as two scrawny kids wrestle with each other, until a lone teacher comes barrelling out to break it up. Boys spit all the time, covering their victims' blazers with dripping saliva. They flush each other's heads down the toilet. Some have knives and chains. The plain girls are called hounds and dogs and barked at; the pretty ones are whores and sluts. Only a select few manage to fall into the chasm between the two – eliciting no attention because they are somewhere between ugly and pretty. But you can't be clever. If you are ever praised by a teacher, one of the tough kids trips you up as you come back from the teacher's desk, does the throat slitting gesture at you or batters you after class. It isn't worth it. So we stop trying. We're just surviving.

Redlands Hospital, Glasgow, Scotland, October, 1971

My third child has arrived early. Unlike my two other children, she has no hair and looks startlingly pale. The doctors say she has jaundice and take her away and put her under light machines while I sleep. But after just a day they return looking grave. They tell me that the jaundice is not getting any better; that she has too much of something called bilirubin in her blood and this can only be treated by a complete blood transfusion. I don't even get to say goodbye – they take her to another hospital, Rottenrow, for the procedure. I try to understand how they will suck all the blood from her tiny body and fill her with someone else's. The nurse attaches a pump to my breast, extracts the milk and sends it to the other hospital. Arif goes to visit her and comes back with tears in his eyes as he tells me what she looks like – so tiny, yellow-brown, with tubes sticking out of her. I spend those days fretting about what went wrong and what I could have done differently. Should I not have refused an epidural? When the doctors told me that the antibodies in my blood were too high, should I have been more worried? Did I eat the right food when I was pregnant?

My mother-in-law has already sent my third child's name. It was delivered on an intermittent phone line and it means brave and bold. I take this as a good omen. A few days later, she has improved and we go to collect her from the hospital and take her home. Her colour has normalised yet she looks small and weak. But she fixes her crinkly eyes on me and keeps me in her gaze.

Aasmah's hair takes an age to grow. Both my other children appeared with huge amounts of hair on their heads, but this one's is patchy and reluctant, only really appearing at the age of one. Slowly her colour becomes healthier and she fills out into a fat little bullet just like my other children. And she sleeps like a dream. When I take her to Pakistan at six months old, my relatives marvel at what an easy baby she is. She sleeps for a solid thirteen hours at night and they joke that I must have put a sedative in her milk. She hardly ever cries; maybe she was saving her tears up for later. As she grows she becomes larger than life – adventurous, mischievous, sociable. When my son appears, she is besotted with him. She pleads with me to let her feed him, but she can't get her tiny hands round the bottle, so I let her put her hand on mine as I hold it. She is always nuzzling into him and stroking his shiny cheeks. She often comes in from the garden with a buttercup and places it under his ample chin. A golden light shines under it.

'See, Mum, he loves butter!'

When it's time for nursery, I enrol her in one not far from my old teacher-training college. We play nicely, then after half an hour I sneak out. Her eyes lock on me as I edge towards the door and she clambers over everyone to get to me, screaming and crying. She wraps her arms round my waist and digs her fingers into my flesh.

'Nooooo! Don't leave me, Mummy!'

The nursery staff slowly prise her off, she is sodden in tears. But she seems to have forgotten this when I pick her up later. The next day I ask her if she would like me to stay for ten minutes. She looks in to my face.

'No. You have to go. You're too big, Mummy.'

Bearsden, Scotland, 1983

My mother is going to Pakistan. She's leaving me behind and I am inconsolable.

Moving house at eleven was traumatic enough, but this is seismic. It has been decided that my mother, my sister and my little brother are going to Pakistan for eight months initially; and I am staying in Glasgow with my dad and brother. Eight months. That's almost a year. It feels abnormal for a family to be split in two and to live four thousand miles apart when there has been no breakdown in the marriage of the parents. But as I have learned, our family is complicated – everyone has competing needs, especially my little brother, who is struggling to find a place that can contain and educate him. My parents think he will be freer in Pakistan and will have the support of a huge extended family. My sister will go to college there.

I have little choice in the matter – my mum promises me that she will be back before I even notice, that she will phone me as much as she can, and that when she comes back she might take me with her next time. I'm not sure I want to go and live in Pakistan, but I just nod mutely.

I cry hard when we return from the airport; the house feels different already. It is cold and quiet. There is no sound of my mum's heels. I wake the next morning and check her room, her wardrobe. All the places that she inhabited are now empty. It's like she has taken all the sound and light with her. How will I get through this?

When she knew she was leaving, my mother cooked huge amounts of food and froze portions of it in plastic bags. Every night when I come back from school, I pick out a bag and defrost it in the microwave. I soak the rice for at least an hour like my mum showed me and then cook it for me, my dad and brother; I become an expert. My dad is grateful that there is food on the table when he gets home from work. After the meal, my dad and brother disappear into the lounge to watch telly and I load the dishwasher and clean the kitchen with Helen. We settle into a rhythm – my dad and I. I feed him, he drops me off at school in the morning, always on the brink of lateness and with Radio One on loud. But I miss my mum, her softness, the way she absorbed the hard edges of my dad and brother. Without her there, I watch the house slowly drain of empathy.

My dad is a good man, still hugely generous and loving. And there are perks to him being in charge. He takes me to Dolcis and buys me two pairs of unsuitable black court shoes with thin pointy heels, the kind my mother would never let me buy.

'Are you sure these are school shoes?' he asks with a frown, as he peels two £20 notes from his wallet.

'Yes, Dad, don't worry. Everyone's got them,' I say, which is true. The school I go to is so wild that girls wear almost whatever they want. They chop their skirts in half, wear white stilettos, fluorescent ankle socks, unbuttoned shirts, half knotted ties. Almost anything goes.

But things inevitably start to shift. My dad is facing all sorts of financial pressure in his business and he misses his wife. I am twelve years old, yearning for my mother as school feels unsafe, my body is changing and my periods start. My fourteen-year-old brother is unhelpful and dismissive. So my dad and I start to clash. We have periods of catastrophic anger, deadly silence and then tearful reconciliation. It is a toxic and exhausting pattern.

I keep my distance to try to limit the rowing. I spend a lot of time on my own in one room; my dad and brother in the other. Thankfully Helen is there every day and I grow closer and closer to her. But I need my mum. I really need her. One minute we were all together in a small house and I went to a normal school and had loads of friends – now I am virtually on my own.

Around this time, I befriend Sandra, who comes from Netherhill. She has tight red curls, freckles and unforgiving, close-set brown eyes. I am staring at her lace fingerless gloves one day and we start talking about how much we love Madonna. I don't care that she is from Netherhill, which everyone says is very rough, and she doesn't seem to care that I am Pakistani. Sandra is funny and warm and just wants to have fun. She smokes and drinks cans of something called lager. She tells me she steals money from her mum and she wears white stilettos and a fake leather jacket. She hates school and can't wait for the day to end. Some days she isn't there – and when she returns, she is quiet; it takes her a few days to return to her normal self. On those days I miss her. She begins to spend time at my house, whistling at the space. We colonise the attic room on top of the garage. We drag two plastic chairs and a box up there and drink Coke and eat sweets. She always has so many sweets for us to share. She chain-smokes cigarettes and looks about forty when she does, tired and expert. She becomes my surrogate sister. I start to dress more like her, borrowing stuff from her – a leather jacket, some zebra-patterned court shoes. School becomes bearable because she is there and she is in with the tough kids. She travels to school on the same bus with them every morning, they are her neighbours, so they leave me alone. Life becomes safer, not so edgy. I start to relax.

One day she arrives at my house on a bike as big as a horse.

'What the hell is that?'

'It's ma dad's old bike.'

She has never mentioned a dad. I have been to her house once, worried as the bus swung out into a road I didn't know, fretting that my dad would be angry with me for wandering about after school.

'Come on, Aasmah, it'll be fun! Live a wee bit!' she always said.

Her mother was a pretty, exhausted-looking woman, who seemed tired of arguments with a twelve-year-old girl and who looked surprised to see me. The atmosphere was strained between them and we left soon after. Sandra kicked the kerb when she came out, swearing softly into the air.

Today she finally persuades me to have a go on the huge bike.

'It looks a bit . . . knackered,' I say.

'It's fine, honest . . . it's just the brakes don't work.'

'What?'

'The brakes . . . they're screwed. But ye just back pedal tae brake. Look, I'll show ye.'

She rides the bike forward and then pedals backwards and it stops.

'Try it,' she says, clambering off.

I am not convinced, but it seems to work. So off we go, me on mine and her on hers. When we get to the top of a steep hill, we swap bikes and speed down the hill. As I approach the end of the road and the busy junction, I squeeze the brakes. I hear her shouting at me:

'Mind? The brakes don't work, Aasmah. Back pedal, for fuck's sake!'

Shit. I back pedal furiously, but the bike is going too fast now and won't slow down. I can see the main road in front of me and I am hurtling towards it. If I have an accident, my dad will be furious. He will find out I have been hanging out with a girl from Netherhill who has given me a dodgy bike, that I am wearing high heels and probably smell of the smoke from Sandra's cigarettes. If I crack my skull open or break my leg, it will be in the *Milngavie and Bearsden Herald* and I will be in trouble for weeks. Or dead. Desperately I put my foot down. It hits the road at speed and tosses off my shoe. My bare foot scrapes along the concrete and eventually slows enough that I can jump off, just yards from the junction. The bike goes spinning into a wall, clattering and bouncing. Kids in gardens come out to see what the noise is about. I look down at my foot which is hurting and see the skin on the inside of my right toe hanging off in a bloody mess. A wee kid comes running to me with my shoe.

'Is this yours?'

I take it from him silently, grimacing at the pain in my foot.

Sandra has abandoned her bike and has run to me, her face is red, her breathing heavy. I quickly jam my foot into my shoe.

'Aasmah! Are ye OK? What the fuck happened?'

She looks at the bike lying twisted on the pavement in front of a post box and then back to me.

'Why didn't ye back pedal?'

'I did! It didn't work.'

'Oh God, whit's happened tae yer foot?'

I look down. There is blood trickling out of the top of the shoe.

'Nothing.' God, it was hurting.

'Aasmah, get yer foot out. Lemme see.'

Her voice is so mature and authoritative that I obey. I slowly ease my foot out of the shoe, a bloody mess. It sticks and is painful to extract.

'For fuck's sake, yer toe is all . . . oh Jeez.'

'It's fine,' I say grimly. 'Sorry about your shoe.'

'I don't gie a fuck about the shoe!'

'But my blood, it's everywhere. I'll wash it . . .'

She looks at me strangely. Then she jams her foot into the shoe. I stare at her in shock.

'What . . . ?'

'There! Yer blood. My blood. It's nae big deal.'

There is silence. She smiles gently as she removes her foot, my blood staining her toes. I try not to stare.

'Ye need tae clean that and bandage it. It might need stitches.'

She sounds like my mum. I feel a pang for her, thousands of miles away.

No way am I going to tell anyone or go to a hospital. I limp home pushing my bike and Helen helps me clean it and put a plaster on it. To this day, I still have a huge lump where the skin grew back on the inside of my right toe. But that day I also realised I had a new kind of friend – one who didn't flinch at my skin, my breath or my blood. She would protect me.

Hanging out with Sandra changes everything. We have nothing in common but we cling to each other. I am lonely, she is angry. Through her I get a pass into the tough gang. The class bully Goldy starts to talk to me, sometimes we hang out in the same circle, sometimes he copies my homework. I feel so relieved to be accepted into this group – even if they are pretty scary. There are so many upsides.

School dance practice arrives and the teacher says those dreaded words: 'Find a partner, everyone'. I stand against the monkey bars and wait to be paired off with a girl or the teacher. To my surprise, I see David McKenzie sidle up to me, looking embarrassed. I stare at him, open-mouthed. And then he says the unbelievable words:

'Er, would you like to be . . . my partner?'

I can hardly speak. I just nod. An actual boy has asked me to be his partner. Why? I look for Sandra, but she is far away at the end of the line and just gives me a wink and a thumbs up. I feel a rush of emotion in my chest. I feel like the warts have finally fallen off me; at last I'm like everyone else. It just happened much sooner than I thought it would.

We look out for each other at the start of the day. We roll our eyes when we are told to sit apart and then come back together to walk to the next lesson. It is such a huge school that there is a lot of walking from lesson to lesson, often from portable cabin to annexe. We walk to French with Miss Harris, who wears peasant skirts and frilly blouses and says that everything is 'ultra easy'. We have English in a sunny annexe with Mr Paton, who is young and balding and is clearly in love with Miss Harris. The dreaded R.E. is in a temporary building too. Maths is inside the school with Mr Elder, who makes up songs about your name and dances around the class. One tough boy called Titch walks around with an industrial scowl and a huge set of keys attached to his belt. One day Mr Elder clips his keys to his own belt and mock swaggers around the class, hips thrust out, imitating Titch. We all laugh because it is spot on, but Titch sits there unsmiling, his face twitching in anger, and later swings his keys into the face of a boy who laughed a little too hard.

Bearsden, Scotland, 1984

It is April and my mum has been gone for six months. I am resigned to it, but it fills me with anger whenever I think about it. I speak to her every fortnight or so on the phone, but the line is so bad and I can hardly hear her. Her distant voice doesn't even sound like her and it upsets me more than reassures me. All I ever ask is:

'When are you coming home?'

'Soon, *beti*, soon . . . I– [crackle] – '

'Mum?'

A hissing noise.

'I can't hear you!'

'. . . is school?' her voice appears again.

'Fine,' I sigh. If only she knew how things really were.

I don't really know what else to ask – I have no interest in anything that is happening out there.

'Is it hot?' I say weakly, something sticking in my throat.

'What? I can't hear you . . .'

'Never mind, Mum, it doesn't matt–'

The lines goes dead and I hand the phone to my dad. I don't look him in the eye. I am angry because he always speaks first and I get the tail end when it always cuts off. Every time. It is cruel enough that my mum has gone: not being able to speak to her privately is worse. I feel like a hostage – I want to break free and shout down the phone that things are actually terrible and please rescue me, but I know this will create a huge fight between my dad and me, so I just keep quiet.

On Friday afternoon we stare at the prospect of R.E. and Science again. That lunchtime Goldy had copied my homework. I had been doubtful, because I hadn't really understood it either. But it gave me such a thrill to be asked. I knew I was in the inner circle and I knew I was safe. He didn't say thanks this time or nudge me conspiratorially – he looked irritable and distracted, his eyes were red as if he hadn't slept. Something about him unsettled me that day.

We pile into the classroom for R.E., little kids falling over as they get their ankles kicked by the bigger kids.

'Right. Enough!' shouts Mr Lang, 'Just sit down and shut up, will you?'

Everyone seems to be in a bad mood today. Chairs are scraped and bags are thrown on the floor.

He hands out a piece of paper to everyone.

'OK, today we are doing Women and Islam.'

My face falls. I stare at the paper. Oh God, not again.

'Awwwww, whit? Ah thought we'd already done Izzlam!' moans Wendy Jardine.

'There's plenty still to learn, Wendy, thank you. You can start reading, please.'

She rolls her eyes.

'Why not just get Aasmah to read it? She's an Izzlam.'

I squirm and look at the clock. Forty-five minutes of this.

'Muslim, Wendy. Islam is the religion. Muslim is the person who practices it.'

He looks expectantly at her and waves the sheet of paper.

She lets out a huge ballooning sigh and slumps on her elbow.

'Muslims believe that men and women should not mix,' she starts. 'They should be educated separately. When they marry, they do not see each other before the wedding – it is called an arranged marriage.'

'Whit? That's mental!' shouts a wee boy in the front row.

'Hahahaha, are you going to get an arranged marriage?' shouts Goldy from the back.

I shoot him a look, feeling confused and betrayed. Then I put my eyes down again. I hate this. Just read it, and get it over with, I think. Wendy starts droning again, not pausing at any of the full stops.

'It is called an arranged marriage Muslim men can have more than one wife–'

'Whaaaa? Ahahahaa. Durty bastards!' laughs Goldy.

'Stuart! You use that word once more and you will be out of this class.'

Goldy folds his arms defiantly. When the teacher looks away, he silently mouths 'Bastard'. Everyone starts whooping and hissing. My head feels heavy, my thoughts gluey. Something is wrong. I look at Mr Lang. Why is he doing this? Can't he see how awful this is for me? But his face is blank, he looks bored. I look at Goldy, who is staring at Mr Lang, a cold smile dancing across his face. The class is in uproar.

'Do I have to keep reading?' complains Wendy. 'This stuff is mental!'

I look at Mr Lang, willing him to stop. Can't he see that something bad is about to happen? But now he is in a battle of authority with Goldy; he doesn't care about the collateral damage.

'Yes, Wendy,' he says levelly, his eyes on Goldy, skinny as a pipe cleaner, legs open, arms folded, chin up.

I just want to get out of the room. I stare at the blue sky and white clouds outside and wish I could taste the air. It feels catastrophic in here. I try to keep the tears in my eyes.

'Muslim men can have more than one wife,' she continues. 'Sometimes Muslims marry their cousins . . .'

My head is in my hands as the class erupts again. There is too much noise and, with every sentence, Wendy is peeling away my soul and exposing me for what I am:

weird, foreign, deplorable. I notice Sandra laughing too
and I feel the sting of betrayal. Goldy's voice carries over
the noise and reaches me.

'Ho, Aasmah, ur ye gonnae marry yer cousin? Naebody else will!'

I've had enough. I snap.

'SHUT UP, GOLDY!'

But no one hears me. They're too busy banging their
desks and stamping their feet. I look at Mr Lang, who is
flustered and angry, and I say in a loud voice the words
that will change everything. If only I had known the
power of my words. If only I had just swallowed them
and left it, let them have their fun until they moved on
to the next person. But that day I felt I had been pushed
too far.

'Why don't you have a look at Goldy's homework,
Mr Lang? I think you'll find it's very similar to mine.'

Goldy's smile freezes, as if he has been shot in the
throat. The class goes quiet. No one speaks for an age. A
light passes over Mr Lang's face, a shadow over my heart.

'Stuart, can you bring your homework here. Aasmah,
you too.'

There is a moment where no one moves.

'Now!' shouts Mr Lang.

I get up and walk wretchedly to his desk and leave
my notebook there. Goldy gets up slowly and passes me
on my way back. I shrink back slightly as I feel the heat
of his fury. There is absolute silence. I glance hopelessly

at Sandra, who is staring at me in horror. But, at that moment, I know even she cannot save me. Mr Lang scans our books and basks quietly in his victory, delivered to him unexpectedly by me.

'Right, Stuart – stay behind after class. You'll be getting detention for this. And, the rest of you – open your workbooks at page forty-five and answer the questions.'

I spend the next twenty minutes staring at my book, keeping my head down, my face hot, my heart cold. I feel like I am writing on water, my words dancing drunkenly on the page; that I am not really here. Occasionally someone shoots a look at me and whispers to their neighbour, but the class is the quietest it has ever been. After R.E., I stumble to the science block.

Mr Doyle is the exact opposite of Mr Lang. He is a serious man, academic, grey-haired, often dressed in tweed and a black teacher's gown. There is hardly ever any fooling around in his lessons, and even less so today. He looks pleased with this. He walks by as I pour a liquid into a test tube, my hands feeling slippy and unsure, and something makes me turn and look deep into his face. He pauses. Please, please help, I think. Something terrible has happened. Then he straightens a test tube, folds his arms behind his back and moves on. I watch him walk away; I am not to be saved.

I keep waiting for Goldy to reappear. I worry he might beat me up at the final bell. But there is a quietness in the air unusual for Fridays and he is nowhere to be seen. Is he still in detention? Where is Sandra? Everyone else is keeping their distance from me and their voices down. I walk through the gates, like a shoplifter, waiting for an alarm to sound, filled with dread for what I have done and what is to come.

That weekend I really need my mother. I turn round what has happened many times in my head. My mother would listen to me and understand my fear. I don't know what she would do apart from be there. There was no way I could tell my dad. He would think it was nothing. And so, ironically, I turn to religion. I write a note.

'PLEASE GOD, make everything alright on Monday. From Aasmah.'

I write it with the triangular red and white biro I got from Help The Aged's Hector Club. I fold it neatly, keeping the corners sharp, trying to make it as aerodynamic as possible. Then I point it at the sky and let it go. It dips behind some trees and I close the window. God will get it. He is my only hope.

*

Monday comes and I walk through the playground as if in a dream, everything feels blurred and tricky. Am I imagining that everyone is turning their back on me? Why would they do that? Where is Goldy? Is he going to confront me? Would he beat up a girl? Would everyone see me cry? Would it hurt? I stand, apart from everyone, and wait for the bell.

Finally I see him. He is surrounded by his hangers-on. His eyes light up and he runs towards me

'There ye are – ya fucking clipe! What are ye looking at, you fucking hound? Ye're finished!'

He spins round to the other children in the playground and jabs his finger at me.

'Naebody's tae talk to her, right? Ever! Anywan speaks tae her, they'll get fuckin' battered!'

I watch as he stamps off, back to his gang, which parts to reveal Sandra. Our eyes lock and she gives me the look of death. I turn away; I cannot bear to see it.

This is the first full day of The Silence. No one speaks to me. My friends, my enemies, the class squares, the tough guys – everyone gives me a wide berth. There is no cruelty, no words – just the turning of backs. The sudden complete silence is more painful than anything. But it's Sandra I miss the most. The scaffolding of my school life collapses without her. I suppose I had grassed on one of her own and that trumped everything. So I take my punishment. But the next day stretches into the next and days became weeks and still nothing. I queue for classes on my own, I sit in lessons on my own. At break time, I circle the massive playground; if I keep moving, it will be less noticeable than sitting somewhere on my own, drawing attention to my isolation. Lunchtimes are tough. Fifty minutes to kill and where can I eat? I can't sit in the canteen any more: I'll stick out like a sore thumb, confirming my pariah status. So I walk and walk and walk. In the rain, the sun, the wind – whatever. I am always on the move. Sometimes I go into a shop and buy a sandwich and eat it walking. Other times I don't bother, I just keep walking, looking busy, like I have somewhere to be, someone to meet. I live in hope that Goldy will forget, forgive, move on to the next victim, call a truce. He soon begins to ignore me, but the kids still keep their distance. Until the fatwa is officially lifted, nothing will change. I am in limbo.

Then one day, it does. A new girl starts. I can't believe it. As she gulps and blushes in front of the class, I see my opportunity. As expected, everyone ignores her and she is left to stumble up and down the corridors of the labyrinthine school on her own. From somewhere I find my voice and, when no one was looking, I sidle up to her.

'Claire? Hi, do you want me to . . . show you where . . . things are?'

She goes red and stutters. 'Y-yes.'

It is the first time that anyone at school has spoken to me in weeks. I blink, check that no one is watching, and whisper, 'OK, but don't tell anyone'.

She looks puzzled but nods anyway.

The next few days are delicious. I feel myself thawing; my voice returns. I keep it as inconspicuous as possible, this illicit friendship. Was I breaking the terms of my punishment? Claire hadn't been there when It happened. So the rule didn't apply to her, did it? And yet, I knew that, if it is too loud or noticeable, if I dare to speak or laugh, Goldy and his henchmen will notice and they will try to destroy it. I have to hold on to it. So Claire and I sit quietly together, but don't talk. Having someone next to me, after months of isolation, is wonderful.

At the weekend I go to R. S. McColls and buy two fluorescent pens, one for each of us. I fly into school on Monday, looking for Claire everywhere. I finally spot her sitting on a wall reading a magazine. I shove my hand in my pocket to retrieve the pen but, as I approach, she looks up, her face changes and she slips off the wall and walks briskly away. I stop in my tracks. I don't even need to ask her what has happened. There is no point. Someone has told her. A messenger pupil or maybe Goldy himself. There is to be no respite, no early release.

My dad still occasionally picks me up from school, windows down, Pakistani music blaring from inside as other children stare and laugh at what they call 'bong-bong music'. Mortified, I slink along the street and get in, hardly looking at him as I reach for my seatbelt and close the window. Why is he so loud? Doesn't he care that everyone is staring? He is frustrated with me too.

'Why do you always look down?' he says, looking furious. 'Look UP. There's no point being a mouse. Be a LOIN, for God's sake!'

I consider telling him, then I remember how he had found my handwritten note to God. He had spied it under some leaves and had read it then thrown it in the bin, telling me not to write silly notes. My dad is a lion. But I am not. He shakes his head in bafflement and we drive off, the voice of Ghulam Ali soaring and dipping through the streets of Bearsden, pulling out my insides and leaving them lying on the road behind us for everyone to see.

Wah Cantonment, Pakistan, 1980

In the night we burrow into unfamiliar quilts that smell of faraway; the cicadas sing while we surrender to sleep; motorbikes rev and car horns scream on the main road. Our sleep is punctuated by the azaan – at first a disturbance, then a magical comfort.

It is winter in Pakistan and it feels like we are visiting the edge of the world. The mornings are crisp, filled with distant smoke and unknown noises, a short flurry of heat at the apex of the afternoon. Everything is bathed in sepia. People speak in long poetic Urdu or in short, sharp Punjabi. Others switch between the two. Everything is upside down; this is not our home. But we sink into this world, this place, because here we are loved.

My mother and I are sitting on the vast parched lawn of my Aunt Samina and Uncle Javed's house in the military cantonment near Rawalpindi. A thin velvet quilt lies beneath us to cushion the uncomfortable day-bed made of knotted rope. Behind us a gardener wrestles with a hose, another man levels and waters the soil. Occasionally they look over at us and stare. At the perimeter of the garden a lush green hedge stands twenty feet high.

My mother is brushing my hair. She spends ages doing it, telling me that I have her hair and I must brush it one hundred times every night. I laugh at the notion. Then she divides my hair precisely into two parts with the sharp point of a comb, and the brushing starts again before she finally loops two hairbands at the back of my head and gathers my springy hair into pony tails as fat as beehives. As she does this, she recounts fables from her childhood. They are like nothing I have ever heard before. There are no beautiful princesses or wicked witches; no beanstalks or glass slippers. Instead her stories are inhabited by magical animals and birds; by warring sisters and jealous brothers. They are sometimes frightening, but their moral always stays with me, picking away at my conscience for weeks.

A long time ago, two childless women find a baby in a basket and both claim him as theirs. They fight over the baby until a local elder says that he will rule on the issue. He asks each woman why she should have the child.

'I will give this child the stars and the moon,' says the first. 'He will sleep on a bed of soft golden threads and drink from a cup of the finest marble.'

The second woman is silent for a moment.

'I cannot give this child any gold, any stars or any riches. But I will give him a coat made of my love and a blanket of my softest kisses.'

I wrinkle my nose at my mum, at the age of nine, thinking I know which answer is better.

The elder frowns.

'Before I decide – is either of you willing to give up this child to the other so he can live in peace with one mother?'

They both shake their heads sadly.

'Then – you will have to share him.'

He signals to his assistant to bring him a sword. He holds the terrible weapon above the child.

'I will cut the child in half and you may have half each. There is nothing else for it.'

The first woman starts to weep then nods numbly. The second woman just stares. As he swings the sword up, a cry rings out.

'No!' says the second woman, leaping forward and putting her arm in front of the sword. 'Stop! Give him to her. Save him!'

The elder stops mid-air, the sword grazes her hand, a few drops of blood trickle on to the earth. He puts the sword down and points at her.

'You will have the child. You were ready to sacrifice your love, perhaps even your life. That is a mother's true love.'

He picks up the child and gives it to her. Then he turns to the first woman.

'You have learned a valuable lesson today, sister. Think on it.'

I turn to my mother to look into her face.

'I don't understand. The first lady was going to give the baby gold and the moon and stars. The other lady didn't want the baby after all.'

She laughs at me.

'*Beti*, what would you rather have? Gold and money or your mummy's love for ever?'

I consider this for a while, taking in my mother's soft pillowy skin, her dimples, inhaling her smell, noticing the way she dips her chin to really study my face. I know that her eyebrows don't lie straight like mine and that childhood vaccination marks on her left arm have stretched with her skin and now look like shiny flattened oyster mushrooms. Sometimes I don't know where she ends and I begin.

'Mummy for ever, of course.'

We sit in silence for a while, the winter sun on our backs, the smoke prickling our nostrils, birdsong gathering in the trees. She rubs my back rhythmically with the flat of her palm.

Pat-pat, pat-pat . . .

I am always on the move. Keep busy. Don't stand still or look lost, even if you are. At lunchtime I disappear. I walk the fifteen minutes to the town centre and buy something hot from the bakers and walk back slowly, sometimes the rain soaking into the paper as I walk. It's all about killing time. Sometimes I sit on the bench near the war memorial outside my primary school, but it is raised and prominent and I don't want to be seen. I hide my loneliness like a stain. If it is raining hard and there is nowhere to shelter, I creep into the outside public toilets at the town hall where, in happier times, I had sat and waited with my little brother for his school bus. It stinks and it is cold, but I am safe, hidden and dry. In those freezing lonely moments, I turn over in my mind how things have come to this.

Since we left the house on the hill, it has been a long slow march to this. Silence at school, constant arguing with my dad, an absent mother. And now here I am in this draughty concrete block, sitting on a wretched toilet lid, eating my lunch, staring at posters about something called V.D. I miss my mum so much. I feel it like the cold in my bones – sharp and deep. She would have fixed this. If she were in the house, she would have applied a balm to my wounds; she would have insisted on hearing my voice, instead of letting it disappear little by little every day.

I creep in to her room most days and settle myself at her dressing table. In front of the triptych mirror, I stare at my face – grey, furious with acne and usually blotchy from crying. There are drawers on each side, which I have gone through already, trying to find something of my mum, a clue as to why she has left me behind or when she is coming back. But there are just hairpins, packets of cotton wool and mismatched buttons.

There is a plastic doily in the centre, and a few perfumes and some old lipsticks. The perfumes smell old and heavy; the lipsticks are rounded and stubby. It is like a museum. She has been away for so long that everything has a layer of dust on it, including the glass bottle of Oil of Ulay. An oval tube of Vaseline Intensive Care lies on its side; she used to rub it into her hands and elbows every night. I smell each bottle and dab some of the contents on to my wrists, conjuring up her scent and her presence, wiping the tears from my face with the heels of my hands.

*

I'm not sure when I transferred the bulk of my love from my dad to my mum. For the first eight years of my life he sought me out and kissed my hands and pinched my cheeks. He told me that, when I was born, his luck turned around and his business became successful; that I was his good luck charm and I would always be lucky. While my dad lavished ice creams and kisses on us, my mum was busy with the mundane bits of parenting – making sure we were washed and dressed, that we had drunk our milk and brushed our teeth. And my mother, although beautiful and loving, could also be as hard as nails. She gritted her teeth when she was angry with you. When she frowned at you, it was as if the sun had disappeared. She was the strict one. And yet I felt drawn to her. My mother was not a big hugger. She would receive one if you threw yourself into her arms, but she rarely initiated one. But when she needed you to have a nap or just to comfort you, she would pat you rhythmically on the arm or back and you instantly felt calm and safe. If you could get her on her own, her attention was delicious. She listened patiently, gave you good advice and always made you feel better without necessarily telling you what you wanted to hear. My mother was fair, not emotional like my dad. When I realised that my dad acted mainly according to his emotions, promising the world but not always delivering, I started to gravitate more towards my mum and her sensible strictness. She told me that I looked like her – the same curly hair, the same flat nose; the same eyes and eyebrows. She told me that I was as determined as her, but possibly more stubborn. One day I came to realise that I just couldn't be without her.

*

Eight months after she went away, my mother is on her way back. She really is. I don't know why or for how long. I confirm this with my dad five times. I smile and hug him for the first time in months. I look at the calendar and feel like I am dreaming. It's like being released from prison. It's over.

I have dreamt of this moment for eight months. Eight months is too long to be without a mother, especially this mother. When she appears, it is strangely underwhelming. I am just numb. Too much has happened. I give her a small hug, nor daring to speak. She looks smaller than I remember, and smells of a different land.

I keep her in my eyeline all day, following her about at a safe distance, listening to her voice from behind doors and through walls, not daring to fall asleep in case she disappears again. If she could do it once, what is stopping her from doing it again? My trust has vanished.

Two days later, I overhear her on the phone to a relative saying that she has reached here safely and that she will see them in six months. The ground slips away from my feet again. She isn't staying. I knew it.

In the evening, we finally snuggle up together properly. She smells of Glasgow again – of Head and

Shoulders shampoo and Oil of Ulay. It feels surreal to be so close to someone you have pined for, for so long.

'You're very quiet . . .' she says.

I squeeze her tiny body, digging my nails into her until she pushes me away.

'What's wrong with you?'

I reach deep down and extract my voice. It comes out like a low growl.

'Mum, please don't send me back to that school.'

'What do you mean?'

'I will not go back to that . . . place.'

'What on earth . . . ?'

'When you go back to Pakistan, take me with you.'

So she did.

EIGHT

Bearsden, Scotland, 1976

Helen makes us sausages and beans for lunch. The theme tune to *Grandstand* is playing on the TV. She leans over me to cut my sausages into quarters and I feel the softness of her body against my ear. She smells of lavender and bleach. My little brother is whacking a toy car on the tray table of his baby chair. I spear a quarter sausage on my fork and another on my knife, then I bang my cutlery upright on the table, shouting:

'Look-a-look-a-Lelly! Look-a-look-a-Lelly!'

She has heard this many times, but she still laughs, throwing her head back and showing me her gums. Most of her teeth fell out years ago and she only has a couple left. My parents call her Helen, but we have somehow arrived at Lelly – no doubt because one of us couldn't say her name properly when we were toddlers and it had stuck.

Helen's hair is dyed the harshest black, her skin is as white as chalk, her eyes grey-blue. But she only transmits warmth. She is four foot ten and built of laughter and scolding, of fluster and patience. She wears a floral smock and a long cream cardigan, the pockets of which are always filled with elastic bands and safety pins. Outside, thin black shoes encase her tiny feet; inside she wears worn slippers with fat rings of fur round them. The jingling of her pockets and the tap-tap-tap of her feet announce her arrival.

My dad brought her home one day when my older brother was a baby. By the time I arrive two years later, she is part of the family. She is our fairy godmother, surrogate gran, mopper of tears and cleaner of bums. She feeds us, bathes us, cuddles us, fights for us. She stays for twenty-eight years. Migration, illness and disapproval try to separate us; they all fail.

Helen drinks weak tea and loves a piece and jam. She adores *Coronation Street* and black-and-white films and only watches ITV. But she reserves a special love just for us. She is always plucking us under our arms and lifting us into her kind face. She is forever hoisting one of us into a large cumbersome pram with big silver wheels. She spits on hankies and wipes whatever requires it – a leaking nose or mouth, a clumsy spill, a bloody scratch. She climbs into an ambulance with my accident-prone older brother, who seldom has his shoelaces tied and tumbles down the carpeted stairs, crashing through the glass door at the bottom. We trail after her everywhere and, when we cannot find her, we seek her out.

'Lell-eee? Lell-eee where are you?'

And yet we drive her to the limits of her patience, bickering and biting each other, scratching and yelling.

On at least three occasions she leaves the house saying that she can't take it any more. We stare at each other in horror as the door slams and we run to the end of the road, begging her to come back, pulling at the sleeves of her cardigan. Our parents will be furious with us if they find out.

'Lelly, Pul-ease! We're sorry, we're so sorry. We'll be good this time, we PROMISE!'

After a while she stiffly walks back to the house, her face pink with annoyance, little strands of black hair dancing in front of her wet eyes. We feel terrible that we have upset her. Until the next time.

Glasgow, Scotland, 1968

My husband takes the terry cloth nappies to the launderette to wash them. While they spin round in the huge drum, he tries to focus on his newspaper, but his mind is elsewhere. It is less than two months until I start my teacher training course and we still haven't found anyone to look after our two children. We have asked everyone; we have even put an advert in the window of the newsagent on the corner. Relatives tell us that we will struggle to find anyone who wants to work for an Asian family, looking after two Asian kids, but I don't believe that. Yet as the days tick by I start to despair.

My husband tells me that the woman in the launderette is very friendly, always asking him how his wife and children are. She often laughs and says that she is pretty sure he is the only man she has ever seen in here and certainly the only man who comes in to wash nappies.

Today she catches his eye and grins at him. But his smile is thinner and tighter. She waits for the right moment and then goes over.

'How are ye the day?' she beams.

'Oh fine, fine.'

'Yer wife OK, kids all good?'

He looks over the paper and meets her eyes.

'Well, to be honest, we're struggling a bit.'

He puts his paper down and she draws nearer.

'My wife is starting college in a few months and we need someone to look after the children. And we just . . . can't find anyone. I've been looking for weeks–'

'Whit? You shoulda telt me. I know just the wummin'!'

He looks at her in disbelief. She glances at the clock on the wall.

'Gie me five minutes, I'll get Carol tae watch the shoap.'

For the next five minutes, he sits and waits, teetering on the edge of an unexpected victory or another crashing disappointment. She takes him three stops on the bus; together they draw strange looks from other passengers – this tall brown man in a suit and this tiny white woman in her tabard. They get off and she heads for a large tenement, several windows of which look blackened with smoke. He hesitates to go in. It looks forbidding and dirty, there is smashed glass and graffiti.

'Come on! Ye want someone tae mind the kids or no'?'

He takes a deep breath and follows her in, trying not to inhale the smoke from the cigarette she is never without.

He tells me he climbed four flights of stairs to the top floor of the tenement, his heart sinking with every floor. And there behind a black door, a tiny dishevelled woman stood, blinking at them both. Shirley blew out some smoke and announced: 'Helen, this man needs ye tae look after his weans.'

Bearsden, Scotland, 1980

Helen walks everywhere with us. To the shops, to the park, to our schools, to the station to get home. She can walk for ever, her tiny legs covering many slow, honest miles. Twenty years before, she walked from Glasgow to Manchester, searching for her husband. She found him in a pub, pressed his two infant children into his body as he looked on open-mouthed, pint in hand, and collapsed into a nearby booth to rest her swollen feet and aching ankles.

Helen grew up with nothing – but she is neither bitter nor envious. Brought up in an orphanage in Ireland in the 1920s, she moved to Glasgow, got married, and worked as a cleaner on a children's hospital ward.

Her tastes are spartan. She likes plain bread and butter, cheese, maybe a bit of corned beef. I discover she likes lemon curd and I pester my mum to buy a jar of it whenever I spy it in the supermarket. When I try to share my chocolate with her or offer her a biscuit, she looks sheepish and embarrassed, as if it were someone else's, not meant for her. For her birthday in August, we buy her cardigans or Rainmates or fancy bubble baths. In our birthday cards she tells us how much she loves us in huge shaky letters and includes a Clydesdale Bank tenner. She is always making cups of tea; she loves custard creams and the Royal Variety Show. She laughs hard at well-upholstered comedians leaning on microphone stands telling mother-in-law jokes; it starts as a yelp, moves to a shriek and ends in a catastrophic cough and a face of tears.

She is virtually always smiling – singing Sidney Devine tunes, or 'Ally Bally Bee'. When the wind blows at the hem of her skirt, threatening to show her thigh, she yelps with laughter and shouts: 'Hahahaha, free show!'

Helen is from another time. She talks about food coupons, stamps, the social, the CalMac, the gas board. She lived through the war and thinks the 80s are excessive and decadent, often telling us: 'You don't know you're born!' We have nothing in common and yet somehow we blend together perfectly. We put our arms out and she comes to meet us.

She is straightforward – when I tidy my room or get my shoes on quickly, she hugs me like a cloud. But when my felt tips leak on to the carpet or I spill my Ribena, her face goes red and she says: 'Och, you're a hang of a girl, so ye are!'

I walk into a room and she looks spooked: 'Oh! You're awfy like your mum, so ye are! My goodness,' she says, her hand on her fast beating heart.

When her teeth finally fall out, the dentist gives her a set of clumsy dentures, but she can't get on with them.

'They gie me the boak,' she tells me. That is the end of the custard creams. But the food she loves the most is my mum's. Her eyes widen as my mum puts a full plate of curry in front of her. Helen is usually gone by tea time, but if my parents are going out, she stays on and we all have dinner together. Those evenings are magical – just the seven of us. She is the final piece of the puzzle.

One day my mum promises me that I can have a tea party with my friend Karen after school. I have it all planned out – I have bought the Mini Rolls and Iced Gems. But when I get home, we can't find the key to the cupboard with all the goodies. I dissolve into tears until Helen rustles up an impromptu spread – corned-beef sandwiches on white bread thick with Stork, cut into tiny squares, glasses of hissing Coke and two Kit Kats. It's not what I planned, but it tastes so good, not least because Helen has made it from nothing. I think she would do anything for us; we would certainly do anything for her.

*

I never question why Helen is there. But it turns out some people do. As I get older, I notice the inquiring looks we get when we are out. Older men and women stop and look askance. A caravan of children with bruised knees and errant socks. Four of us of varying sizes, one with what looks like an Afro, a baby hidden in a pram, all of us definitely brown, led by a woman the colour of snow with an inky beehive studded with hairpins who is not much over four foot tall. We don't really go together. And yet there is a familiarity between us that comes from years of cleaning bottoms and wiping noses. Some people find it baffling.

Years later she tells me that she fell out with friends because they didn't approve of her coming to work for us: she didn't want to elaborate about exactly what the reason was, but one of her favourite words was 'ignorant'. She did tell me about one encounter on a bus into Glasgow.

She was on her way to a department store in the city centre to buy a wedding present. She looked out of the steamed-up windows, glad of the plastic Rain-Mate tied under her chin that we had given her, feeling sleepy in the sizzling heat of the bus. In her dwam, she heard snatches of the conversations around her.

'Aye, she's a right wan . . . thinks she's Elizabeth Bloody Taylor . . .'

'Ah telt her it wisnae gonnae work, he was a bad yin . . .'

'. . . and ah telt him to no' tae buy it fae there and did he listen . . . ?'

'My man cannae get a joab. And look at them, swarming all over the place.'

She snapped out of her daydream, her spine cold.

Two women were staring out of the window, faces angry, arms folded, at two Asian men unloading boxes out of the back of a car and into a cash and carry.

'Thaim Pakis are pure coining it. How's that fair?'

Helen shifted in her seat.

'Disgustin',' spits the older woman, 'smell of curry too. My God, the stink! Cannae speak English. Just keep to thersel's.'

'Aye, keep their wummin at home, millions of kids–'

'THAT'S NO RIGHT.'

They spun round to see a small woman with a big voice, sitting on a seat with her feet barely touching the ground. She has sat forward, hoisting herself up, her face is pink and her hair is messy.

'Er excuse me, hen?'

'Whit yer sayin' is no right. About Pakistanis.'

'Oh aye, and whit would ye know aboot it, hen?' said one, unfolding and folding her arms, raising her chin and narrowing her eyes.

'I work for a family, a Pakistani family. They're good people. Beautiful kids. You've no' got a clue.'

The women looked incredulous. Helen was so angry she rang the bell to get off, even though she wasn't even halfway to where she needed to be.

'Mair fool ye, hen. They're no like us, ye shouldnae be working for thaim,' shouted the women after her as she got off the bus. 'Look after yer ain!'

But Helen was already on the street and couldn't hear

them any more. She glared back at them through the windows, walking off her anger as she stamped through the puddles of Glasgow.

*

Helen is always defending us, from little kids who follow us down the street calling us wogs or Pakis, spraying the backs of our legs with pebbles; from parents who come to the door complaining that we have done something or said something when we haven't. Indoors she is tough; to the outside world she always takes our side, her voice growing louder and angrier on the doorstep as she defends us. She is our armour, our connection to a world in which we are trying to find our place.

I come back from school one day, furious and tearful. A boy has told me that my hands are dirty and black and that he will have to soak his in water and bleach because he brushed past me. At home, I find Helen spraying a cleaning product on a surface as usual. I take off my blazer – it feels as heavy as my heart – and sit down to drink my Coke and eat my Wagon Wheel. I stare at her hands as she wipes the table.

'Whit's wrong, pet?'

I sigh.

'I hate being this colour.'

There it is. I just say it. Now it lies on the scrubbed table in front of us. Her face falls.

'Whit? Don't be silly. You're a lovely colour.'

'No, I'm not. At school, everyone has white skin and some of them don't want to touch me. Because . . . I'm brown.'

My voice cracks as I realise I cannot pretend it isn't true any more. Tears fall on to the table and she swiftly mops them up with a blue J-cloth. She sits down next to me and puts her hand over mine, her nails soft and translucent from always being in water. Her hand is so small and pale, next to my monstrous brown paw. I feel like King Kong and pull it away. Her face grows pink, her eyes harden.

'There's nothin' wrong with your skin. We're all the same, the same blood, the same hearts, some people are just too ignorant to see that.'

She must be right, but what about everyone else? Why does she think that but others don't? She is so small that she has to stand to hug me. I smell the familiar floral and detergent scent that I have known since I was born. Helen has a way of making me feel better, human. I always feel that there is hope because she loves us, cares for us, doesn't wipe her hands after touching us or hold her nose around us. After all, she had changed our nappies and blown our noses, she had wiped our faces and kissed our cheeks. And she hadn't caught any diseases. One day, maybe other people would touch us too. Then we wouldn't be monsters any more.

*

Helen grew up in an orphanage with her brother and she always knew that her origins lay in Ireland. She has never been on a plane, but loves looking at them as they roar over our house. I often ask her where she would go in the world if she could and she always wrinkles her nose when I suggest Spain or France.

'Too hot fur me! And whit would I eat?' she says. 'Ah dinnae like foreign food.'

Then she would look at me wistfully and say: 'I'd love to go to Ireland, though. See where I'm really from.'

When my brother and sister start their jobs, they club together to send her to Ireland for two weeks. My sister books it all and then puts an itinerary together with photos and places it in an envelope. When Helen arrives that morning, she looks puzzled. I tell her to open it and she spends ages reading it.

'What do you think, Lelly, isn't it exciting?' I say.

She has her glasses on and looks flustered and annoyed, her face is pink. She is turning the pages over and over.

'So what do I have to do? Do I stick the pictures on?'

I look at her in disbelief. She has no idea.

'No, Lelly . . . you're going to Ireland! You've got to get on a bus and then a ferry . . . and it's all booked. There's a hotel . . .' I trail off.

Helen is looking at me in shock. I realise that perhaps this is too much of a surprise for her. Her face crumples and she bursts into tears. I feel my heart break. I've never really seen her cry and it's devastating. It all feels like a silly idea now; we shouldn't have surprised her.

'Lelly, I'm sorry. We thought you'd . . . I'm sorry, please don't cry.'

She has her head down and is pulling a tissue from her sleeve. She's mopping at her blue eyes. I don't feel equipped to deal with this. But there is no one else around. She pushes back her chair and heads to the bathroom and locks the door. I sit there for about ten minutes, wondering whether I should phone my mum. When she returns, her eyes are red and she is sniffing.

'I'm sorry,' she whispers. 'It wis just a shock, a surprise . . . it's a lovely present. You're good kids.'

She pats me on the head, picks up her cloths and Jif and heads upstairs.

Two months later, Helen goes on the trip. She befriends a woman on the coach and they hang out. An elderly gentleman takes a fancy to her. She says it was the best trip she has ever taken.

Bearsden, Scotland, August, 1996

Unusually, the phone rings out for an age before I decide I had better come down and pick it up. I don't hear all the words, but I get the message. I am angry that my parents, who normally fall over themselves to pick up the phone, didn't bother this time when it was really important. I crash into the living room.

'Why didn't you pick up the phone? It rang for ages!'

My parents look flummoxed. The TV is on loud.

'We didn't hear it . . .'

'Of course you didn't, the telly is on so damn loud!'

My dad switches the TV off. He looks angry at my rudeness.

'Well, who was it?'

'It was Helen's daughter-in-law. She's dead!'

I throw the phone on the sofa and slam the door. Then I run upstairs and cry my eyes out. Helen was in her seventies and her health was failing, but it all felt so sudden. I wasn't ready.

By now she was living in Dunoon, but would get the ferry then the train then the bus then walk, because she didn't want to give us up. She stayed over during the week. She'd had a heart attack when she was sitting down to dinner with her family. I am relieved that she didn't die on the street, or at a bus stop or on a freezing train. I am relieved that I did not see it happen, this end that I knew would come one day. Because she was part of our family. She wasn't our blood, but I cried more for her than my grandmothers. I had known her all my life; she was there every day, seeing my high points and my lows, my milestones and my disasters – everything. She hugged me when I was upset at school and laughed with me at silly adverts on the TV. She kept me sane when my mother went away to Pakistan. She was so proud when I got a job on her favourite channel – STV – and used to record my bulletins on the VCR. She saw a photo of my first boyfriend and told me that 'he looked like a footballer', which I think was a compliment.

We make the heart-breaking trip by ferry to Dunoon for the funeral; it is August and the sun is bouncing off the water. In the church, the floral tribute reads MUM, and I am thrown. I suppose I never thought of her as a mum. She was Helen, or Lelly or gran. I realise today that I will have to let her go; that because we weren't her real family, we will be forgotten. I bite my lip hard to stop the tears. But they tumble out anyway. Twenty-eight years; now just one hour to say goodbye.

I have never seen my parents in a church; they look incongruous. The priest speaks of Helen as a mother, grandmother, sister, auntie. Then he pauses and says that she was also someone who formed a special bond with a Pakistani family for twenty-eight years, which many may have frowned upon. I stare at him. We did matter after all. I look along the church pew at my parents – my mother's cheeks are sodden with tears, her tiny nose is red. My father's concrete face looks as though it might cave in. He found her. I bet he never thought we would cling on to each other for so long.

At the wake, her daughter-in-law grips my hand.

'She kept so many photos of youse as kids. We put some in the coffin with her.'

A strange sound escapes from my throat and I clamp my hand over my mouth, mortified. We have to go now; it's done. I think how I'll never feel those soft floral hugs again, never look into those watery eyes or hold those tiny hands, never hear the tap-tap-tap of her tiny feet in those thin-soled shoes. I'll never have to slap her on the back when she laughs so much she has a coughing fit, she'll never come to the school gates waving my forgotten P.E. kit, and she'll never cut up my sausages again.

Look-a-look-a-Lelly, Look-a-look-a-Lelly.

Gujranwala, Pakistan, 1956

Maqsooda is something not usually seen in a servant – an outgoing teenage girl who smiles a lot and likes to have fun, much to the annoyance of my stepmother, who imitates her girlish laughter whenever she hears it.

'*Heinhein heinhein!* Why do I hear this sound in every corner of this house? Is there no work that needs to be done?'

But Maqsooda is no slacker. She cleans the house, launders the clothes, makes the beds, washes the dishes. She has been put to work early by her parents, so has never been to school and cannot read or write. She is slightly younger than me, slightly shorter. But she is like my shadow; every time I look up she is nearby, cleaning a floor or folding some sheets. I often find myself staring at her face, which is as round as the moon, her eyes are big and bright, she wears a gold-coloured nose stud with a sparkling dot of glass in it. Her hair is thick and brown and woven into a paranda that trails down to her hips, swishing as she goes.

We are many sisters, but she is like another. And she loves being in a house of so many girls, many of whom are her age, and she especially likes being around me and my sister Naz, because we are very particular about our appearance and clothes. She puts our pressed shalwars on our beds and runs her hands over them longingly, saying how beautiful they are.

'*Bhaji*, can you do my hair like yours?' she implores, her eyes wide and admiring, when once I put ringlets in my hair. I twisted pieces of cloth into wet hair, tied them tightly and slept in them. My stepmother said they looked nice; my mother barely noticed.

There is nothing extra in our house. No fripperies or meaningless items. Everything has a practical use. Magazines are banned; books are encouraged. The one exception is soap. For most everyday jobs, we use Lifebuoy. But to wash our faces we are allowed Imperial Leather. It is a treat, an indulgence. A sharp-edged rectangular cake of amber wax, it lathers magically and peels the day's dust and grime from our skin. That moment each morning and evening is ritualistic for us. We hook a towel over our heads and behind our shoulders, looking like nuns, then we splash water over our faces. We pick up the soap and start to turn it over in our hands until it lathers, but not too much, because we want it to last. We apply the cream in small circular movements to our skin, leaving it on for a few moments to let it really soak in, our dark eyes staring out of our unfamiliar white faces, then we rinse it all off and pat our faces dry, invigorated and clean. I often see Maqsooda watching me in the background, folding something. One day I find her using the expensive soap. My mouth forms an 'O'. But I can't stay annoyed with her for long

'I just want my skin to look as nice as yours,' she pleads. 'I'm sorry, Bhaji.'

She leaves the house at seventeen, because her parents want her to get married. We cry and hug her and give her some nice clothes; wrapped in the middle of the package is a bar of Imperial Leather soap.

It is not surprising that the happiest people in our house are the servants. Although loyal, they have no blood investment in the feuds and vendettas that continue for thirty years. When my mother and stepmother stop speaking directly to each other, the servants convey messages between them; they live off the gossip and high drama of that rivalry; they are often deployed as spies or scolded for being indiscreet

My stepmother summons me one day in June. Her eyes are hard and cold with anger.

'Your mother has been speaking to the servants about me again. Tell her she is not to. I don't care for that type of behaviour. This is not Lahore.'

Not sure what to do with that request, I turn over in my mind how I should approach my mother. My first loyalty is to her, but I don't want idle gossip to inflame an already difficult situation. So after a while I go to find her. She is rinsing daal in a bucket of water.

'Ummi, I've been speaking to Bebe.'

'Ohhhhhhh,' exhales my mum, 'What's wrong now? Do I walk too loudly in my own house?'

'No, Ummi, she says that you were . . . saying things about her to Maqsooda – and she says please don't.'

My mum carefully tips out the water then fills the bucket again.

'I bet she didn't say please.'

She takes my silence as proof.

'Ummi, you know how it is. She's very . . . proud. Best not to say anything to the servants, because they can't keep anything to themselves.'

My mum clangs the bucket down angrily.

'I'll say what I want to whom I want in my house. She will not silence me. I know she wants me to lie down and die. So she can be free.'

My mouth falls opens in shock.

'Why are you looking so surprised? It's true! That woman has made my life a misery. She has made me invisible in my own home! She shouldn't be here! Why is she here?'

She moves closer, her face twisted in anguish. 'She might want me dead so she can be free. But it's not my death that will free her, it's your father's death that will free me!'

'Ummi! Don't say that!'

I am utterly scandalised. Women of my mother's generation live through their husbands. Once they die, the life of a widow is thin and purposeless.

'You think I want your father to die? Of course I don't. I have begged him for years to put her in a different house. And he has refused. But when he dies . . . she goes!'

And there it lies in front of us, the terrible truth. I can barely look at it. My heart is still beating fast as she finishes washing the daal and leaves it to soak. Then she readjusts her dupatta, hooking it behind her ears, and goes to do her evening prayer.

*

By July the heat is tormenting us again. I go into my stepmother's room to get a book she had borrowed from me. The day is so catastrophically hot that I forget to knock. She is sitting on a low stool, a glass of water on the floor in front of her. I just have time to see her immerse a piece of paper with writing on it into the water and stir it with a teaspoon before she jumps up and hides the glass behind her. Water drops splash around her feet.

'What are you doing in here?' she snaps, her face flushing deep red.

'Sorry, I just . . .' I motion to my book.

'Well? Take it and go.'

I pluck the book from the shelf and leave, unsure about what exactly I have seen. I sit in the hall with the book, where it is cool, and see her float past two minutes later with the same glass. She glares at me, then opens the door to my father's room and goes in.

This is not the first strange behaviour I have witnessed. Once I went up to the roof to retrieve my embroidery. But as I opened the door I saw her there. She had her back to me and was sitting on the ground. I could tell from the shape of her body and the way she had her chador around her that she was doing something private. A sudden movement and I saw a small object shoot to her left, then another to her right. Then, to my horror, she threw one behind her and it rolled within a metre of my feet. I looked down: it was a small polished black stone. I froze, hoping she wouldn't turn and see me. Something felt wrong about the whole atmosphere – it was too still and too heavy. To my relief, she threw a stone in front of her and bent her head as if in prayer. I took the opportunity to move away and backed quietly down the stairs.

The servants know about the black magic. I hear them talking about it in low voices while they are washing the clothes. Some of them think it perfectly normal; others say that it is un-Islamic. They all know why my step-mother dabbles in this nonsense. They know that she has written suras from the Qu'ran on pieces of paper and has let the ink mix with the water in a glass, before removing the paper and giving it to my father to drink. They know that the stones represent the devil and she is trying to cast her out.

Gujranwala, Pakistan, 1958

The day begins quietly enough, but it ends in ruins. Another family is coming to visit to see if I am interested in marrying their son. I tolerate these occasions, but my heart isn't in it. My dreams of being a doctor were snuffed out a long time ago. Next, I pin my hopes on doing a master's degree in philosophy in Lahore and becoming a college lecturer, after I get my bachelor's degree. But my brother rules this out, saying that I cannot stay in student lodgings in Lahore; that it would be scandalous and, anyway, it was time for me to get married.

But luckily for me my brother does have high standards. He has connived with me to get rid of one unsuitable match already. He similarly vetoed a proud, boastful family who said their son was a lawyer. Khalid found the address and went to have a look. He located a dingy office down a filthy back street and came home furious, saying that no sister of his was going to marry someone like that.

The rishta arrives one evening. They come in and sit down and start to make gentle enquiries of me. I sit quietly and regard my prospective in-laws. They seem nice enough. Good Kashmiris, everything looks right on paper. As ever my stepmother has managed to make herself the most senior person in the room; my mother demoted to second string. She sits there quietly, her hands folded in her chador so they don't touch anything dirty.

I notice that my stepmother has become locked in deep conversation with the mother of the prospective groom. Occasionally, my stepmother flashes her eyes in my mother's direction. She catches my eye and looks away. Maybe they don't like the look of me after all. There are several conversations going on at once and I can hear them all, except for my stepmother's. She keeps her voice low, her body folded in towards her guest, locking us out.

After the guests leave, she comes to find me in my room. She sits on the bed.

'Well, they seem to like you very much,' she announces.

'Oh, that's good,' I say, non-commitally, almost bored.

There is a silence.

'But of course you cannot marry their son.'

She picks up one of the books by my bed.

'Oh. Why not?'

She raises her thick eyebrows and waits. Seconds pass.

'Because one failed marriage between our families is enough.'

She says it very softly. There is an even longer silence. I can hear the irritating whine of a mosquito nearby.

'I don't understand.'

She turns a page of the book.

'What . . . failed marriage?'

'Your mother's, of course.'

None of this makes any sense.

'It's not failed, things are complicated, but–' I begin.

'No, you misunderstand. Your mother was married to that woman's cousin.'

'No. That's wrong.'

My stepmother looks quietly triumphant. My face feels hot. The mosquito screeches past my ear.

'Sorry, *beti*, but it's true. Did your mother never tell you that she was married before your father?'

I stare.

'It was not a success. Didn't last long.'

I feel queasy. I need to find my mother. It all sounds outrageously untrue.

'No, Bebe . . .' I start.

'I'm surprised she never told you. It was very generous of your father to marry her after . . .' she searches for the words, '. . . after she was . . . sent back.'

Slap.

I crush the mosquito in my trembling hands and head for the door, my face unbearably hot.

*

I search the house for my mother. She is folding clothes in her room when I go in.

'Ummi, is it true?'

She barely looks up.

'Bebe says that you were . . . married before? To that', – I gesture towards the now empty drawing room – 'family'.

She is still folding, but her movements have quickened.

'Ummi. Is it true?'

'So what if it is?' she says in a deathly monotone, her back to me. I draw closer. I have to see her face. It is flat and grey. So, it is true. Suddenly things start to fall into place.

'But why didn't you tell us? What happened? Who was he?'

'What's there to tell?'

Silence descends on the room; a thousand questions more perish in my mouth.

'Ummi,' I put my hand on her arm.

She stands up and looks at me, suddenly looking a thousand years old, her hair unkempt. Her face is blank, but I see the years of anguish under her skin. She shakes my hand off.

'We were married. He sent me back to my parents after two months. There is nothing more to say.'

She opens the wardrobe, places the clothes inside and leaves the room.

After a moment, I follow her out. My stepmother

is loitering near the staircase, surveying the damage, looking flushed and sheepish. In those terrible seconds, I believe that if my mother had any strength in her tiny body she would have thrown her down those stairs. They dare not lock eyes. There are no words either, but a ghastly message passes between them like electricity. Wait.

NINE

Lahore, Pakistan, 1984

High up behind the faded red stone arches, she rules over this ancient Mughal city. A grid of smart well-kept streets opens up in front of her, revealing hedges of bougainvillea and jasmine in full bloom, driveways regularly swept by crouching servants with tightly-bound bundles of straw, swish-swishing away at the tiniest leaf or twig. Beyond this quiet enclave she can see the line of trees, which border the famous canal that bisects the city. Along it spin the sleek white Hondas ferrying the rich kids to school. Motorbikes carrying entire families weave in and out of the traffic towards Gulberg, Liberty Market, Anarkali and the city limits.

Today the sun is razor sharp, not hazy; the sounds of the neighbourhood are loud and deep. Car doors slam, gates open with a squeak and bang shut, bolted by the chowkidars. A fear of crime fuelled by occasional stories in the papers means that gates are opened and closed as hastily as those at the Wagah Border between India and Pakistan – with no more than a fleeting glimpse of what lies on the other side.

But for her there are no barriers. She can see every-thing: the peaks and troughs of family life, the feuds and reconciliations. She observes us, the smart houses with their large noisy families and retinues of servants. She watches the cooks and the gardeners and the drivers; the matriarchs, the teachers, the company men in their English suits, the beloved sons who do as they please and the difficult daughters who will not bend. She learns the shape of the day, the commuter frenzy in the morning and the sleepy dips of the afternoon.

Her eyes settle on me. I feel the stillness of her gaze and turn. I am only recently arrived, so I cannot stop staring; everyone else finds her unremarkable. I try looking at her out of the corner of my eye, pretending to casually shade my gaze from the sun, but she is always looking straight at me – her eyes hard and blank, but at the same time demanding to know who I am and why am I here.

*

Babaji pushes a perilously wobbly gold trolley laden with tea and savoury and sweet snacks into the drawing room. A procession of guests, mostly female, sit on hard sofas with wooden backs and indulge in light and formal conversation. Enquiries are made about houses and land and education and distant family connections. Dupattas are rearranged, mouths are dabbed with napkins, forks clink politely against plates.

Babaji pours the steaming hot tea and distributes the freshly fried food. I notice his hands shaking as he does this and I wonder how old he is. No one knows exactly, of course; he could be anywhere between sixty and ninety. He is a small thin man who wears a shalwar kameez, a knitted tank top and a hat. He has a kind, patient face that breaks into a smile easily, a fishing net of lines criss-cross his forehead and his darting eyes often convey that he is beginning to lose his grip on things. But he has a family to provide for, so he will work until he scalds someone or drops dead, whichever occurs first.

He cooks the food, clears up, receives the guests and organises the groceries. I have never seen him sit down; he is always either upright at the cooker or the sink or moving at a lightning pace to answer a phone or make some more roti. Three times a day he disappears to his quarters to say his prayers. The rest of the time he is there, servicing our every need. He cooks our breakfast eggs and makes our milky coffee; he presides over huge pots of lunchtime curry; he looks sad and redundant when we pile into the car to get a burger from Salt 'n' Pepper in Liberty Market or to eat Chinese food at Tai Wah.

He may be elderly, but he is efficient. He can juggle competing tasks at the same time – cooking, cleaning, fixing things and answering the door. I never have a meaningful conversation with Babaji – we are worlds apart with no common language – but I am aware that this elderly, partially deaf, slight man is my buffer, a layer of protection against malign and sometimes comedic occurrences. He once removes an errant parrot from my bedroom. I tell him in halting Urdu that there is a bird in my room and he returns with a huge knife. We look blankly at each other for a few seconds, until I realise that we have confused 'chiriya' (bird) with 'churi' (knife). Quite what he thought a thirteen-year-old girl wanted with a gleaming meat knife is beyond me. He catches the bird without the knife and releases it outside. Neither of us is sure whether the misunderstanding is down to his poor hearing or my abysmal Urdu.

When the phone rings, my instinct is to answer it as I would have done in Glasgow. There, it would be someone from the petrol station to speak to my dad, or a relative for my mum or an official involved in the ongoing complications of my brother's education and treatment. Here, picking up the phone is like picking up a snake by its tail. You may get trapped in a conversation with a distant relative who only speaks Urdu and launches into a speech about your linguistic failings. Or it is a random oleaginous man speaking in halting English who has bribed someone to get your number and now wants to meet you or propose marriage. It is easier to leave it to Babaji, whose elderly male voice is sufficient to get the unwanted callers to hang up. There are a lot of ghost calls. Today the phone rings for an age, then Babaji appears and sprints to pick it up.

It is someone for my mum, who is woken from her afternoon nap. I feel a tightness in my stomach and come out of my room to find out what is important enough to disturb her. This is how I learn that, in Delhi, just two hundred and sixty six miles from where we are standing, the prime minister of India has been assassinated by two of her own guards.

*

Mrs Khan is imperious and unsmiling, her clothes are good, her nails and eyes always painted. She mostly sits, but when she moves around she totters on her too thin heels, which threaten to snap under her not inconsiderable weight. She is grand and haughty, her chin is always raised, her nostrils large. She is zealous about the subject she teaches – English. She brings the class of girls to attention by tapping her glossy fingernails on her desk and tells us to write down the following sentence and incorporate it into a story:

'*And then the first drop of rain touched the earth and the flowers seemed to sing with joy.*'

Mrs Khan has thin arched eyebrows and her hair is cut into a modern short style. When she gets annoyed or exercised, which is quite often, her curls dance around her face and her eyes gleam with anger.

'Saima, how many times have I told you, for God's sake!'

'Kulsum, why are we waiting for you to open your pencil case? You're not the maharani, you know!'

She always seems one centimetre from an outburst, irritable and impatient but also magnetically confident and supremely refined, with a voice that is sometimes sensuous, other times cold with fury.

Although she is fearsome, I enjoy her classes. English is one of the few subjects I understand. There are other baffling ones: Maths is like no Maths I have ever studied – hugely advanced; Physics is borderline impenetrable; and something called Islamiat, which I just stare at, as it requires an understanding of Arabic. I have been parachuted into an unfamiliar syllabus in a country four thousand miles from home. I am lost, but nothing feels impossible or overwhelming. Because every day I go home and my mother is there.

Physics lessons are held in the lab, which is a circular-shaped brick room near the entrance to the school. The teacher, Mrs Lal, is the opposite of Mrs Khan. She is shorter than all of us, with a long plait that snakes down the back of her sari. She wears thick glasses, which make her bulging eyes look like those of a frog. She is silent and expressionless, her voice so quiet I have to lean in to hear her. She moves slowly, she talks slowly, she answers slowly. Where Mrs Khan is fiery and dramatic, Mrs Lal is calm, almost soporific, blinking at us from behind her huge glasses.

School starts at 7:30 a.m., so by 10 o'clock we are starving. There is a dhabba in the school grounds that sells snacks. I sit in class dreaming of the naan-kebab that I will eat. A spiced potato mixture rolled up in a butter-soft naan. Apa serves us – she must be around forty, with shoulder-length hair, green eyes and a silver nose-stud. I go there with my new friends – Saima, whose mum is a six foot two white Brummie with blonde hair and whose dad is Pakistani; then there is Mehreen, whose hair is cut into a long mullet framing her green eyes; Naurin, who has a middle parting and two plaits and is always pushing her glasses up her nose; there is Hana, who is American and who can't stop peeling apart her split ends; there is Ayesha, who is a Cockney; and Maryam, who is studious but warm. There are rich girls, scholarship girls, girls who hate studying, clever girls, girls who only talk about getting married and going to the beauty parlour, and girls who want to be doctors and scientists. Some wear shalwars and some wear jeans. We are all different; we are all the same.

The only teasing occurs when they laugh at how I pronounce my surname – the anglicised two syllables – Mee-yer. I start to say it properly – Meer. I learn to stop apologising and whispering. Here I grow into my actual size.

*

It is Sports Day. We are all wearing white shalwars and cornflower blue dupattas that are looped around our shoulders and knotted at the waist. It is sunny and dusty, I can smell smoke and spiced potatoes and jasmine. The games pitch where we play badminton looks parched. I compete in the races but just can't run like I used to – my shalwar flaps in the wind as I try to find some pace. I sink into mid-table oblivion.

But not my mother. She is ready to take part in the parents' race. I catch her eye as she lines up in her shalwar and cardigan next to a couple of confident-looking men whose blackened hair is younger than their faces. I see that competitiveness, that setting of the jaw and I brace myself. She kicks her shoes off and stares ahead. The whistle blows and she is off. She reaches the first post and starts eating the orange segments that have been left on a plate. She tosses the empty rinds on the ground. Then she sprints to the next post, steps into a hula hoop and pulls it over her head. She throws it behind her and it rolls into a man still bending to eat his oranges. But she is off again. My mouth drops open. She sprints for the finish line. There is no one behind her for ages. Some of the men have given up and are strolling about slapping each other on the back and gasping for air. Others are still tangled in hoops or huffing along the grass. She crosses the line and a huge whoop goes up from all the girls who have been watching transfixed.

Open mouths turn to me:

'*Arre yaar*, is that your mom?'

'Wow, Aasmah. How come she runs so fast? Was she an athlete?'

I shrug, mystified, proud. My mother doesn't do anything half-heartedly. When it's time for the prizes, she climbs on to the first place position on the podium in her huge sunglasses and smart handbag. The woman who came second high-fives her.

Gujranwala, Pakistan, 1952

I become an aunt at the age of eight. Samina's first child is a boy, Mossadeq, and I and the rest of my sisters combust with joy and fight to hold him. He is fat and sleepy, with a thick head of black hair and arms like a wrestler's. As usual, my sister Naz and I are arguing – this time over who gets to look after him and who loves him more.

'I love him more than the stars and sky!'

'I love him more than all the gulab jamun in the world!'

On and on we go all day, grabbing him, scooping him up and running off with him when the other is not around, until there is a shriek of discovery and an argument. The first grandchild, the first nephew, the first of the next generation.

One day we are fighting over who will change his cloth nappy. I am holding her off with my body and one hand, undoing the nappy with the other. His father, Javed, is laughing at us.

'For goodness sake, stop arguing. Your love is too much!'

His nappy is off and he starts to pee. Naz looks at me, her eyes narrowing.

'If you love him so much,' she shouts, 'let him pee on your hand!'

Her eyes are glittering. I recoil, disgusted at the idea. Then I remember how much I want to beat my sister and I put my hand in the remaining stream of his pee. It is surprisingly warm. He chuckles, thinking it's a game. My sister looks on disgusted, my brother-in-law shakes his head. I hold my hand up, the pee dripping on to the floor, victory in my face. My sister, vanquished, widens her eyes then opens her mouth and shouts towards the kitchen: 'Um-mi! You won't believe what Baby has done . . . !'

Lahore, Pakistan, 1984

Everything is upside down in Pakistan. School starts early and finishes early. We don't go on Friday and Saturday. The most basic things taste different to how they do in Glasgow– the bread is sweet, but the biscuits lack sugar; cheese comes in a tin, eggs yolks are a lurid orange. I stare as my mum puts salt and pepper on orange halves or scoops a thick gloopy cream on to her toast. Her face lights up if relatives suggest making a late-night pot of green tea – but it looks pink and milky and smells salty when it arrives. The biggest shock, though, is that there is no proper chocolate here. There is a Pakistan-made bar called Jubilee, which is soggy and underwhelming, like chewing on a log. There are versions of Mars Bars, but they taste odd and are expensive. For the first few months we eat little of anything and my Nano follows me around the house entreating me to eat something.

'*Toast kaalo, toast kaalo.*'

At school everyone speaks English, but in shops no one does. We go to bed late and wake up crazily early. My mum makes us sleep after lunch like toddlers, which we resist. The clothes are a battle. The compromise is usually a long shalwar top and a pair of jeans. Two of the bathrooms in the house are like the ones at home, but two are tiled holes in the floor that you have to squat over. There is no bath, just a shower head; you have to sit on a low wooden block while the water goes everywhere and you freeze to death. The blankets are thin but heavy and smell of here.

Imran is now ten and is at yet another new school. There is a less strict system for educating children with special needs. He learns his Urdu alphabet and Mum makes him repeat it when he comes home.

'*Alif, bai, pai . . .*'

But his behaviour hasn't improved on the plane journey over. He is still the same, still battling with his demons, still doing inexplicable and often aggressive things. At school he terrorises his teacher, Master Ji, constantly knocking his hat off and exerting his growing physical power over people in authority. He changes school again. Babaji loves him, he calls him chota saab – little sir. But Imran abuses him too. While he is praying in his quarters, he jumps on his back. When he ventures into the garden, he unleashes the hose all over him. My brother has huge freedom in Pakistan, fewer questions are asked but nothing gets better. The spring heat makes him worse. He is still obsessed with cars, so he throws stones at the neighbours' car windows because he says it is too old; the next day the man whose car it is comes by and asks us if he can take him for a Coca Cola. My little brother does a poo in his pyjamas, panics and throws them over the high wall into the next garden. One of their servants brings the pyjamas back saying: 'We think little sir may have lost these.'

One day a visiting relative asks how come one of the tyres on our car is a different colour. After an investigation, we discover that the back tyre had been replaced by the spare from the boot. We have no idea how it could have happened – my sister, my mum and I look at each other blankly. Then my little brother walks by, scowling, talking to himself. Luckily he has done a good job – he has watched it done many times at the petrol station – but we all feel vulnerable. A few weeks pass and my mum starts the car and it makes a strange noise. She gets out and discovers sheets of newspaper jammed into the exhaust pipe. She removes them and, after school, asks my brother why he did that. He replies that dirty smoke was coming from the exhaust so he blocked it up. My mum is starting to look stressed again.

*

There is something about this place that could get into your bones. It smells of open fires and sewage, of jasmine petals and roasting spices. In winter I am shocked at how cold it is in the mornings and the evenings. It shifts from a piercing cold to an easy, spring-like heat, which evaporates again as night falls. But the cold is so different to that of Glasgow. That is constant, damp and bites at your toes. This is sharp and misty and short-lived. Winter here is also a time of weddings – long strings of fairy lights coiled around houses and trees, the bonnets of fancy cars thickly coated with flowers, men playing trumpets and banging drums moving through stationary traffic.

Here in Lahore we are surrounded by family. Not just my uncles and aunties and cousins but my great-uncles and aunts and whole new families related through marriage. Hardly a week passes when we are not packed into the car to go and visit someone. They fuss and pinch my cheeks and say how I've grown since I was a baby. They try to speak Urdu to me and I give it a go, but usually it is met with howls of laughter, so I soon give up. Luckily most of my close relatives speak English. We loll around on the floor with cushions and blankets, drinking tea, eating nuts, cutting our toenails, rubbing oil into each other's hair, staying up until the small hours. There is a lot of laughter and tears of joy, my aunts and cousins are comfortable together, low and high fiving each other when someone says something funny. The children nod off on the floor and are covered in blankets as raucous conversations rage around them. Then some-one arrives with an entire roasted spiced fish, places it on a tray on the floor and we all dig in. I watch the easy way my relatives are with each other – no barriers, no feuds, no separation – and it reminds me of the house on the hill.

I have a particular love for my Uncle Khalid – who is generous and fun-loving and yelps and weeps with laughter all the time. His English is good, he is keen to hear about British football and he is a chain smoker. He loves playing cards and performing small magic tricks. Many times he takes a tiny piece of paper, places it in his mouth, shows it to us on his tongue, then closes his lips. Then he presses one finger against one nostril and sneezes the paper out of the other. We scream in wonder and make him perform it five times more. I must have asked my mother why his skin is completely white, his face covered in freckles, his thinning hair, eyebrows and eyelashes almost platinum, but I can't remember the answer.

My Aunt Naz is intoxicating too. She is small and round, almost a carbon copy of my mother but with much more emotion. She can be laughing loudly at a joke, then suddenly she starts to cry. We tease her for her huge emotions and her loud snoring. When she comes to stay, everyone first establishes where she is sleeping so they can settle as far away from her as possible. Her love for us is huge; she just has to look at me to make me laugh. She giggles at our attempts at Urdu, but despite my mum telling me that she was really clever at school, she insists that she cannot speak English very well.

We live a middle-class life but I am shocked by the poverty. There are beggars as thin as paper everywhere. I see my first as we exit the airport building – a woman banging on the door of a car, her clothes faded against the bright plant pots of marigolds and aggressive hoardings advertising toothpaste and cigarettes. There are men with no arms, no legs, who propel themselves alongside cars on rough planks of wood with tiny wheels attached. There are elderly blind women standing in the road with their whole lives etched on their faces and young women with thin children, their eyebrows and hair thick with dust, begging you to save their lives. I have never seen such catastrophic poverty and desperation. But the worst thing is the lone children wandering around.

'Where are their parents?' I ask my mum.

'I don't know. They might not have any. They might have died, got lost,' she says. I think of the temporary loss of my mother and feel ridiculous. At least she existed, at least I found her again. At least I am not wandering around alone and barefoot, in rags, begging for scraps and sleeping in the dust at the side of the road at the age of six. Just half a mile from the main market, we drive past lorries unloading marble pillars to be fitted to the facades of homes that will be as big as museums – bursting with glass and gold. Driveways are built wide to accommodate four or five imported cars. Swimming pools are excavated that will barely be used.

Everywhere that there is a beggar or a tiny child pulling at your clothes, there is a policeman with a ribbed jumper, a beret, a moustache and a baton moving them on. But they turn a blind eye to the young rich boys speeding past, revving their Honda Civics or doing a screeching handbrake turn in the middle of the road, Michael Jackson and Whitney Houston playing from wobbly cassettes in their car stereos. They grow their hair long and wear baggy jeans and intricate belts. They look bored and agitated with their money and privilege.

Faces are always upturned to me, searching, curious. My clothes don't help me blend in – I eschew the shalwar kameez and wear jeans, long shirts or shalwar tops, a dupatta slung across my shoulders. But it's not just my clothes: it's my hair – a grown-out mullet, and, of course, my skin colour. Once it was too dark, now it's too fair. But you can never be too fair in Pakistan. The women selling soap powder on TV are fair; the men advertising cigarettes and Coca Cola are almost white. If you are fair, shopkeepers are more attentive, relatives coo over your complexion, men on motorbikes slow down and stare. The only way I could attract more attention is if I were blonde. I have been jettisoned from one end of the spectrum to the other. Horribly dark and pitied to desirably fair and superior. A family friend asks my mother if I would be interested in filming a commercial. I am dumbfounded by the turnaround in how I am perceived here. My confidence is too shot to say yes, but I digest the offer with a smile.

The newspaper, *Dawn*, arrives every morning and we usually flick through the *Readers' Digest* and *Time Magazine*, especially the People Section. Today I see my mum fold the paper and push it away. When she goes into the kitchen to get something, I open it. My mouth dries up. Somewhere in India. An explosion at a chemical plant. Thousands of people died. I try to understand why people live so near to something so dangerous. I try to imagine if thousands of people were suffocated to death by a poisonous gas leaking out of a factory in Glasgow. I can't stop staring at the photo on the front page of a woman lying on her side, frozen in the dust, her dupatta twisted around her body. There is a doll lying face up on the ground just centimetres from her stilled outstretched fingers. I read the caption and understand that this perfect doll with its eyes open is in fact her baby, choked of its short life. And I see the love of a mother in those desperate fingers – trying to reach her child and pull it out of the poisonous air.

Lahore, Pakistan, 1985

We haul the last of the suitcases into the boot of a second car; we have accumulated so much stuff here. As it slams shut, I wave at the servants who have lined up to see us off. Babaji has tears in his eyes. My mum has said we will be back, but I can see in his sloping shoulders that he doesn't believe he will ever see us again. It was odd to say goodbye to my school friends – I only knew them for eight months, but they were like sisters. I stay in touch with them for years. On my last day, I take in my autograph book and they all sign it. The American girl, Hana – she of the split ends – writes drily:

> *Have*
> *Horrible*
> *Husband*

And we roll about laughing.

I look up at the asylum – two houses along, which has loomed over us for the last year. She is still standing there, watching through the rusted black bars, her long plait hanging forward over her shoulder. Her face is blank. I think about waving at her but something stops me. We get in the car and I look up for a last glance. She is still there, a statue. Perhaps she never saw me. Perhaps she sees like my little brother – he looks but he isn't really taking anything in.

A few hours later the plane folds its wheels in and climbs into the pink sky, nosing its way north then west. We are on our way back. This is how it always is. We seem to lurch from one crisis to another, always pushed and pulled by my little brother's needs or some financial catastrophe. By the time I am sixteen, I will have changed school six times, trying to start over each time. There is no stability, just constant change. But maybe Glasgow will be different this time.

Glasgow, Scotland, 1966

I find my new home up six flights of stairs and behind a peeling red door in an old draughty building. The flat is on the top floor of a tenement off Argyle Street. The floors are bare and cold, the ceilings high, the view long and grey.

As I step off the plane into the freezing February air, my eyes water so much that I think I must be imagining snow on the hills behind Prestwick Airport. But no, Arif assures me that it is indeed snow and laughs nervously that I will see a lot more of it. The airport is bright and busy, but the roads are like nothing I have ever seen. Clean and grey and smooth with broken white lines separating the traffic. No one honks their horn or dives in front of you. There are no horses and carts or bicycles trying to squeeze through tiny gaps. It is like driving on the moon. Outside the day is ending and everything is grey and straight, teetering on inkiness. We are on a road called the A8. And I immediately wonder where the A1, 2, 3, 4, 5, 6 and 7 are. Then we enter a tunnel and, as I adjust to the twists and darkness, my husband informs me that this tunnel snakes under a river called the Clyde.

I squeal and lift my feet off the floor, gathering up the edges of my silk shalwar kameez in case the car floods and I get soaked.

Once we reach the terrace of run-down flats, I notice two things. The air is cold and damp and there is a terrible smell in the corridor of the building that must be urine. For all the beauty of its roads and hills, people still do the toilet out in the open, it seems.

We arrive on a Saturday and, having already taken six weeks leave, my husband goes back to work on Monday, leaving me to try to keep warm in the cold flat and suspiciously eye the gas cooker. But just one hour later, he is back. His boss has told him that he cannot possibly leave his new bride on her own in a new house in a new country. So we spend the day shopping frugally for groceries, as my husband has already used one month's advance salary to pay for the wedding and flights. We go to Grandfare and buy our food, opting for potatoes to make a cheap meal. Our bill is fifteen shillings, which feels like a reckless fortune. Many people stare at me in my sari and coat – one woman is gawping so much she walks into a pyramid of cereal packets – but it doesn't feel unkind and I am staring too. I have never seen so many women wearing skirts, knee length and above, so much flesh. I try to get used to the voices, speaking English but in an accent that is both flat and animated at the same time.

At night we walk along Kelvin Way, which binds Argyle Street to the West End, buying a single fish and sharing it as we walk. If we are feeling rich, we buy chips too and I try to feed as many as possible to Arif while saving the delicious fish for myself. We eat every scrap slowly, keeping the pleasant vinegary taste in our mouths for hours after.

At the weekend we take the car we share with my brother-in-law for a trip to somewhere in the hills. We go to the Campsie Hills, the Trossachs, Balloch, Tarbet. My favourite is Glen Fruin, near Loch Lomond. We arrive there one day to thick snow. I have never seen snow before and leap out of the car in my shalwar, coat and slingback sandals. Before long I am gathering bundles of snow in my bare hands and throwing them at my husband, my half-naked feet sinking into the snow. He looks amused at first, but his face turns to shock when he sees my determined expression. He hasn't quite grasped that I am competitive – the college badminton champion. Two massive snowballs bang into his face, causing a red mark. When he gathers himself together, he protests, but it is too late. Another snowball is heading towards him, but he manages to duck in time. In the uproar I realise that one of my feet is bare – I have lost one of my beautiful sandals. We search for ages until I can't feel my hands anymore and we retire to the car. I am devastated – I loved those sandals, the ones I had worn on the plane from Pakistan. I worry quietly that I have lost a connection to home. All the way home my bare foot mocks me, my teeth chattering.

In Glasgow I spend my days walking the streets, window shopping mostly, and sitting on park benches. I drink it all in – the grey sky, the people, the voices. The difference is stark and pleasant. I had felt stifled back home – here I am left to my own devices all day. I can read, sew and plan. I know I want to work, but I don't know as what. But an idea is forming in my head. I tell my husband that I do not want to have children straight away, that I want to get a job, possibly as a teacher. He agrees, but within three months of our wedding I discover I am pregnant.

We take in lodgers to ease our finances – an Egyptian doctor and his wife and two young children. We operate a rota to use the kitchen. The woman feels the cold and is always sitting in front of an electric fire with her coat on. The little girl looks at me from under her fringe and squeaks: 'Is Mr Mir home?'

If I say no, the two children run around the flat chasing each other, banging and clattering up stairs and down corridors. If he is home, they sit quietly.

Just before the baby arrives, I buy a second-hand sewing machine and lots of material from the sale at Pettigrew on Sauchiehall Street. I make baby gowns and bed sheets out of flannelette and nappies out of terry cloth in anticipation of its arrival. I knit yellow and white sets of cardigans, hats, mittens and socks. When she arrives just before Christmas, she is two weeks late, with a full head of hair and a placid, knowing smile. I leave her outside the tenement in her pram for fresh air along with all the other prams, checking on her intermittently from my top floor window.

As she grows, we take her shopping for groceries in Grandfare and I notice a female customer takes a shine to her. She's always there – maybe a regular. My husband says: 'Oh, look, that lady is there again.'

I smile at her and she smiles back and think nothing more of it. But she is always there, just watching and smiling, and then I think maybe she works there.

She always says to my daughter:

'Oh, aren't you a wee button?'

I notice she always has the same few things in her basket – three tins of beans and a cucumber. I think she must live on her own or maybe not have kids, so I don't mind the unique attention she gives us; we are the only ones she seems to talk to. Three months pass before she tells us that she is a store detective.

Gujranwala, Pakistan, 1952

Three years after I am born, Neelam arrives, then finally Kaukab. Two more girls. My mother has been birthing children for sixteen years and has only managed one boy out of six children. It weighs heavily on her.

Kaukab looks like me – small eyes, curly hair, a good temperament. But my little sister Neelam doesn't really look like any of us. Her eyes are huge and unblinking. Our hair varies between thin and limp or wiry and curly. Her hair is smooth and straight and her skin is fair. She is younger than me but we still play together. She has a collection of rag dolls that she loves to play with. She makes them go to school, argue, make dinner, go shopping. She shares them with me; she is good-natured and easy to be around.

Neelam is six when she gets measles. She deteriorates and has to be taken to hospital, where my mother stays with her for a month. I visit her a few times and am shocked at how ill she looks. She has no hair and she looks like the life has been sucked out of her. Many children get measles, so I am confused as to why she is so ill. After a month she comes home, but it is not my little

Neelu who comes home, it is a baby. She cannot walk
or talk or sit up or eat. Everything has to be done for
her. Gradually my mother teaches her to do everything
again, but her speech remains slurred and she can't walk
well. She wobbles and weaves and sometimes falls, but
we persevere. After six months she is sent to school, but
the teachers are impatient and the pupils unkind and she
says she will not go back. She just wants to stay at home.

My mother is so worried, even though the doctors
assure her that Neelam will gradually get better. Slowly
over the years her speech improves as does her walking.
She grows stronger and her hair grows back even thicker
and blacker. I am protective of her, but there is something between us now – perhaps a difference. She will
probably never go to school. My mother and my sisters
and brother worry about what is going to happen to her.
Who will she live with when my mother is gone? Will
she be able to get married, have children? The future
is not written. I often look at her walking uncertainly
through the house and sometimes it feels as though she
is already walking away from us.

Glasgow, Scotland, 1986

This sickness affects my throat, my eyes, my spine. It clings to me like a cloud, obliterating the person I am supposed to be. My voice deserts me when I have to speak in public; shopkeepers stare or grimace or run out of patience as I fail to answer their questions or mumble my answer. I never look anyone in the eye, keeping my head down so often that I bump into lamp-posts and trip over steps. I watch the pavements slipping by, balling my fists further into the depths of my blazer pockets, scratching at the crumbs in there. My shoulders are always collapsed and rounded in. The truth is I hate being here. And I hate everything about myself. I hate the noise my shoes make on pavements, I hate it when I see my arms swinging by my side. I hate catching a glimpse of myself in a shop window – or hearing my infuriating voice.

On the rare occasion that I have to go into a shop – perhaps to satisfy my buzzing need for sugar – it's excruciating. I try to creep in but the bell above the door sounds loudly. Looking at the floor, I trudge up to the till and grimly wait my turn. Already I am feeling faint with nerves. There's a loud high-pitched squealing sound – like an alarm – can't anyone else hear it?

I pray that this is an invisible day not a visible day. To be so undesirable and insignificant that no one notices you is wonderful. But when other kids notice you, when their cruel eyes settle on you, that's when you know you should have stayed in your room.

Today is such a day. There's a line of kids crowding around the tills, asking for sweets in the jars behind. I wait my turn. They each confidently ask for a quarter of this and a half of that. Then the lady turns to me:

'Yes, dear?'

I hesitate and the crowd of teenagers turn to look. This makes it worse. A pretty girl with perfect hair, blue eyes and a rosebud mouth looks me up and down. She nudges the handsome boy with spiky hair next to her, who smirks.

'I, I, a quarter of sherbet strawberries, please.'

'Squeak, squeak, goes the mouse,' giggles the boy. I feel the heat stab my face.

'A bit louder, dear. A quarter of . . . ?'

'Sherbet strawberries.'

'Say please, mousey!' says another voice. They are all resting against the rack of chewing gum now, fully focussed on me. My mouth is dry and I am curling my toes inside my school shoes.

The woman behind the till turns to get the jar of sweets, sighing. I know these are dangerous seconds –

when adults disappear – so I brace myself. The boys' faces harden, they chew imaginary gum.

'What the fuck are you staring at?'

He eyeballs me.

'Well?'

I feel something strange and new in my throat – not just fear, possibly anger.

'Nothing special,' I hear myself say.

His eyes widen, the girl gasps.

'You ugly, smelly dog-wog,' he whispers.

'Yeah, don't stare at us. We're not the freaks, you fucking freak.'

He lunges in a pantomime way and I keep looking levelly at him. The girl pulls him away.

'Leave it, she's no worth it, Ben.'

'That's 25 pence,' says the woman, tutting at all the noise.

I hand my change over. I am scared now – annoyed at my big mouth. Haven't I learned my lesson? But I'm also angry. Will it always be like this? I've been so close to the bottom that I am starting to feel as if there is nothing to lose, that all this hiding and not existing might be a waste of time. It doesn't change anything. I might as well live, mightn't I?

I walk out of the shop and, as I cross the threshold, the boy pushes me from behind. I stumble but keep standing. The girl is trying to pull him away again. I say nothing – but I raise my chin just half an inch and look him in the eye. I see in his face the same anger that was in Goldy's eyes when I crossed him; in the eyes of the boy who wouldn't hold my hands in school dance practice. It's fully loaded. He tries to pursue me, but the girl and the rest of his friends are telling him to leave it. As I walk away, I hear him spit at me, my heart beating horribly fast.

I try to process these encounters, which are occasional but painful. I know these kids are in the wrong. I know it is something about my awkwardness and the way I carry myself that attracts them; I know my skin colour marks me out. I know that some children can be cruel; that I may have been guilty of that cruelty too. But I also know that it won't, it can't always be like this. I've got plans. I can't wait to get away from these people.

From that day on, I stand a bit straighter, my chin is a bit higher. I still hate going in shops and speaking in public. But something minuscule has finally shifted.

TEN

Glasgow, Scotland, 1970

We grew up in petrol. The smell lives in our nostrils, it colonises our hair and takes root in our clothes. Everything in the petrol station is covered in a greasy film of black dust – the door handles, the filing cabinets, the banknotes. Sofas grow large grey or black patches where my dad sits every night, transferring the grime of the working day to our home. We drink our milk and orange squash from free promotional glasses; drawers are full of boxes of credit card counterfoils and multi-coloured rubber bands for bunching notes together.

Petrol station work gets into your bones: it is cold and dirty. Sitting under fluorescent tubes in a kiosk manning the till, cleaning the pumps, supervising the tanker deliveries, restocking the cans of engine oil, cigarettes and chocolate. In the early days my dad fills the customers' tanks, inhaling the smell and monitoring the display on the pump from under his increasingly long fringe.

He started managing a petrol station a year before I was born. He had no idea what it would involve or any experience in the area. Ten years earlier, he worked as an internal auditor for a company in Glasgow. The office was full of young men with long hair and short coats who got on well and who were always playing practical jokes on each other. They would wait until the last one of them had jumped on to a moving bus, then as he clung to the handle at the back, they would chop away at his hands until he had to let go and jump back into the road. But after ten years with no promotion in sight, my dad applied for a job in London, got it, and says that he was let go soon after because the firm hadn't realised he was Asian; they had thought his surname was Myer. He was jobless and frustrated for four months until, one day, he opened the paper and saw an advert for a petrol station franchise in Clydebank. He picked up the phone.

My little brother and I were born into petrol stations. We never saw our dad do anything else. To us he always looked comfortable – tall and broad, unloading boxes or marching solidly across the forecourt. My dad saw it as a comedown – a steady desk job to petrol station manager – but it gave him a flexibility that he would never have had otherwise. He was his own boss, his children could come and visit him and sit on his knee and eat too much chocolate, and he often got to work alongside my mum. She tells me that before they took over their first station they would park outside on the main road and count how many cars went in, terrified that this venture would fail. Luckily it didn't – but the petrol stations consumed our family life: at one point we had three across Glasgow – and my dad managed them seven days a week. He was always busy, stretched, on call twenty-four hours a day, dashing between the three. The oil price was volatile, so my dad did well. He worked all hours and managed to buy us a big house and put us in mostly good schools. But as he took on more and more sites, we spent less time together as a family; we took fewer trips and made fewer home movies. It was rare that my dad could come to a school concert or prizegiving, but he tried.

My dad liked to work – but he was sociable too. So he started a lifelong pattern of nocturnal timekeeping. He worked all day, came home, ate dinner, fell asleep until 10 o'clock, and then announced that he and mum were going out. They would come home in the small hours, get up at 7 a.m. or 8 a.m., and it would start all over again. This gets into our bones too; we become night owls. Even when we are young, we stay up later than we should because there is too much fun to be had downstairs – the telly is on, someone is on the phone, we are playing cards or snakes and ladders, eating oranges, shelling nuts and drinking gallons of tea.

Our weekends are also ruled by the petrol station. More often than not we have to shuttle between them, delivering omelette sandwiches to my dad or picking up or dropping off my little brother, depending on whether he has had a good day or a swearing and screaming outburst in front of the customers. My mum drives fast, skipping over hills and bumps, periodically putting her left arm out to stop me from sliding forward and hitting the dashboard.

We might have wished for weekends like our friends – spending it together as a family – but when we are young we never tire of going to the garage. It is exciting; being able to duck under the oily counter and into the back office makes us feel like VIPs for once.

Over the years my dad has his share of dramas, enemies and incidents. Some male customers don't take kindly to him being in charge, calling the shots, employing Glaswegian women. Often they try to make trouble and throw punches. The police are called many times. I never witness any of these incidents, but my brother recounts them with feverish excitement and they pass into family folklore, to be retold tens if not hundreds of times over the decades.

In fact, there are mostly men in the petrol stations. Men fill the cars and whistle loudly across the forecourt if whoever is in the kiosk takes too long to reset the counter to zero. Men open their car bonnets and stare lovingly at the innards of their cars for ages, plucking and polishing until they are satisfied.

From inside that kiosk, I must have watched hundreds of men jingling their car keys, expertly opening the petrol cap, and swinging that silver nozzle from the pump to the tank like a hefty fishing line. A whirring noise starts and they stand authoritatively, one foot on the ground, one on the raised island that houses the pump, chewing gum and looking inscrutable, while occasionally narrowing their eyes as the display ticks up to the required amount. Then the game of nerves commences. I stare as they ease their finger off the trigger and the numbers slow to an occasional click. £9.95, £9.96 . . . click . . . £10.00. They beam, put back the nozzle, toss the thin plastic gloves into the bins and stride, chests out, into the kiosk to pay. Some fat-fingered men miss the golden amount and 'Ooooyahhhh, ya wee bandit!' echoes around the forecourt.

Once inside, they are either chuckers or lingerers. 'Ten pounds, number four' and a grimy tenner is thrown on to the counter and they are gone. Or they stay and peruse the few shelves we have; gawping at cans of Castrol GTX for ages, sniffing air fresheners shaped into trees for the right level of sickliness or stocking up on chocolate bars and clinking bottles of Irn Bru.

For a child of eight, it is fun to stand next to one of the ladies on the till, perched high on a stool in a big coat, her feet freezing in strappy sandals and tights while a two-bar electric fire sizzles away on the floor. She pinches my cheeks and asks me about school while buttons flash red and green, the till bangs and beeps, and the bell over the door rings every time someone comes in. The East End Lotharios hitch up their trousers and smooth down their moustaches before they push the door. Some do a little waltz with an invisible partner and then lean on one elbow on the counter.

'Hul-loooooo, pet.'

'How ye daein', doll?'

'Achhh, it's my wee darlin' – yer lookin' stunnin' the day.'

'Lemme take ye away fae all this, hen . . . Why ye workin' in a place like this?'

If they are taking too long and there is a queue, the men behind shout: 'Ho, Romeo, getta fuckin' move on, will ye?' and my eyes pop out of my head.

Then my dad appears, tells me to go in the back and tries to move them on. They straighten up, their eyes hardening, taking in my dad, all six foot three of him, his black hair and his brown skin.

'Can I help you?' my dad asks.

'Er, no, pal, I don't think so.'

They eyeball each other for a while and then the phone rings in the back and my dad goes to answer it, leaving a sticky silence.

'Who the fuck is that?' the man growls. I shrink back into the chocolate bars hoping he can't see me.

'That's the boss,' says the lady on the till, matter-of-factly.

The man's eyes harden; he whistles softly.

'Is it now?' he says, his face tight, looking at where my dad has disappeared to.

He rummages about in his pockets, shaking his head, throws his money down and leaves, stopping to spit ostentatiously on the ground just outside the kiosk.

'Disgusting wee jobbie,' the woman says, then remembers me and puts her hands over my ears.

The only women there are generally my mum, me and the lady on the till. Occasionally a woman drives in to fill up and I watch her with wide eyes. How does she know what to do? Will she be able to lift that heavy nozzle? I'm not the only one watching. All the men on the forecourt are too. Sometimes the women get things wrong and park on the wrong side of the pump or can't get the fuel caps open and the men fall about laughing before offering to help.

One day a woman drives in, screeches to a halt and gets out. She has red hair and wears a navy trouser suit with sailor stripes on the huge lapels. She lifts the nozzle and a man shouts: 'Need any help, pet? Know which bit goes where, do ye?'

Other men titter around him. Without taking her eyes off the display she shoots back: 'Aye, ye put the thin ugly bit in the hole, ye should know that.'

The man nearly chokes on his gum and starts to cough furiously as she effortlessly fills her car up, replaces the nozzle like she has been doing it for years, and walks into the kiosk. She pushes the door confidently, pays, notices me with eyes as wide as a football pitch and winks: 'Shitey bastards.'

Baljaffray, Scotland, 1979

On that estate, the centre of every child's world is the burn at the bottom of the hill. By the time we are five, we know every twist and turn of that stream – the shallow bits, the best stepping stones, the jaggiest rocks, the places that older kids have tried to chuck us in. We know where the nettles are that will sting us and the dock leaves that will soothe our angry skin. We spend hours there, mostly with our bare hands, sometimes with twigs and branches or forks stolen from home that become bent or snapped.

But even more magical is the Bluebell Woods behind our houses and over the main road that runs round the whole estate. My mum often packs me and my little brother off there for half a day with a few Chocolate Digestives. I walk around making dens and picking flowers while my brother wanders aimlessly nearby, silently chomping on biscuits and conducting invisible battles in the air.

I know three things about the woods. They are magical, possibly enchanted. My cousin broke his arm swinging from a tree there. And lots of rough boys go there but they usually leave us alone. We are walking through the woods when three boys block our way.

'Ahhh, hullo,' says one of them in a voice older than his face.

I look at him blankly. What does he want?

'I said hullo.'

Emboldened by my silence, he continues: 'Can. You. Understand. Me. Good-ness grac-ious me,' he says, in a weird voice, his head waggling from side to side.

His friends snigger. I feel confused and wait for them to get to the point. I have heard people doing that voice before at school and on TV, but I don't know what it is or why he is using it to me.

'What is it?' I ask, impatiently.

'Do you eat curry?' he asks

'What do you mean?' I reply.

'Do. You. Eat. Curry?' he says it slowly and loudly, as if I am deaf.

His friends stand nearby picking their noses or spots. They look bored and harmless.

'No,' I say impatiently, eager to get on. 'Do you?'

His friends shoot him a look and whistle at my impertinence. The big boy frowns and looks annoyed.

'Shut up, you cheeky bitch, or ah'll batter ye.'

The air changes. The bad language wakes up my little brother.

'Aasmah, let's go. He's a bad boy,' he says.

'Hahahahahaaaa, Ass-mah. What kind of fucking

name is that? Ass-mah. Are you an ass? An ass-hole?
Do you have asthma?'

He clutches his throat and drops to the ground,
writhing hideously.

'Help, I've got asthma, help! Haw haw.'

His friends are in hysterics. I look around to see if
there is anyone else coming, but the woods are deserted.
I try to move on but he springs to his feet and blocks
my way.

'Haud on. Did I say ye could go?'

I sigh. Out of the corner of my eye I see my brother
raise his hand to wave it in front of his face and I grab it
and hold it tight. They must not know.

'He's a bad boy,' repeats my little brother, looking off
into the distance.

'Aww, the wee boy wants tae go. Are ye gonna wet
yourself?'

My brother looks blank and starts to mutter to himself.

'You must not swear in restaurants, Imran, how
many times have I told you,' he says randomly.

The boy stares.

'Hang on . . . is he OK?'

I start to panic. We've been rumbled. The boy's eyes
widen. A light goes on. Bingo.

'Oh my fuckin' God – is he a . . . a spastic?'

He gives a low whistle and moves in for a closer look.
This I can't bear. I don't mind when people tease me

about being smelly or having brown skin, but they can't touch my brother. I consider my options. I could wait until he comes a bit closer and then punch him, but he is much bigger than me. I can't let him do anything to my brother though. I have this sudden fear that he might be really cruel to him. I look at him, his brown eyes, his beautiful face and curly hair, swaying away and I feel something building in me that I have not felt since he disappeared with his pram at the age of three.

'He's only six. Leave him alone.'

It's a warning. I put my arm round his shoulder.

'Or whit? Whit ye gonnae dae? I'll fuckin' batter ye. An' wee Ali Baba here.'

He prods my brother in the shoulder and leans down to look at his face.

'Are ye? Are ye a mongol?'

In that moment I feel so much. I don't know what my brother is – no one has really explained it to me. I just know that he is not like other children, that he talks to himself, has no friends, can't read or write much and never really has conversations. He mostly makes demands and observations. But I love the bones of him – his voice, his face, his tiny fat hands, the smell of Vosene from his hair. I am my brother's protector. We have been put together. We share a room, he is my silent buddy, we are always seated together at tables and in cars. I won't let anyone harm him.

'I do eat curry!' I interject desperately, tears tumbling down my face and dipping into my mouth.

The boy looks at me, triumphant.

'And my name *is* Aasmah.'

'Jeez, whit a pair you are.'

He sniffs at the air around me:

'Aye, ye smell of it too.'

I wonder how this is going to end; I feel like I have been standing here trapped for half an hour. How I long to press my face into my mother's body, to feel her comfortingly *pat-pat* on my back or arm. Suddenly I see a movement to my right. It's two adults walking by. They see my pained face, my head bent; they see the strange stance of the boy looming over us and they stop.

'Everything OK over there?' the woman asks.

The boy straightens up, pats my little brother on the arm. My brother jerks it away.

'No touch!' he mutters.

'Och aye, we're brand new. They just got a bit lost and ah wis giein' them directions, that's all.'

The couple look dubious. The woman takes me in, muddy and tear-stained.

'Where do you want to go, pet?'

'Home,' I say, 'I just want to go home.'

Without asking me which way is home, they motion to us and we approach. They peer at both of us, but there are no words as we pick the path out of the woods.

I wipe at my muddy tears and lead my little brother with me, pulling him to safety. We get to the main road and I thank them. As we walk home, the sharp wind cuts into my face. My little brother hums happily and asks if there are any chocolate biscuits left. I reach into my coat pocket and give him mine.

*

There is always music in our house. A brown- and straw-coloured radiogram as big as a trunk sits on the sideboard, there is a record player in my parents' bedroom, a car journey is never taken without my dad pushing a thick cartridge into his car stereo, unleashing the soaring strings and mournful voice of Mohammed Rafi or Ghulam Ali. My parents sing along enthusiastically, their voices inhabiting different keys, meeting somewhere in the middle. My dad tells me that he would sing all the way to college on his bike and all the way back. My mum says there wasn't much music in her house when she was growing up and she is making up for lost time.

This music means little to us; it feels incongruous as we drive through the cold, grey streets of Glasgow, but we become used to it; it acquires a comforting familiarity. My parents love Bollywood songs and ghazals and sing them like songbirds – but that tunefulness deserts them when they attempt to sing anything in English. They adore Abba and Boney M – but their accompaniment to those songs stops us in our tracks. They launch in confidently then drop like a stone from one tuneless key to another until we beg them to stop or one of us starts crying. Over the years my mother massacres nursery rhymes, my dad's rendition of 'Happy Birthday' or any Beatles song bears no resemblance to the actual tune. Just as my parents struggle with the 'w' sound, which doesn't exist in the Urdu alphabet, they can only sing in Urdu and Punjabi. And so that's what they do. My dad sings all day. In the shower, in the garden, while cleaning his ears with a cotton bud, walking up the stairs, to my mother while she is washing the rice, to any passing child. His face is always covered in tiny bloody dots and bits of toilet roll from where he cuts himself shaving because he can't even stop singing when he is sweeping the razor across his cheeks.

I find my dad's obsession with music more tolerable than his obsession with cricket. He loves poetry and adores ghazals. He talks about Ghulam Ali all the time and plays so much of his music in his Volvo that my little brother memorises all the words and the melodies and sings them very precisely to us if he is in a good mood.

One day Ghulam Ali arrives at our house. We are used to Pakistani people coming to visit, never quite sure whether they are relatives or friends or famous. The Pakistani bowler Abdul Qadir once stayed for a few days. But today I sit on the stairs and watch a small, balding unremarkable man and his musicians file into the living room. They settle on the carpet cross-legged and there is a lot of throat-clearing and tuning of strange-looking instruments I have never seen before. My uncle and aunt and their kids arrive and we all sit and wait. When he opens his mouth, all the years of wobbly cassettes and cartridges from the car come alive. For someone used to a three-minute pop song, this is too pure and indulgent, but I enjoy the spectacle as various adults randomly shout 'Vah!' or 'Amazing!' They close their eyes and are transported. After the first song, my little brother, who has been listening while staring into the middle distance, gets up and sits beside Ghulam Ali. My mother explains that he would like to sing. There is some doubt as to how a ten-year-old boy will manage to convey the meaning of the words, the cadences, the stretching of the notes. We hold our breaths and watch him, in his tiny tank top, as he closes his eyes and in a deep voice sends the notes into the room. My mum's eyes are shining. For five minutes, he is at peace and so are we.

Gujranwala, Pakistan, 1959

I and all of my sisters adore clothes. We obsess about material, stitching, patterns – everything. We want our entire outfit to match and, if we had our way, all our clothes would be made of silk or georgette. My aunt – who unofficially adopted my sister Naz for the first six years of her life – was the family dressmaker, but when she dies, that mantle passes to me. I pull apart a kameez, copy the shape of the pieces and make a replica. I make another and another. Before long I am making my own shirts and my sisters are begging me to sew things for them too.

I spend hours copying designs and stitching clothes. I spend the entire summer making all our outfits. So it is no surprise that when the time comes for each of us to wear the dreaded niqab, we turn it into another dressmaking event. We reject the full length perforated all-in-ones worn by older women. We opt instead for a two-piece outfit made of silk not cotton. A coat with buttons, topped by an all over veil that has a square of thinner translucent material over the face. We also go for black because we think this is stylish and chic rather than grey or white. Despite all that, it is still a trial to wear it on a long day out. In the summer the black silk gobbles up the heat and turns it back on us, leaving us crimson-faced and sweaty. Often I sit in a horse and cart and flip my niqab back so I can feel the air on my face for five minutes. But as much as I hate it, I recognise that I do need some protection. If I ever go shopping in the markets of Gujranwala with my sisters, men push into us intentionally so they can touch us. We go to the market less and less.

Glasgow, Scotland, 1982

These clothes crackle on me. They are too stiff or too thin, with fussy collars and sleeves that pucker too tight; drapes of thin silky cloth you have to fight to keep from sliding off your shoulder. Sequins are sewn meticulously into transparent gauze and look beautiful but transform into a river of thorns scratching against your skin as soon as you put them on. I tolerate Asian clothes as a young child but, as I get older, I realise that I am engaged in a battle with them. They don't sit right or look right. Relatives shake their heads and tug at the shoulders and hems, saying I am not wearing them properly; that they should be accompanied by a smile not a scowl; that this bit is too long or short. On the rare occasions that my mum insists I wear them, people in the street stare, children laugh, Pakistani people tut. And I feel cold in them. I have always been taught to dress modestly, to cover myself – within reason. Knee-length skirts and dresses are fine; shorts and miniskirts are not encouraged. These clothes are meant for another climate – they only look good with open-toe sandals, not swamped in a big coat or accompanied by socks. In the cold greyness of Glasgow, they look incongruous and I feel ridiculous in them. I have been born into jeans and sweaters and skirts; flimsy and fussy Asian clothes irritate me. My mother has a way of carrying herself in shalwars and saris that I can never emulate. She is effortless, floaty, ethereal. I am clumsy and crumpled, always dropping something or trailing part of it into puddles; I can't wait to get home and rip the clothes off, climbing back into my jeans or pyjamas and feeling the familiar soft cotton clinging to my body. Things would have been different if we wore these clothes every day, but we don't. Our Asianness is like fine china stored in a cabinet. It is kept for best but rarely used. Our parents only speak English to us, then bemoan our lack of Urdu or Punjabi. As we grow, we end up in a place that is confused and unsatis-factory: outside the house we are too Asian; inside the house we are not Asian enough.

'Do we have to eat Pakistani food every day?' I ask my mother and she relents. We start having burnt steak and chips or some awful casserole made from a powdery packet mix. The food is nowhere as joyful as my mum's, but it makes me happy that I can eat more than just one type of cuisine; and not have to go to school the next day with my hair smelling of coriander and with scrawny boys edging away from me and pulling their school jumpers up over their dripping noses.

As I dip into my teens, I begin to feel the weight of the outward markers of my heritage. The food is too

smelly and peculiar, the clothes too gaudy and impractical and the language too difficult to learn. I move to
inhabit an unhappy nexus halfway between here and
there, where no one is happy – not me, my family or
my friends.

*

I adore my parents. They are small and tall, petite and
broad. But we inhabit different worlds; we do not
understand the same things because our childhoods are
so distinct. Where we shrink and are unsure, they are
sure-footed in a way that sets us apart from them. They
have never experienced our problems of not fitting in or
being made to feel different, lower, worth less on a daily
basis. My parents enjoyed secure childhoods and school
environments where not only had they been educated
among children who looked exactly like them, they were
the elite, marked out by their intelligence or looks. My
dad was tall and fair with hair so light that when he was a
child he was called 'Golden'. His fairness eased his social
path throughout his school and college days. My mum
was the middle-class daughter of a respected retired
businessman who excelled at school and became Head
Girl at college. Their school days were halcyon; mine
were ruled by jeopardy. So when I went to them with
complaints about name-calling or pushing or spitting,
they saw it differently to me. They tried to be pragmatic,
they couldn't fathom that it cut me to the bone.

My mum tells me to 'ignore it', that I shouldn't give people the satisfaction of showing I'm upset and that I must not sink to their level. My dad says the same thing but occasionally exhibits a flash of anger: 'I'll punch them!', which doesn't help either. So we are stuck between inaction and violence. I know the answer must lie halfway between the two but I don't know how to get there.

It takes several years for me to tell my parents what is going on at school. I become inured to it, it is routine. I see other kids being targeted because they wear glasses or have a stammer; my difference is my skin. I have my friends, but there are kids who prod me with classroom scissors and compasses because they want to see what colour my blood is. Others run their fingers over their tongues and try to rub my skin, so sure are they that the colour will come off. It goes on and on until I tell my mum. She tells me to rise above it and I try, but by the fifteenth time I am fizzing with anger and tears. I am not sure whether my parents are in denial or they just can't empathise. One day I cry to my mum so bitterly that she phones the school and complains to the head teacher. I am both mortified and curious as to whether this will change things. The next day I look at my teacher's face for clues. Is it softer? Is she on my side? She tells the class that they should not be unkind to each other. That day passes quietly and I exhale. A few days later, a boy shoulder barges me and calls me 'a smelly bloody nig-nog' when I beat him at football. He spits on my shoes. I go and tell the teacher. He has to write out fifty lines. But he corners me the next day. He is seething.

'See if ye tell the teacher on me again, I'll get ma big brother to batter ye. He'll be waitin' at the gate for ye. And then I'll use this on ye.'

He pulls his jumper up and pulls a penknife out of the inside of his waistband. It doesn't look terrifying but his face does. I have no doubt that he would use it on me, perhaps to check the colour of my blood once and for all. I think of the safety of home and the vast unprotected expanse of a school day and I decide to give in and give up.

The teacher calls me over the next day.

'How are things? OK? Any more trouble?' I look into her face and see both concern and impatience. I think of the penknife.

'No, it's fine,' I lie.

'Good, excellent.'

We stare at each other.

'One thing,' says the teacher. 'Name calling isn't nice, but it's just that. I was teased at school for having red hair. You have to be able to ignore it, brush it off, yes?'

I nod.

'Just remember – *sticks and stones may break my bones but names will never hurt me.*'

I shift on my feet.

'Off you go.'

I turn this over in my head. She must be right. Name-calling upsets me, but it's not like kicking or punching. I spend the next ten years trying to ignore the words and the way they make me feel.

Glasgow, Scotland, 1967

I come across Mary as I walk along the street with the pram. She is standing in her garden, in a powder-blue jumper and grey miniskirt, watering some plants. Her eyebrows raised, she stares at me for quite some time until I draw level with her. She softens her face.

'Ah, hello,' she exclaims. 'You must be the new people at 61. I'm Mary.'

She doesn't offer her hand.

'Oh hello,' I say enthusiastically.

She takes in my clothes, my shalwar kameez.

'What's your name, dear?'

'Oh . . . it's Almas.'

'Lovely, dear,' she declares. 'And what a beautiful baby. And how are you getting along with everything?'

We talk about houses and babies and the weather and how she moved twice in the same street before she suddenly catches sight of her watch.

'Oh my, I have to be at the badminton in five minutes and I'm not even changed. I'll have to go, dear.'

'Badminton?' I say.

'Oh, yes, I play every week in the church hall.'

'Oh, I'd love to play.'

Her eyes widen.

'You . . . play badminton?'

'Oh, yes, a bit.'

She claps her hands together.

'Well, you can come with me next week. Now I must fly, dear.'

Next week I pitch up at the local church. Mary is there with several other women, who have brought their babies and parked their prams in the corner. I add mine.

'Ah, hello,' she casts around for my name, '. . . dear.'

She looks at my trousers and top approvingly.

'Excellent outfit. Shall we double up?'

Mary and I become fast friends. She pops into my house and runs her hand over the sofa. She comes to my daughter's first birthday party and brings her husband and children. She is a helpful and polite woman who fills me in on bin collections and local nurseries.

Other neighbours are just as civil but less forthcoming. Most of them smile and nod but never really stop to chat. There are young and middle-aged couples in chequerboard tank tops with impish children; an older man with a walking stick who stops in his tracks as I pass him and just stares. A woman called Donna lives across the road. She nods but never speaks, always in a pinny, or coming back from the shops with her groceries in a net bag. One day as I push the pram back from badminton, she is standing on her doorstep.

I nod at her as usual and she approaches, looking nervous, weighing me up through her fringe.

'Hello . . . hi. How are youse all gettin' on?'

'Very well, thanks.'

'I see you're big friends with Mary.'

'Yes, she told me about the–'

She lets out a long, loud unhappy breath.

'And is she OK with ye?'

'Yes, of course.'

She is studying the broken paving, grinding her slippered toe over the cracks and the weeds.

'Ye know she used tae live next door to ye, right?'

'Yes, yes I do.'

'Did she tell ye why she moved?'

'I think she said that she needed a bigger house, what with two–'

Donna snorts.

'Oh aye, did she now?'

I wait. The baby is stirring, trying to wriggle her arms free from the blanket I have wrapped tightly round her. Donna folds her arms and looks over her shoulder. The road is empty. She lowers her voice anyway.

'Well, the real reason she moved, hen, is 'cause she heard some foreigners, excuse me dear, were moving in, and she was worried that the value of her hoose was gonnae go doon the swanny. So she shifted sharpish, know whit I mean?'

She looks triumphant.

'Right. I see.'

This is not the bombshell that Donna expects it to be. I have heard that some people don't like living next door to Pakistanis. But Mary has been kind to me. I can't reverse out of our friendship.

'Noo, dinnae tell her ah telt ye that. She'll have ma guts fae garters, so she will.'

She does a zipping motion across her mouth.

'See ye, hen.'

She skips up the steps and into her house. The baby awakens.

*

When my first child is born, we are living in a top-floor tenement. I bump the pram down six flights of stairs and walk to Kelvingrove Park. I sit on a bench with my packed lunch and watch people go by as the baby sleeps. I study the couples, the students, the old ladies, the mothers with babies. And they appraise me too. They peek at the baby and tell me how cute she is. I feel happy, there is oxygen to breathe for miles and miles. But when I see a new mum with her baby and her mother, I think of my own. What I would do to have her here with me and her grandchild in this open, green country. I would show her the hills, the parks, the shops, the straight lines; make her take huge gulps of the fresh minty air free from dust and smoke. I would feed her fish and chips and Coca Cola. I would switch the TV on and we would watch *The Golden Shot*. We would go shopping and she would shake her head at the cheap material, the ready-made clothes, the half-naked mannequins.

A telephone call to Pakistan has to be booked and is scandalously expensive. I love hearing my mother's voice, but she immediately starts crying because she misses me. She goes to our neighbour's house who has a phone to receive the call. But our calls usually consist of her crying and asking how the children are before one of us is cut off by the hiss of many thousands of miles.

It is less upsetting to write her a letter. When my mother receives the thin blue aerogramme, she falls on it ravenously and gets my sister Kaukab to read it twice, immediately. Once fast, then once slowly. Then she folds it back up immaculately and places it under her pillow. That letter is read aloud every night until a new one arrives. My sister begs me to write more often as she is fed up reading the same words for four weeks. But the post is slow and I have little time. It takes two weeks for the letter to arrive. By then my news is old, but no less enthusiastically received by my mother.

Wah Cantonment, Rawalpindi, Pakistan, 1960

Neelam starts feeling pains in her side when she is thirteen. At first we put it down to her previous ailments
and fragile condition, but she insists that it is a new pain.
My mother takes her to the doctor, who prescribes some
pills. But the pains get worse and my brother Khalid
takes charge. He has a friend who works at the Army
Hospital in Rawalpindi – one of the best hospitals in
Pakistan. There they take an X-Ray and diagnose kidney
stones. We are all relieved it is nothing more sinister. She
will have an operation to remove them and then we will
give her some time to convalesce in Wah before taking
her back to Gujranwala.

In the meantime we take advantage of the proximity
of Rawalpindi to Wah, where my oldest sister Samina
lives with her husband and three young children.
My sister Samina's husband Javed is the most perfect
brother-in-law we could wish for. Caring, funny, loyal,
with a mouth that is always stretched into a gentle
smile. We didn't know husbands could be nice – we
had witnessed the coolness of our father towards our

mother. Our expectations of husbands rise sharply. We often stare at him, not quite believing it. We make any excuse we can to stay at their house. It is so much fun, the atmosphere is delicious, nothing like the house of unhappiness that we lived in for years. Even my mother changes when we go there. But as we near home, her face falls and she draws the storm clouds around her again.

Those days in Wah are so carefree. We sit on charpais on the verandah, we loll around on the floor – kids, adults, grannies – we eat oranges and pistachios and pine nuts. We drink sabz chai until the late hours, while the children sleep between us on our laps or in the crook of our arms. We massage oil into each other's hair and press each others' tired legs.

We yearn for these breaks from the oppressive atmosphere of our home. Wah provides that, as do trips to other people's houses. I become inquisitive, envious of other people's homes and families. I admire the colour and order of houseproud Auntie Sarfraz's home. And I cannot stop inhaling the lightness of the air at the house of my college friend Yasmeen. We strike up a friendship because we are the only two girls who come to college in a car. She invites me to her home after classes one day. I am curious, but nothing prepares me for what I find there. The house is full – eight people live there: her parents and six children. There are colourful pictures on the wall; the house is full of noise and life and the adults seem to encourage it. Her mother is smartly dressed and smiles a lot; her father is neither grumpy nor old. Her parents seem to like each other, which I find baffling; they fetch things for each other and look at each other while speaking. We eat lunch and then Yasmeen brings some glass bowls out. Into each one she places two peach halves from a tin. I have never had peaches from a tin – they are glossy and sticky and soft and I eat them slowly, chasing the last drops of juice around the bowl. If no one had been looking, I would have tipped the bowl into my mouth, hoping the sweetness would stay with me for ever.

*

In Wah, we have eaten too much and are heading heavily to our rooms for a post-lunch nap when we hear an unexpected car in the driveway. It is Bhai-Jaan Javed. Usually a smart man, he doesn't have his jacket on and his hair looks uncombed.

'Hey, why are you here? Have you forgotten something, Bhai?'

'Hey Bhai, you want me to beat you at rumi again?'

The gentle smile that usually sits on his face is nowhere to be seen; his features are stiff and frozen as if he has just walked into a door, his mouth is tight.

My sister touches his arm: 'Has something happened? Something at work?'

He collapses into a chair as if all his bones have broken and I can feel the bad air ooze from him. My back feels cold.

'I'm so sorry. I just heard from the hospital. Khalid called me.'

The air disappears. I want to stop him. I don't want to hear it. But we must hear it.

'Something happened . . . in the operation. There was too much blood. Something went wrong. The blood.'

I grip on to the side of an armchair. My legs are folding beneath me. We wait for the words that will change everything. They take too long and not long enough to arrive.

'She passed away.' His voice cracks. 'I'm sorry. She's gone.'

There is silence. No wailing or crying. Just shock. Alerted by the sudden silence, the children look up at the adults questioningly. He still hasn't said her name. It's not real unless he says her name, I think. But then he says the words that confirm it.

'*Inna lillahi wa Inna ilayhi rajioon.*'

I sit down and cover my eyes and think of my sister. Her pale face appears before me, her big innocent eyes, her rag dolls, her unsteady walk, her indecently short life. No one had prepared us for this. There was next to no risk, a routine operation, they told us. And here we had been gorging ourselves on food and laughter while she had bled to death on an operating table on her own. I am disgusted. I taste the acid of anger and shock in my gullet and try to swallow it, but it refuses to budge. I feel like it may burn my throat.

*

Neelam lies on top of a charpai in the back of the rusty rented truck. Her body is wrapped tightly in a cotton sheet. We sit on the benches on either side as we drive in ghastly silence from Rawalpindi to Gujranwala. The roads are treacherous and noisy; no one knows nor cares about our precious cargo. My mother occasionally mutters that this is God's will, that Neelam will be looked after now, and what kind of life would she have had anyway? I try to look away from the tiny shape under the sheet, how incongruously small she looks and how death has stilled her. But I cannot. These are my last hours with her. I will never see her jerky walk again, never see her huge bright eyes. There is no roof on the truck and the wind keeps whipping at our clothes. It disturbs the sheet wrapped around her too, making it constantly flap and fall. Bewitched by the movement, I will her to sit up, to pull the sheet off and leap into my arms. How I would hug her, keep her with me. But it is too late; I have lost her. For six long grey hours, I sit and stare, my mouth dry and bitter.

ELEVEN

Glasgow, Scotland, 1986

A face stares back at me from the mirror and I examine it closely. I take my glasses off; they have left a deep red indentation on the bridge of my bony nose. I push with my tongue on the brace in my mouth. It lifts out to reveal both too many teeth and huge gaps. I touch my hair, which feels greasy and hard at the same time. No matter how much I pull it with a brush and hairdryer, it never lies straight. I run my hands over my rough skin, furious starbursts of acne around my mouth, soft dark hairs on my upper lip and between my brows.

I think about why I have this face of all faces. How it is decided. Everything feels stretched, exaggerated. I place my palm sideways on my large forehead. My mother often tells me that in Pakistan a large forehead is a sign of beauty, but Pakistan feels a long way away and I certainly don't feel beautiful. My face and body are growing in all directions and I cannot contain them anymore. I don't know where it will all end. I feel ungainly, a giant in a doll's house, all feet and hands and shoulders. And then there is my skin – raging with spots and a colour I despise. If I press my fingers into the flesh of my thighs or arms, it momentarily goes a shocking white, giving me a glimpse of how things could be. But this is my face, this is my skin; and I must go out into the world with them.

I wonder how you become beautiful and where all the bad stuff goes; how you speak to people in a loud, clear voice; what it is like to be popular, to be invited to Saturdays on Sauchiehall Street and sleepovers and pizza. How to embrace the world and everything it holds instead of hiding in your room; how to become one of those people who lights up a room when you enter it instead of sucking the joy out of it.

Once I played in streams and parks, I knocked on doors and played with friends, I filled my space. Now my world has shrunk to the four walls of my bedroom, where my books and dreams meet and I am a heroine plucked from the thin pages of a Thomas Hardy novel, my unruly chestnut hair fastened into a low bun, a shawl wrapped around my sharp shoulders. By day I shepherd animals across a Wessex moor and by night I rebuff the marriage proposals of wealthy landowners and handsome blacksmiths. Or I am the girl in the video, with a soft spiky hairstyle and a satin face, dressed in bubblegum pink, surrounded by boys in baseball jackets with yellow hair. Every night my dreams wreak havoc with my mind, pulling me this way and that, before delivering me with a bump on to a damp sandy shore at dawn, the familiar salty taste of disappointment on my lips.

In my dreams I am loud and certain. But when I wake, I leave my voice behind on that beach. I lost my voice during those awful silent months at school and I just don't know how to get it back. Hardly anyone outside my house hears it. Hardly anyone outside my house sees me. The thought of going anywhere sends me into a terrible panic. On the rare occasions that I am persuaded, as the car weaves its way from the driveway to the main road, heading into town, I feel sick with fear. I spend a lot of time sitting in cars, waiting for my mum to drop things off or buy stuff, shrinking in the front seat, hoping no one will spot me. I yearn to be invisible. But in the meantime I enjoy the delicious masochism of being shown what I cannot have. It thrills me. This is because I know, as difficult as life has become, this is not the way it ends. I drown myself in the awfulness and become obsessed with extremes and regeneration. You have to really suffer before things get better. The before and after, the bad then the good.

'Are you coming in?' Mum asks, to which the answer is always a shake of the head. My legs wouldn't work. And I would be mute, burning with embarrassment and wanting to chop off my head so no one could lock eyes with me. It's easier to stay in the car, staring at people's easy interactions, their small talk – all the stuff I have lost the ability to do. I spend years doing this, retreating, making myself small, curling up in bed and hiding from the world that I have forgotten how to navigate and that does not want people like me – awkward, silent. I have become 'difficult', 'eccentric' and 'a loner'. I like these words; I have made my peace with them.

The inability to go into shops and interact with strangers is gradual. I persevere for a while although I find it excruciating. Sometimes I get away with a silent transaction in a newsagent; but other times they ask me questions and I have to force the air out of my throat and squeak an answer, which often makes other customers laugh or stare.

'Speak up, hen! You lost your voice?'

'She must be in love!'

'Seller of sweets I am, reader of minds I am not.'

Sometimes I stand in the queue, dreading my turn, awestruck by the easy confidence of other children my age as they negotiate and choose and laugh easily. I want so much to be like them, not turning purple-faced and sweaty with embarrassment if someone asks me a question. Often the dread overpowers me and I rush out, the door slamming behind me.

My mum persuades me to come with her to a department store. I spend most of the time wanting desperately to fold myself into the car and speed home to safety. She is going through a bargain bin of material remnants and I am staring at the floor. I look up and catch sight of a girl with dark hair and a school uniform staring at me. I look away, annoyed, only to look up again ten seconds later and she is still staring at me. I huff loudly and my mum glances at me:

'What's wrong?'

'That girl,' I hiss, 'she just keeps staring at me. Can we please leave?'

My mum follows my stare and then goes back to the bargain bin.

'Mum! Did you not hear me? I want to get away from her. Please.'

Not looking up, my mum says levelly: 'That isn't a girl, that's your reflection. Why don't you ever wear your glasses?'

I squint at the girl, who is also squinting and frowning at me, from what I now see is a mirror, and realise that I have in fact started an argument with myself.

Soon it becomes too painful to go into shops, so I stop buying things, or if I am desperate I ask my mum to go for me. She does it, but I can see that she feels it isn't normal, just another thing for her to worry about.

*

I open my new A4 pad and press the blue biro onto the first page. It feels pleasing and soft. I write:

> *Clare is not ugly. Clare just needs some help.*
> *Here we have listed all her negatives:*
>
> *Bad, spotty skin*
> *Thick glasses*
> *Small, peeky eyes*
> *Buck teeth and braces*
> *A big hooked nose*
> *A fat round face*

A Glasgow Girl

A moustache
Sticky-out ears
Lank, greasy hair
Big bum
Fat thighs
Big feet
Hairy legs and arms
School skirt is TOO long
Shoes are not fashionable
Her skin is TOO brown

Once she has been through the Teen-a-fix
transformation, she is like a different girl.
She is now called Sophia. Look!

Her skin is clear, shiny and peachy
She has contact lenses, no glasses
Straight white teeth
A face lift
High cheekbones
A new smaller ski jump nose
Liposuction on her bum and thighs
Smooth hairless arms and legs and face
Her clothes and shoes are fashionable now
Sophia is popular and has lots of boyfriends.
Everyone wants to be her friend now. Another
satisfied customer. Do YOU want to be like
Sophia? We can help.

*

Life at home is comfortable and manageable. I can stay in my room, reading and writing stories. I can come down and watch hours of TV in a room on my own. I eat dinner and help my mum wash up. I have become interested in cleaning. I like nothing better than to be left with a filthy kitchen, rice all over the floor, stacks of dirty dishes and pots, and to transform it into a perfectly clean space. It is something controllable and achievable and I want to compensate my mum in some way for not being a normal daughter.

The other things I become obsessive about are books and writing. I accumulate books and read as many as I can. I start to write letters to make a connection with people. To bemused and distant older relatives, to loners at school who live just streets away. I enter every competition on every tin label and cereal packet. I don't want to win. I just want to get something in the post. To feel connected, loved. These people don't know me, they don't judge me, they just send me my free pens and treat me like every other kid who writes to them, albeit with a funny name. I scour magazines for offers and pour silver ten pence pieces into envelopes, secured with Sellotape, and wait for my stickers or books. I write relentlessly to my penfriend in Finland, although he is as boring as me and I struggle to fill a blue aerogramme. But because I am so industrious in my letter writing, at least one letter comes in the post for me every day. These letters are my oxygen; I don't know what I would do if they stopped.

I am tidying my books and notice a tattered old blue Bible. We had half an hour of Bible class every morning in primary seven, so I presume it came from there. I open it and see on the first page in girlish cursive: *Annette M Mackie, age nine*. And then an address, somewhere in Ayrshire. A thought grows in my mind. I quickly write a letter to Annette, saying that I have her bible for some reason and would she like me to send it to her in the post. I chew my pencil and add: 'Maybe we could be friends?' I post the letter the next day, along with a few competitions, and hope for the best. Maybe Annette wouldn't want to be friends with a Pakistani. Maybe she is twenty now and might think me too young. I praise myself for being so brave. If I am rejected, it will be swift and it will be on paper.

A week goes past and nothing, so I forget about it. Then one day when my parents are out, I hear my brother calling me from downstairs.

'What is it?' I shout down, annoyed.

'Er, there's someone at the door for you.'

He sounds as surprised as I feel. Who on earth would come to my door? I tiptoe down the stairs and see a smartly dressed man with a grey suit and black cap on. When he sees me he steps back and signals to someone in the huge Rolls Royce behind him. My brother, sister and I watch open mouthed. From the back seat of the car gingerly steps a tall, frail, immaculate woman of about eighty. She uses a stick to walk up the shallow steps to the front door. She looks at me imperiously and I shrink back. Is she a witch?

'You.' She looks at me, 'You have my Bible?'

I say nothing.

'My Bible,' she repeats. 'You wrote this . . . this letter!'

She seems angry and holds it in her gloved fingertips as if it is wet or dirty. Slowly I realise that this is not Annette Mackie's grandmother or mother but Annette herself. She is certainly not nine anymore.

'May I have it, please.' Her face is as blue as ice, her voice lacks moisture.

I can't even speak and run upstairs to get it. I want this to be over. I am upset at how cold she is. I thought I was at least doing a good deed. But she just takes the Bible from me and gets back into the car. My face is burning. This is not how I had expected it to go. The Rolls Royce does a messy three-point turn in our driveway and speeds off. I think how upset my mum will be that the gravel is all over the lawn again.

But mostly I feel shock and humiliation; there had been no thanks and I felt small and the cause of trouble again. I try not to cry because my siblings are watching me closely. My brother whistles and says: 'Wait until I tell Mum and Dad what you've been up to!'

My sister nods sagely: 'And what a waste of a first-class stamp too!'

Gujranwala, Pakistan, 1955

I shouldn't like my brother – he is arrogant, entitled and likes to stir trouble between me and my sisters – but he is the only one I have. I idolise him. I would do anything for him.

That is why I often stand at the top of the stairs leading to the roof, one eye on the bottom of the steps, watching for my father, one eye on my brother illicitly flying kites. Sometimes he lets us hold the string, shouting instructions or grabbing it back when another kite looms over us to try to cut ours down. He knows if my father catches him indulging in this 'waste of time', when he could be studying, he will be punished. He is not supposed to spend time swimming in the muddy canal either, but he does. He creeps back in with wet hair and my father pounces, berating him for neglecting his studies and hitting him twice with a stick that he keeps in his office. We stand outside and cry. We are his biggest fans, his protectors.

That is why I sometimes creep into our father's bedroom to sneak the car keys off his bedside table and give them to my brother. He knows that if he wakes up to see him, there will be no time for an explanation; but if it is me, he won't suspect anything untoward. I had an innocent face; I was beyond reproach.

That is why when he needs to finance his farfetched idea of staging the first floodlit football tournament in Pakistan, I don't hesitate to scoop my scholarship savings of two thousand rupees into his grateful hands. He promises that not only will I get my money back, but that he will make so much profit, I will probably get double. The outlay is huge; but the returns are non-existent. No one wants to pay to watch a match when they could duck under railings or hang from trees or buildings to watch instead. He looks defeated and sheepish when he comes to tell me that my money is all gone. But still I don't mind.

And how he loves to wind up my sister Naz and I. We hadn't got off to a good start and he finds the insecurities between us tantalising. When there is an argument, he says to me: 'Why are you letting her win? You're bigger than her.' Then he sidles up to my sister and says: 'You're older than her, are you going to let her tell you what to do?' So round and round we go locking horns until we get wise to his ways. When Naz and I finally understand that he is trying to make us fight for his entertainment, the steam comes out of our tricky relationship. We suddenly see that we are more similar than we thought. We mellow with each other. There will always be annoying brothers in the world. But if you can love your sister, that is a lifelong friendship.

Khalid toys with us at sport too. He is good at everything – football, swimming, running – and, of course, cricket. We beg him to let us play cricket up on the roof. Eventually he relents but insists on batting first. Then we try for an hour to get him out. When we are fed up, he gives us the bat, bowls us out with the first ball and performs a victory dance in front of us.

Glasgow, Scotland, 1985

I am enticed back to Glasgow by the offer from my parents of a new school in August and a feeling of unfinished business in my own head. But when we arrive back in April, there are still two months of school before the end of term, so, to my horror, my parents tip me back into the fire – the same school. I kick up a huge fuss, but they say that it's only for two months and my mum is here now, not four thousand miles away. There is no alternative, so I have to do it in the end. I dig out the uniform I thought I would never have to wear again. My stomach flips at the sight of the diagonal stripes on the tie. My mum drops me off at the gate and squeezes my hand.

'Remember, *beti*, just two months.'

I get out of the car and try to remember where my class is. This is crazy. Six months, thousands of miles, a completely different education system, a different culture – and now, here I am, back where I started and almost ended. I wonder how people will be with me. Will they still not speak to me? What will Goldy be like? Will I get through these two months unscathed?

What I find is less toxic than I feared. In the six months I have been away, people have moved on, friendships have ended, new feuds have begun, kids have left, arrived. Children, unlike adults, don't tend to hold grudges; they forget why they hated you; why they couldn't speak to you. Goldy completely ignores me and his legend fades in my mind, like the Wizard of Oz. There are seven classes in my year. In my class of thirty, the children are still a bit cool with me – but this is more to do with the fact that I disappeared for so long to a country they'd struggle to place on a map. So I make friends with children in other classes in my year. It is tolerable. I see the end of the line, I know I can cut all ties with this awful place in two months. A vile boy who is known to carry a knife round with him says: 'Susan says you were asked to be a model in Pakistan! Who the fuck would use you as a model? You're a fuckin' dog, hahahaha . . .'

I smile to myself. Sticks and stones.

I see Sandra queueing for a lesson. I try to avoid her but she locks eyes with me and we take each other in. Her hair is now blonde but still curly, her eyeliner is blue, she looks older, around twenty. I go to turn away and she says: 'I really like your earrings.'

I stare.

She comes up to me and gingerly touches the red plastic hoops. We are so close that I can smell the familiar whiff of cigarette smoke. It is painful to look in her eyes, to inhale that familiar smell. I think she's trying to make amends. But I do hold grudges. I can never forget those months of isolation, those endless walks in the rain, that neverending silence.

'Thanks,' I say tightly, my eyes dead, finally standing up for myself.

She looks at me hard, then rolls her eyes. That's the last time we ever speak.

*

My next school is old and crumbly, just how I like them. It is two or three large terraced houses knocked together. You can only cross between buildings on certain floors so I spend a lot of time climbing then descending squeaky staircases. After the huge anonymous 60s buildings and baying mobs in the playgrounds of the last school this one is more manageable, like being in someone's house. There are just girls here and they are politely dismissive of me, rather than feral. They are all very neat and tidy. Skirts are below the knee, shoes are heavy and black. No leopard-print court shoes here, no jewellery and certainly no make-up. Apart from me of course. I have finally discovered a perk of being Asian. The teachers can't tell that I have eyeliner on; they think that's just how my eyes are. On my first day, I stand at the front of the class and feel the same buzzing terror as twenty pairs of eyes scan me then look away again in disinterest. I am the new girl. But I have no history here – no one knows what happened at the last school so I can start afresh.

I have missed almost my entire second year; a strange six month international sojourn in the middle of the academic year, bookended by two spells at an unfathomably awful school. I am just expected to catch up so I do. On the first day, the teacher takes me through my timetable. Maths, English, Physics – whatever that is, Chemistry, Extra English. My eyes widen at the last one. How do they know I'm good at English already? I bound along to the lesson and park myself at the front. Only four more girls appear – and they are all in different years. And they are all Asian. I've never been in a Scottish classroom with four other Asian girls before. It feels exhilarating. The teacher arrives and hands out a book – but it's like something from primary school. She instructs us to read it through and she will ask questions after. I flick through the book, then look at her, mystified.

'Is there a problem?' she asks.

'This book is for . . . it's like a kids' book.'

'Is it now? Well, why don't you read it out for us . . .'

The other girls look timidly at me. So I do. She looks at me, frowning.

'Right. So your English is quite good?'

I look at her blankly. Of course it's good. I'm fourteen, not eight. I look round at the other girls and the penny drops.

'Do you speak English at home?'

I blink at her.

'Do your parents speak English?'

'Yes.'

'What kind of books do you read?'

I think of the book in my bag.

'*Jane Eyre*.'

Her eyes widen.

'Right, I don't think you're in the correct class. You can go.'

I can't get out of there fast enough but as I leave I glance at the other girls, meekly reading their baby books. Has she asked them if they can read books for their age or has she just assumed like she did with me? I feel a flash of anger, for me and for them.

This assumption that I might be 'a bit slow' follows me around like a fly. Some teachers take me at face value and let me show them what I can do. But others look at my education record, with weird gaps in it, and draw their own conclusions. Just two months into my new school, I sit a mock exam in Physics – a subject I have never studied – and get seventeen percent. The physics teacher shakes her head at my mother at Parents' Evening and says that I will never pass a physics exam; I don't have the aptitude for science; and that she can forget about me becoming a doctor. After just sixty days, she is unequivocal in her dire predictions.

My mum comes home red-eyed and humiliated. I have never seen her like this. I know that she wanted to be a doctor – but her brother said she couldn't go to college and study medicine. It was almost unheard of in Gujranwala. My father's sister was able to study Pharmacology at Glasgow University in the late 1950s. But there were no such open minds in my mother's family back then, so she parked her dreams. She kept trying to reignite them through us. My older siblings had already punctured her expectations; she had foolishly pinned her hopes on me. I knew I wasn't going to be a doctor, but I didn't want my mother to be made to feel so small by a careless teacher. I also knew that I could be clever – I was just steadying the ship after a rocky few years. It broke my heart when she kept wiping her face with a wretched thin tissue too soaked with tears to be effective. That night I stared at my physics textbook trying to decipher its code. They presumed I couldn't read or write English properly; they presumed I would never pass a physics exam. They wrote me off. Something was stirring in my chest.

Up until then I had been average in most things – apart from English. That night I draw up a study plan. I stay in my room every night and get myself into the top sets for every subject the following term. The next physics exam I sit I get seventy-five percent. I just keep going, wanting to be the best at everything – a scorched earth policy. Previous records fall, top students are overtaken. It becomes an obsession. I'm doing it for all the

Asian girls (and boys). And for my mum. At my old school, we were too smelly. Here we are too stupid. I finally feel I can control something, change something about the way people perceive me. I get all As in my O Grades including Physics which I then drop from a great height; I've proved my point.

But I'm not finished. It's normal to sit five Highers – I ask to do six. The teachers are dubious and ask me if I realise how much work it will be. I tell them I have nothing else to do and have loads of time to study. I sit my six Highers and wait for the results. The day before, I take a ride on a quad bike that belongs to my uncle and of course I fall off. I twist my ankle and can't go down the stairs to pick up my results from the doormat. My mum comes running up the stairs with the envelope, flushed with excitement, her hair even curlier than usual. She stands while I tear it open. I feel sick. I want to be perfect. Anything less is going to upset everything. A horrendous Maths exam which made some of us cry on the day has unsettled me. I could hardly finish it. I slide the laminated certificate out diagonally. The first subject is English.

'English . . . A.'

My mum cheers.

'French . . . A.'

She punches the air.

'History . . . A.'

Her eyes widen.

'Economics . . . A.'

'Whaaaat?' She looks shaken, and sits down on the floor with a bump, her slipper comes off and she bangs it on the floor in jubilation.

'Latin . . . A.'

She is now banging the shoe so hard that the little cloth heel almost snaps off.

I pause. I know this is going to spoil everything. I don't want to continue.

'For God's sake, hurry up!' pleads my mum.

'You know it's Maths, right?'

'Yes, yes, who cares – you've got five As, FIVE As. My daughter got five As.'

I grit my teeth. Still pulling the certificate out diagonally, I see the execrable word MATHEMATICS. I start to pull the other end. And then I see something weird. The apex of a letter. I keep pulling and then I stare at it, blinking.

'WHAT?' screams my mum. 'For God's sake, tell me.'

'It's . . . an A.' I say in a puzzled voice.

Her eyes widen, her mouth opens and she screams. She bangs her slipper so hard on the floor that the heel snaps off and does a little loop before settling on my bed.

'Oh my God. How . . . ? I don't . . .'

She starts to cry. I just stare blankly at the paper,

checking it again. My elation is cancelled out by my confusion. Helen appears looking worried, saying she heard shouting. I hug her and tell her.

'Mum, don't cry.' I hate it when she cries, and especially if I have made her. Even if it's something good. My mum doesn't show a huge amount of emotion so when she does it feels overwhelming.

'I'm so happy,' she says through clenched teeth, trying to stop her tears, but it's no use. She grabs me by the shoulders.

'You've got six As. Six. You said you would. I should have believed you.'

Mum wipes her eyes with the corner of her dressing gown. Helen has sat down on a chair, mopping her face too with one of the many tissues she carries in the huge pockets of her cardigan.

'You can do . . . anything, *beti*,' mum whispers.

I look at her and realise that it is over. And it has begun.

*

News of my exam success spreads quickly. Relatives phone to congratulate my parents; some of their friends think it's a lie and spread doubt. When I tell my mum that I am going to be the Dux of the School for 1988, she almost passes out. My name is engraved in gold on a huge walnut board in the reception of the school. It is the first Asian name, but it won't be the last.

At Prizegiving I am rarely off the stage, feeling self-conscious, collecting little trophies and book tokens. My parents are in the audience, seated in front of a couple who are getting more and more befuddled by my monopoly.

'Who is that girl? She must be half caste. Can't be fully Asian, surely?'

At which point my mum cannot contain herself any more. She clutches her handbag to her stomach and turns round beaming. 'That's my daughter and she is one hundred percent Pakistani!'

*

I am regaining my voice at school, but it is still a squeak publicly. I am able to devote most hours of the day to studying because I have had no social life. Things are shifting – I have a group of good friends – including Beatles super fan Felicity – but the idea of being in a public place like a cinema or restaurant still makes me feel queasy. As a result I miss out on all the milestones of my teenage years. I cannot make eye contact with anyone I don't know or even eat a crisp in public. I stare after the girls in the loos at the end of the day drawing on eyeliner and lipstick and heading to Oliver's in town to meet boys. To this day there are huge gaps in my cinema knowledge. While most teenagers were watching movies at the weekend, I never went. The result is a list of films as long as the Clyde Tunnel that I have never seen.

AASMAH MIR

The Breakfast Club
E.T.
Top Gun
Dirty Dancing
Star Wars
The Goonies
Ferris Bueller's Day Off
The Never Ending Story
Good Morning Vietnam
Superman
Indiana Jones
Stand By Me
Ghostbusters
Footloose
Gremlins
Pretty in Pink
St Elmo's Fire
Police Academy
Groundhog Day
Back to the Future
Flashdance
Alien
Scarface
Platoon
Full Metal Jacket
Nine and a Half Weeks
Beverly Hills Cop
When Harry Met Sally

A Glasgow Girl

Rocky
The Karate Kid
Uncle Buck
Bill and Ted's Excellent Adventure
Edward Scissorhands
Robocop
Romancing the Stone
Blues Brothers
Weird Science
Short Circuit
Bladerunner
Home Alone
Big
Splash
Cocktail
Lost Boys
Working Girl
Trading Places
Die Hard
Mona Lisa

Glasgow, Scotland, 1986

I never fully get to the bottom of what happened when I went to Pakistan. But the child I left and the child I came back to are markedly different. I never had any worries for her – she was sociable and boisterous as a young child, striking up conversations with strangers on ferries and parents in parks. As she moved into her teenage years, she became quieter, but that was to be expected. When I come back, she hardly speaks and doesn't want to leave the house, and sometimes her room. Her relationship with her father is in shreds. She finds it impossible to go into a shop to buy anything because she feels 'embarrassed' and 'hates people looking at her'. I put a lot of this down to being a teenager. But something doesn't sit right. She looks uncomfortable and pained all the time and her social skills have disappeared. She is defensive at home and awkward when relatives visit. She never goes out with any friends or asks for any money to buy clothes or records; she wears black all the time. It's like she has given up. All I can do is wait for my daughter to return – pushing

a heavy lawnmower across the grass when she was
seven, beating all the other children in the hundred
metres at Sports Day or twirling away for her dad's
movie camera.

The Hospital, Scotland, 1990

We drive for forty-five minutes to get here, out of the living breathing city, plunging into the flat post-industrial landscape, the inhospitable hills, the A-roads, the roundabouts – a postcard devoid of any beauty or warmth. Everything is the colour of concrete or straw; there is no life here. We spot the collection of unremarkable buildings from far off then it disappears behind a hill, only to re-appear five minutes later – surrounded by fences and wire and barriers. The gates are triple height and the colour of pain; the paint is peeling and rusted. One set has to close before the others can open. There is no putting it off. We must park our car and queue up to go through the metal detectors. If the alarm goes off, thick-necked men with tattoos and epaulettes search us, telling us off for leaving hairpins or a stray five pence piece in our pockets. We squeeze on to a minibus with other families – similarly edgy and ashen-faced, clutching gifts of sugary comfort from the outside world.

Everything takes an age; there are so many layers to penetrate before we can see him. We are baffled by rules and obedient in the face of authority. The whole trip takes five hours. We are anxious and nervous before; we are drained and upset afterwards. But at least we are free. We do this three times a week without fail for sixteen years because this is where my son is.

By now I have become used to officialdom, rules, bureaucracy, assessment panels, hearings, psychiatrists. But there is something so nightmarish about ending up in this place that I try to detach myself from it. I clench my teeth and make the journey, once, often twice a week – sometimes to get nothing other than a sulk or silence. But this is my boy, my Imran. He is no longer curly and cute – he is six foot solid, with huge arms and legs, deep dark circles stamped under his eyes, pumped with lithium and tranquilisers. He lumbers towards me, sleepy but excited. He gives me a bear hug, grabs the bag of treats with his paw and starts to eat straight away, while someone brings a tray with an enormous dented metal teapot of watery tea. He doesn't speak while he eats, shovelling McDonald's and chocolate bars into his mouth. I pour a cup of the tea, glad of something to do, while the security guards watch on, and other families try to make small talk through the grimness. There is no privacy but then there is nothing here – just containment. The truth is we couldn't contain him any more. And that is why he is here.

It all became too much. The tantrums, the throwing things, the squaring up to us. Once he lunged at the steering wheel when Arif was driving him somewhere and they almost ended up in a ditch. The final straw came when he lost his temper with my daughter and pushed her to the ground. His anger, his demons became insuperable. I had to give in and make the dreaded phonecall. Three men arrived later that day, with huge arms and white shirts. He was sectioned and went willingly. We had reached the destination we always knew we would.

Now he sits opposite me. Sometimes he is in a good mood – cracking weak jokes and nestling his head on my shoulder; sometimes he looks exhausted and irritable, complaining that someone has stolen his toothpaste or shaving foam. Other times he turns his body to the side, his face like thunder, and hardly says a word.

I have never seen his room, his bed, his walls. But I know they are spartan and bare, largely because that is how he likes it. He will take essentials like toiletries and clothes; but anything beyond that and his eyes flare in panic. On his birthday we bring a cake and cards, but he sends the cards home with us. He doesn't want to keep anything – either because of his obsessive cleanliness or because he fears his belongings will be taken. I'm never sure which of these it is. This may also explain why he eats every scrap of food we take him; he doesn't want to take anything back to his room. So we bring less than others – no two litre bottles of Irn Bru or six-packs of crisps. He eats so fast – he has always done that – I don't even know if he tastes it. When I tell him pleasantly to slow down a bit, his grin freezes then the corners of his mouth drop and his eyebrows knit into a scowl. He cannot tolerate any kind of advice or criticism. It can send him into a fury. At home he would have found something to throw by now; but here I see the flash of anger in his eyes, he shoots a look at the security guards and instead he goes into a sulk.

Visiting time is two until four. When they shout: 'That's the bus', I feel both relieved and guilty. I get to walk out of here. He has to stay. I can leave this clinical, desolate place – and go back to the land of the living. But he cannot. As I drive home, I flick on the radio and listen to some pop music. I chew on some Fruit Pastilles, sucking the colour back into my cheeks. In those early grey days, it never even crossed my mind that he would stay in this place for so long.

Bearsden, Scotland, 1990

The house grows quieter, calmer without my brother. But it echoes with guilt too, that we let him go. I carry my own guilt for years; I was after all at the centre of the incident that finally made my mother pick up the phone. Maybe I should have just told him what he wanted, but we were all worn down. Mum tells me that it would have happened anyway. They were drained, they had exhausted every type of treatment, facility, medication; and things had taken an ugly turn where some of us occasionally felt scared of his physical strength, unsure what he was capable of. I suppose I always knew this day would come; the first time he scowled at me and gritted his teeth in anger I knew I had lost him. I would have to let go of the little boy I had shared a room with for eight years. I only remember my brother in two incarnations – the forever toddler and the hulking six footer. Sometimes it feels like there were no years in between.

TWELVE

Oxford, England, 1988

My dad once told me I was lucky, but my luck runs out when I reach the porter's lodge of an Oxford college for my entrance interview. I have sailed through the exam but now I have had to get on a train for six hours to a place I couldn't find on a map, stay overnight in a deserted hostel and face the terrifyingly blank face of a tutor in his intimidating study. I sit with the other candidates and feel worlds apart. They are immaculately dressed, with loud confident southern voices and A Levels in Law. I curl my unpolished shoes under the chair and feel embarrassed in my childlike clothes. They have all swept their good woollen coats over the backs of their chairs; I haven't even brought one despite it being December because I'm from Glasgow and it's always warmer down south. The boys unbutton their suit jackets every time they sit down and do them up again when they stand up. The girls are wearing smart skirts and jackets and their clothes are uncreased and luxurious. I cannot stop staring at these mini-adults who just know what to do. I am nothing like these people. I may have gone to a good school and got high marks, but this is not my world, this place of big voices and long corridors. I recognise that I am not ready for this, that it will crush me. And yet I keep hoping that my luck will hold as it had for all my exams, the results of which have brought me here to these vast quadrants and stone arches. But this isn't really a test of my brain, it is a test of my personality – something I have yet to acquire.

In preparation I had bought a copy of the *Independent* for the law report. I read it through twice and absorb nothing, so distracted am I by the obituary of Roy Orbison. In my early teenage years I had divergent musical tastes – the pure shallow pop of the 80s and the mid-century randomness truly befitting an introvert – the Beatles, The Kinks, the Everlys, Frank Sinatra, Ella Fitzgerald – and Roy Orbison. His voice and lyrics had collapsed my heart so many times but I kept returning to them whenever I wanted a sound for how I was feeling.

I am shown into the study to meet the professor who will interview me. He doesn't smile and motions vaguely to a chair.

'Sit,' he says, and a dog sleeping at his feet pricks up its ears.

He asks me why I want to study law and I flounder. I wonder if I should tell him that it's because my parents think there are only two honourable and stable professions – medicine and law; that because I would cry at the sight of blood from the age of about five and was always squeamish about bodies, the only option really left to me was law; that I was just sixteen when I had to apply to university and I had no idea what I wanted to do as a degree let alone a job; that *L.A. Law* always made practising law look exciting and fun; that I had to pick something and because I have acquired a fiendish taste for the impossible I decided to take a punt on law. At Oxford. Instead I recover and give him some prepared waffle about wanting to uphold the law and help people. It seems a ridiculous but necessary question and I wonder whether, in all his decades in this airless room of toppling books and stained coffee mugs, interviewing a procession of cocky and terrified teenagers, anyone has actually delivered an answer that made him sit up and look less bored.

He doesn't give me any eye contact and I feel nervous and under-prepared, my voice fading. The dog moves and I notice a large yellow harness on it and realise that the professor is blind. He poses a hypothetical legal question, which I have never even considered, and I give a ludicrous answer. I haven't really thought about this interview at all and talking isn't my strong point. I keep trying to push my voice out of my throat.

Now I realise why all the smart candidates outside have done A Level Law. I bet they have never struggled to make friends or panicked about going in to a shop. I bet they talk to adults all the time at family dinner parties. I feel stupid and out of my depth, keen to get out of that room and back on to the train to the cold clear air of Glasgow. This was one step too far. I tell my mum that it went badly, but I can see she still has hope in her eyes. My dad is fit to burst and will not be deflated. He thinks a successful exam and the offer of an interview means the deal is done. But I know there is a huge gap between me and the other candidates. Days pass and then the letter finally drops through the letter box. It is thin and spiteful looking: bad news is always brief. And yet until I read it, I still harbour a hope that I am going to go to Oxford and lay all the ghosts to rest once and for all; that I can prove to those teachers that I am clever, worthwhile; that I am going to send my parents into the stratosphere. My mum who wanted to do a masters but wasn't allowed, who would have breezed into somewhere like Oxford with her brains and her confidence. My dad who used to cycle thirty miles a day through fields and streams to and from college in Lahore singing his heart out. He would boast about it for years. He often cried about his own father, who died too soon at the age of fifty-six; and how he would have been so proud that the granddaughter he never met had even got beyond the gates of Oxford.

But it was not to be. I saw the long unmistakeable word 'unfortunately' before I saw anything else. I was winded for days, but I knew I had done a terrible interview. I hadn't been cheated of anything; I still had a way to go. We had pinned all our hopes on Oxford. We were so stupidly sure of ourselves that we had thrown an offer from Bristol University in the bin. I rummage around and find it, then I smooth the paper out. We get the

Road Atlas out of the car and, just as we had searched for Oxford, we now search for Bristol, following the route along the A74, the M6 and the M5.

'Wow, Mum, that's . . . a long way away,' I say.

At seventeen I have started to fill every corner of my brain with my thoughts and plans instead of my anxieties and phobias; years of having to put on a brave face and walk past a sea of hard stares have given me a straight back and a high chin, although some people mistake this for aloofness. I still have a fear of unfamiliar social situations, but I can go into a shop, even sit in the cinema on my own or with my new solid school friends. Going four hundred miles away to university and having to fend for myself, to speak to people I don't know, is an intimidating prospect. But the idea of starting over again in a new city with new people, of finally shedding this skin, is intoxicating.

Gujranwala, Pakistan, 1968

'When. When is she leaving?'

The question arrives exactly forty-one days after my father dies.

My mother looks into my brother's face expectantly, her fingers twisting at the ends of her dupatta.

'Ummi, she's lived here for thirty years. We can't just throw her out.'

'Oh yes, we can.'

'But she is an old woman!'

'So what? We are all old now. At least she got to enjoy her youth. When I came here, she was already here like an ancient tree, sucking up all the moisture, taking everything slowly-slowly. Now you want me to forget all that and look after her . . . because she's . . . old?'

The ridiculous question hangs in the air. My brother considers the awful awkward conversations ahead. Why he hadn't foreseen them no one knows. He opens his mouth to make a suggestion, sees the unextinguishable fire in my mother's eyes and decides against it.

My younger sister who remained in the house tells me that the atmosphere changes that day. It had already been shifting throughout my father's short illness. The mourning provided a neutral period. But now the house feels and smells different. My mother is walking at a different pace. At just fifty-seven, her second life lies ahead of her, the life she should have had.

After weeks of protracted and bitter negotiations between my brother and my stepmother's children, it is finally decided that they will all leave. Some of the children are married too by this point, so the family breaks up and moves to different places.

Years later, my mother tells me that she sat by herself in her room as the family left. She didn't stand and crow, or push any luggage down the stairs. She didn't throw anything from a high window or dance joyously as she once promised herself she would. She felt light-headed, drained. She listened to the suitcases being dragged, the cars being summoned and loaded, the doors banging, voices receding and the engines starting then fading. It was finished.

Glasgow, Scotland, 1994

Helen is slowing down now – she is in her seventies but she insists she wants to keep coming to the house to work. I can see she is struggling, not just with the weight of things like the laundry basket or getting the hoover up the stairs, but with her health too. She has moved to Dunoon now to be nearer her family and the journey is ridiculously long. She sleeps over most nights, but she says all the walking is what keeps her healthy. I suggest that I take on someone else to help her with the heavy stuff. She doesn't say anything but the next day, when I come down for breakfast, she has left me a note.

In it she asks me not to employ anyone else, that she knows the next step will be that I will let her go. She says she can't give up this job, that she wouldn't survive without it, that it keeps her going, that she cannot bear to leave us. She says that she knows she is old, that she can't do the stuff she used to, but to not give up on her yet.

I abandon the idea of getting someone else in and start doing more of the housework myself. I don't want her to leave either; how would we survive if part of our family left? Helen is so quiet and unassuming, but there

349

is always a storm of emotion going on underneath. Ten years before, when I discussed going abroad to live in Pakistan permanently, she told me that she would come with all of us and live there. Luckily this never happened – she would have loved the food of course, but I'm pretty sure she would have struggled with the heat.

Glasgow, Scotland, 1979

It has been more than ten years since my father died. Soon after I left, my remaining sister married and went to live elsewhere too. The house feels different – quieter, less oppressive – but it is too big and empty. When my sister has twins, my mum goes to live with her to help out and ends up staying for years, as the family moves around the country on army postings in Rawalpindi, Quetta and Gujranwala. Then she spends periods of time with my older sister in Lahore and my brother in Karachi. She never puts down roots. She has become so used to a life lived in the shadow of my step-mother that she struggles to embrace what comes next. When she arrives in Glasgow, she still exhibits the habits and manias I had witnessed before – the obsessive cleaning, the talking to herself and the sighing. I shouldn't have expected them to disappear. She still feels useless too, as she had been made to feel. In the evenings she doesn't want to watch TV – largely because she can't understand English – so I suggest she knits something.

'I can't even knit properly,' she sighs, her face collapsing.

Undeterred, I give her knitting needles and two balls of wool, cast on a row of stitches and leave her to it. She produces two vests for her latest grandchildren and almost looks pleased with herself. Then I set about fattening her up. I ply her with a can of Coke every day, shortbread, Ritz crackers, Wotsits, bananas, before pushing her on to the scales and noticing with some satisfaction that she has put on a stone.

My mother is happier around the children; sometimes they make her laugh. Despite not speaking a common language, they have a strong connection. She even bonds with Helen – two women with nothing in common except for this family and their age. My mother tells me that Helen is a treasure and that I must never let her go. One day we are in front of the house, filming another home movie in the August sun. My children are all performing for the camera. One of them is dancing, another is waving, another is standing on one leg to show off their balance, Imran is staring off into the distance. My husband spots Nano looking out of a window on the top floor. He tells us all to wave to her and they do, beckoning her in their high sweet voices to come outside. I turn to look too, but she just waves, a strained smile on her lips, her eyes dark and blank.

As summer ends, my mother feels the chill in the air. She tells me it's time for her to go back to Pakistan. I try to keep her with me but I can't hang on to her. She is too restless.

Karachi, Pakistan, 1992

A sound escapes from my mother's throat that I have never heard before. I have hauled her up to dance at my nephew's wedding, refusing to take no for an answer. At first she seems irritated at my persistence, then she hobbles on to the dancefloor and stands there protesting. Around her my family beg her to dance, but her mouth is set in a straight line and she won't move. When we try to take her by the hand, she swats at us like flies. The younger children lose interest in this statue and go and dance elsewhere. She keeps trying to escape back to her seat. And yet it seems half-hearted to me. There is a strange energy in the air, a look in her eye, something unsaid.

'Come on, Ummi, now's your chance!' I shout above the music, sweat gathering on my forehead from the effort. A thought crosses my mind and I lift her arms to show her what to do with them. She repeats the movement like a child learning to clap its hands and finds it so funny that she starts laughing. Hard. I have never seen her dance or heard her laugh. Everyone's mouth falls open, a cheer goes up, but I keep going, pretending it's nothing because I don't want her to become self-conscious and stop. I know this is her only chance and mine. I encourage her to move her feet and she does a little shuffle, which delights me, but she keeps flapping at her dupatta, which falls off her head and around her shoulders.

'Leave it, Ummi!' I shout over the music. I pull it from her and hold it in my hand. It is white and reminds me of a dupatta lost and found forty years ago.

Tears are running down her face as she laughs and waves her arms; something has tickled her so much that she cannot control herself. She is eighty-one years old and it's like she has been waiting all her life to do this. And I have been waiting all my life to see it.

The next time I see her is in hospital in Lahore; she has just weeks left. Perhaps she had known it was her last dance.

Lahore, India, 1932

The bridegroom arrives on a slow white horse just after eleven o'clock. The animal stands in the street, pawing at the dusty ground, expelling air from its vast nostrils. When he jumps down from the horse, the strings of flowers on his sehra swing but not enough to reveal his face. He straightens his kameez, pushes his shoulders back and strides inside, followed by a few male members of his family.

I have been ready for hours, heavy with clothes and jewellery, my skin and hair oiled to a sheen. The nikah is done quickly. When it is time, I climb in to the doli and cling on as four men raise it up on their shoulders and transport me the mile and a half to my new home.

Now we sit quietly next to each other. My veil is heavy and beneath my clothes I am sweating slightly. My back is bent and my neck feels sore under the weight of material and jewels. I am desperate to glance at my new husband but dare not lift my gaze. I spend a lot of time looking at his hands trying to discern his character from the length of his fingers. I notice that he is impatiently drumming the fingers of his right hand on his knee.

Soon it is time to go. I stand up slowly, helped by my mother and sisters, the weight of my jewellery and clothes threatening to topple me. For a few seconds we stand together. I hear prayers. His name is Jahanzeb. Jahanzeb and Hameeda – three syllables each, our names have a pleasing rhythm together; we are well-matched. If I were not laden with jewels, I would walk more quickly out of the room, and there would not be such a gap between us. He walks ahead fast and I follow him out slowly to start my new life, a wife at last.

I am twenty-one, he is twenty-five. I wonder how long we will live our married life together. Fifty? Sixty years? And how many children we will be blessed with. I pray for four. Three boys for my husband. And one girl for me.

Glossary

atta traditional wholewheat flour used to make flatbreads like chapati, roti, naan, paratha and puri

azaan a Muslim call to prayer, heard five times a day

bebe pronounced beh-bay – Punjabi word for mother

beti daughter

chador a cloth used as a head and body covering by women, for warmth as well as modesty

charpai literally four legs – a traditionally hand woven, usually jute, bed supported by four metal or wooden legs

chowkidar a gatekeeper or watchman

dabba a street café or stall, literally a 'box'

dhoti a long unstitched piece of cloth used to cover the lower body of men and women

doli a traditional, usually wooden, chair or bed that was used to transport women, especially brides, from one place to another, often covered on all sides with material

Glossary

dupatta a long, thin decorative or plain scarf worn over the chest and often the head

gharara an elaborate, two-legged traditional long skirt worn by women mostly on festive occasions, specifically weddings

ghazals a rhyming poetic expression of intense feelings, usually of love, pain and loss, set to music. It originates from seventh-century Arabic poetry

jungli a wild and uncultured person

kajal black eye make-up, usually worn on the waterline

laddoo a traditional Asian sweet made of sugar, cardamom, nuts and chickpea flour. It is yellow and round and symbolises good news and festivities

mashki a water bearer who carries and delivers water in a leather water pouch usually shaped like a stomach

mithai assorted sweets made with milk, cream, dry fruits and nuts, a bit like a very soft fudge

nikah the religious contract of Muslim marriage containing rites followed by a signing ceremony

paan a betel leaf wrapped round lime paste, areca nut, fennel, coconut. Used as a stimulant and a digestive

palloo or *pallu* the loose end of a sari, worn over the head or over the shoulder

Glossary

panchayat a gathering of elders in a community that
preside over matters of mutual and individual discord
and pass judgment over them

panj ungla literally five fingers – a piece of jewellery that
adorns the wrist and extends to all five fingers

paranda three long pieces of silk or cotton woven into
the hair to support a plait to make it look longer and
thicker, some are plain, others are bright with bells
and tassels at the end

rishta a proposal of marriage usually from the family of a
man towards that of the woman

sehra a head-dress pinned to the groom's turban or head
covering with strings of flowers or beads hanging
from the front covering his face. This was to ward off
the evil eye and hide the groom's face until after the
marriage

shalwar kameez a long knee-length shirt with loose,
baggy trousers worn by both men and women

suras verses from the Qu'ran

tonga a horse-driven carriage

Acknowledgements

Thank you for reading my book. Seriously. You clicked a button and entered your card details; you traipsed to a bookshop and peeled it from a shelf; you borrowed it from a library. That's more than a transaction – we are forever connected.

This book shouldn't have been as hard to write as it was. But as I embarked upon it with the clear blue water of a whole year stretching out before me, everything collapsed around me in a pretty nasty and shocking fashion and I had to cling on to things to stay upright. I finally started the book five months later than I was supposed to and raced to finish it in seven. It was hard and lonely work; I typed away too late at night for someone who had to get up at 3am, with cardboard boxes of someone's possessions packed up and piled up around me, my daughter's writing scrawled over them. I wrote about being a six year old while a six year old danced around me, occasionally wriggling on to my knee and reading bits aloud. It was surreal.

While I wrote, I phoned my mum in Glasgow and made inky notes. Things she hadn't thought about in years came

360

back and made her throat dry and her eyes water. Thank you Mum for being so willing and enthusiastic to help me do the thing you always wanted me to do; and to do it with you was even more special. I'm sorry I was such a weird and awkward teenager; you didn't need any more stress. Thank you to my dad, for providing so much love and noise over the years. We had our sticky times but I love you so much. Thanks to my big bother, I mean brother, who helped me with facts and dates and had to revisit experiences and emotions he had packed away for decades. And I'm sorry I scratched your face and left a mark when I was seven.

I am indebted to my cousin Ayesha (silent 'e') in Lahore who answered my constant questions about schools and flowers and food and kept me straight on a world and a country I had almost forgotten. And a special thank you to Ravail who found a photo of my mum and I that I had never seen before and posted it to me. It stares out from the front cover.

Big love to my agent Nick Canham who always said I should write a book and made it happen; to all the friends, neighbours and colleagues who urged me on and kept squeezing my arm when I felt like I was about to come apart at the seams. You know who you are.

Thank you to the team at Headline – Bianca, Holly, Rosie, Patrick and Iain. I'm normally quite good at deadlines.

Acknowledgements

The second biggest thank you goes to the person who told me not to write this book, that no-one would want to read it. You are gone from my life now; but the book exists. Whether people read it or not is not in my hands. Like the teacher who said I would never pass an exam, thank you for making me even more determined to do it.

But the biggest thank you of course is for my daughter. Just when I thought I had everything, you came along. You told me to write here that you are really tickly behind your knees but I will write this instead: I really hope your mummy made you proud. You'll always have me, you'll always have this.